WOMEN'S INFLUENCE ON CLASSICAL CIVILIZATION

This volume explores how women in antiquity influenced aspects of culture normally thought of as male, such as economics, politics, science, law and the arts.

The contributors look at examples from around the ancient world, asking how far traditional definitions of culture describe male spheres of activity, and examining to what extent these spheres were actually created and perpetuated by women. It is shown that women, through marriage and motherhood, tended to perpetuate traditional male values, yet also made significant contributions of their own.

Written by a range of internationally renowned academics, *Women's Influence on Classical Civilization* provides a valuable wider perspective on the roles and influence of women in the societies of the Greek and Roman worlds.

Fiona McHardy is Lecturer in Classics at the University of Reading. Her research interests include ancient and modern Greek literature, folk poetry, anthropology and culture. She is co-editor of *Lost Dramas of Classical Athens* (forthcoming).

Eireann Marshall is Research Associate in the Department of Classical Studies at the Open University, where her research focuses on Libya and Cyrenaica in the Roman period. She has previously edited (with Valerie Hope) *Death and Disease in the Ancient City* (Routledge 2000).

WOMEN'S INFLUENCE ON CLASSICAL CIVILIZATION

Edited by
Fiona McHardy and
Eireann Marshall

Routledge
Taylor & Francis Group

LONDON AND NEW YORK

TO RAPHAEL

1 004042777

First published 2004
by Routledge
11 New Fetter Lane, London EC4P 4EE

Simultaneously published in the USA and Canada
by Routledge
29 West 35th Street, New York, NY 10001

Routledge is an imprint of the Taylor & Francis Group

© 2004 selection and editorial matter,
Fiona McHardy and Eireann Marshall;
© individual chapters, the contributors

Typeset in Garamond by
Florence Production Ltd, Stoodleigh, Devon
Printed and bound in Great Britain by
Biddles Ltd, King's Lynn

British Library Cataloguing in Publication Data
A catalogue record for this book is available from the British Library

Library of Congress Cataloging in Publication Data
A catalog record for this book has been requested

ISBN 0–415–30957–3 (hbk)
ISBN 0–415–30958–1 (pbk)

CONTENTS

ILLUSTRATIONS

Figures

Tables

CONTRIBUTORS

Suzanne Dixon has published widely on Roman kinship, gender, patronage and law. Her many publications include: *The Roman Mother* (University of Oklahoma Press 1988), *The Roman Family* (The Johns Hopkins University Press 1992) and *Reading Roman Women* (Duckworth 2001).

Judith P. Hallett, Professor and Chair of Classics at the University of Maryland, College Park, has published widely on Latin literature, and on women, sexuality and the family in classical antiquity. She is the author of *Fathers and Daughters in Roman Society: Women and the Elite Family* (Princeton University Press 1984), and the co-editor of *Compromising Traditions: The Personal Voice in Classical Scholarship* (Routledge 1997), *Roman Sexualities* (Princeton University Press 1997) and *Rome and Her Monuments* (Bolchazy-Carducci 2000).

Mary Harlow teaches Roman History at the Institute of Archaeology and Antiquity at the University of Birmingham. Her research interests are the life course and family history; dress and identity in late antiquity. She has co-edited *Growing Up and Growing Old in Ancient Rome* (Routledge 2001).

Rebecca Langlands is a lecturer in the Department of Classics and Ancient History at the University of Exeter. She has worked on Valerius Maximus and Roman *exempla*, and is currently writing a book about Roman sexual ethics.

Fiona McHardy is Lecturer in Classics at the University of Reading. She is interested in ancient and modern Greek literature, folk poetry, anthropology and culture. She wrote her PhD thesis on revenge in ancient Greek culture and has co-edited *Tragic Fragments* (University of Exeter Press 2004). She is currently researching the ancient Greek wedding song.

Gráinne McLaughlin teaches Latin and Greek language and literature in the Faculty of Arts, University College Dublin. She wrote her doctoral thesis on Greek lyric poetry. Her research interests include: panegyric technique, gender in Pindar, the myth of the Danaids and Presocratic philosophy.

Eireann Marshall is a Research Associate in the Department of Classical Studies at the Open University. Her main research interests are the history and art of ancient Libya and Cyrenaica. She has co-edited *Death and Disease in the Ancient City* (Routledge 2000) and published several articles on Libya and Cyrenaica in the Roman period.

Nancy Sorkin Rabinowitz is the Margaret Bundy Scott Professor of Comparative Literature at Hamilton College; she has published widely on Greek tragedy, including *Anxiety Veiled: Euripides and the Traffic in Women* (Cornell University Press 1993). She is the co-editor (with Amy Richlin) of *Feminist Theory and the Classics* (Routledge 1993) and (with Lisa Auanger) of *Among Women: From the Homosocial to the Homoerotic in the Ancient World* (University of Texas Press 2002).

Jane Rowlandson is a lecturer in the Department of Classics at King's College, London. Her main research interests are in ancient social history, particularly the culture and society of Greek and Roman Egypt. She is the author of *Landowners and Tenants in Roman Egypt: The Social Relations of Agriculture in the Oxyrhynchite Nome* (Oxford University Press 1996), and numerous articles on Ptolemaic and Roman Egypt.

Margaret L. Woodhull teaches Greek and Roman art history at Rhodes College in Memphis, TN, where she holds the James F. Ruffin Professorship in Classical Art and Archaeology. Her recent publications include 'Engendering Space: Octavia's Portico in Rome', in *Aurora: The Journal of the History of Art*. She is currently working on a book on women and architectural benefaction, entitled *Women Building Rome: Architectural Benefaction in the Early Roman Empire*.

ACKNOWLEDGEMENTS

This volume originates from a conference entitled 'An Alien Influence' held at the University of Exeter in 1998. The original idea for the conference was dreamt up by Deborah Gentry who was much involved in the preparations for the conference. We thank Nancy Rabinowitz and Judy Hallett for their constant support throughout the time of planning the conference and the preparation of this volume for publication.

We would also like to thank the British Academy for their generous grant towards the expenses of our international speakers at the original conference and the University of Exeter for their donation of a publication grant.

Finally, thanks go to the staff of the Department of Classics at the University of Reading, in particular Jane Gardner, Barbara Goff, Helen King and Ray Laurence, who offered copious support and helpful comments.

ABBREVIATIONS

Ancient authors

A.	Aeschylus
Andoc.	Andocides
Aug.	Augustus
Cic.	Cicero
Dem.	Demosthenes
E.	Euripides
Hdt.	Herodotus
Hyg.	Hyginus
Is.	Isaeus
Liv.	Livy
Lys.	Lysias
Olymp.	Olympiodorus
Plut.	Plutarch
S.	Sophocles
Suet.	Suetonius
Tac.	Tacitus
Thuc.	Thucydides
Xen.	Xenophon

Reference works

AE	*L'Année Epigraphique*
BM	British Museum
CE	*Carmina Epigraphica*
CIL	*Corpus Inscriptionum Latinarum*
CT	*Codex Theodosianus*
DMA	*Dictionary of the Middle Ages*
DSB	*Dictionary of Scientific Biography*
ILS	*Inscriptiones Latinae Selectae*
NS	*Notizie degli scavi*

P. Adler	*The Adler Papyri*
P. Mil.	*Papiri Milanesi*
P. Oxy.	*The Oxyrhynchus Papyri*
P. Petrie	*The Flinders Petrie Papyri*
P. Tebt.	*The Tebtunis Papyri*
RE	*Paulys Real-Encyclopädie der Klassischen Altertumswissenschaft*
SB	*Sammelbuch griechischer Urkunden aus Ägypten*
SEG	*Supplementum Epigraphicum Graecum*
UPZ	*Urkunde der Ptolemäerzeit*

Journal titles

AJA	*American Journal of Archaeology*
AJAH	*American Journal of Ancient History*
AJP	*American Journal of Philology*
ARCA	*ARCA: Classical & Medieval Texts, Papers & Monographs*
AW	*Ancient World*
BASP	*The Bulletin of the American Society of Papyrologists*
BCH	*Bulletin de correspondance hellenique*
CA	*Classical Antiquity*
CPh	*Classical Philology*
CQ	*Classical Quarterly*
CW	*Classical World*
EMC/CV	*Echos du monde classique / Classical Views*
GLQ	*Gay and Lesbian Quarterly*
GRBS	*Greek, Roman and Byzantine Studies*
HSCP	*Harvard Studies in Classical Philology*
JEA	*The Journal of Egyptian Archaeology*
JHS	*Journal of Hellenic Studies*
JRA	*Journal of Roman Archaeology*
JRS	*Journal of Roman Studies*
JSAH	*Journal of the Society of Architectural Historians*
MEFRA	*Mélanges d'archéologie et d'histoire de l'Ecole Française de Rome*
PCPS	*Proceedings of the Cambridge Philological Society*
QAL	*Quaderni di archeologia della Libia*
REL	*Revue des études latines*
RIDA	*Revue internationale des droits de l'Antiquité*
TAPA	*Transactions of the American Philological Association*
YCS	*Yale Classical Studies*
ZPE	*Zeitschrift für Papyrologie und Epigraphik*

INTRODUCTION[1]

Over the past few decades, scholars have increasingly turned their attention to discussing the lives and activities of women in antiquity.[2] This kind of ancient history aims to look beyond the world of politics and warfare, with which ancient historians have traditionally been preoccupied, so as to investigate the activities and lives of ordinary women who could not hold political office or perform military feats.[3] In this volume, we intend to turn the question around and ask whether ancient women were more involved in these traditionally male areas of culture than has previously been thought.

Successful work in this area has been achieved by anthropologists who suggest that women may have been more powerful than we think, either as the driving force behind their male kin or by exerting influence on public policy in indirect ways (cf. Rosaldo and Lamphere 1974). In 1986, Jill Dubisch wrote in the preface of *Gender and Power in Rural Greece*:

> It is no longer possible to take for granted a male-orientated view of society or see culture as a male-created, male dominated phenomenon.
>
> (Dubisch 1986: xii)

It is this view which we are addressing with the chapters in this volume.

For the classical world, this kind of study is inevitably hampered by difficulties. As Walters (1993: 195) notes, it is necessary to read a lot into tiny amounts of evidence. Nevertheless, a small but growing body of work by classical scholars has begun to take this kind of approach. Works which address the concerns of this volume and on which our contributions build include: Walters (1993); Fischler (1994); Hawley (1994); van Minnen (1998); Lardinois and McClure (2001). Fischler (1994) discusses how the interference of imperial women in the dealings of their families (in a similar way to the women discussed by the anthropologists) leads to an inappropriate level of power falling into the hands of women, because their families are the rulers of Rome. Walters (1993) also discusses how ancient women (this time in Athens) get involved in areas of interest to their families and can

1

manage to influence decisions about inheritance or citizenship, even though they are not permitted to present the issues in court themselves. The ability of women to exert pressure on the public behaviour of their male kin, especially by persuasion, and the tendency of women to influence areas of culture through their relationships with men is addressed by several of the contributors to this volume (Hallett, Harlow, McHardy, McLaughlin, Marshall, Woodhull). McLaughlin, following on from Hawley (1994), discusses how kinship with, or marriage to a philosopher or mathematician could allow women to work in that area themselves. These women had a more direct impact on the male cultural sphere through their publications and teaching, although little if anything of their work now survives to prove it. Van Minnen (1998) also discusses the evidence for women taking a more active role in the public sphere than has previously been thought. He suggests that it was possible for freeborn women in Egypt to be involved in learning (and teaching) crafts for business purposes. The direct involvement of women in business or creating craft, art and architecture for the public space is addressed by several contributors to this volume (Dixon, Rowlandson, Woodhull). Most recently, the edited volume of Lardinois and McClure (2001) has addressed (among other things) the issue of how women's voices were represented within male literature. As is frequently noted, the evidence of antiquity is almost exclusively recorded by men (as is reflected in the titles of books about women, e.g. Foley (1981) *Reflections of Women in Antiquity*, Cameron and Kuhrt (1983) *Images of Women in Antiquity*). Hence, we are compelled to look at ignorant, disinterested or even hostile representations of women and we have little or no evidence of what real women actually thought or did. Moreover, we are hampered by the tendency of authors to avoid referring to women (especially in democratic Athens), or to 'idealize' their behaviour according to the morals of the time. In several of the pieces in this volume, contributors try to look beyond the male author of the text, to detect ways in which women impacted upon their thoughts while composing (Langlands, McHardy, Rabinowitz).

The ancient sources are not the only problem in approaching the study of ancient gender. The unwillingness of some modern scholars to accept that ancient women played active roles in the public sphere has also proved an impediment in the past (cf. Dubisch 1986: 5). Scholars have been inclined to inflict their own culture's gender views onto their interpretations of antiquity, or to assume that women cannot have had any impact on the public arena, because of the political systems and laws at the time when they were living. The tendency to claim that works attributed to women must have been written by men is one instance of this behaviour. Inappropriate assumptions based on gender expectations are at the heart of two of the contributions in this volume (Hallett, McLaughlin). In part, this problem has been caused by the predominance of traditional male-style scholarship in certain fields. For example, Nixon (1994) claims that field archaeology has long been male-dominated with a resulting effect on the research produced. In such circumstances the application of feminist scholarship can offer new insight (McLaughlin, Rabinowitz).

The problems caused by the faulty assumptions of modern scholars are at the heart of Gráinne McLaughlin's chapter on female philosophers and scientists. Even where manuscript evidence has suggested the existence of an influential female mathematician (Pandrosion), modern scholars have refused to accept that a woman could take this role and have concluded that she must really have been a man. In such an atmosphere, it is unsurprising that women have suffered problems in gaining acceptance as scientists throughout the ages. McLaughlin puts forward the view that the influential misogyny of Aristotle was, at least in part, responsible for this attitude. However, where women received the support of their male relatives, they could make some achievements in the fields of philosophy, mathematics and physics.

The problems caused by the disbelief of modern scholars are also raised by Judith P. Hallett in her article on the letter attributed to Cornelia, mother of the Gracchi. Hallett points out that the tendency in recent times to attribute this letter to a man because of its content is dismaying, given the fact that the Romans themselves believed it was written by a woman. Although Gaius did not follow his mother's advice, her letter shows that she played an active, if indirect, role in politics. The fact that Cornelia wrote to Gaius on political matters shows that it was acceptable for mothers to advise their sons. Furthermore, as Hallett shows, Cornelia's advice is different from that offered by fathers. In other words, it appears that women not only advised their sons in a sphere which is quintessentially identified as masculine (politics) but did so in their own way. Cornelia also influenced culture to the extent that later writers drew on her letter and depicted women giving similar persuasive speeches.

The fear of the possibility of such powerful influential women was a great preoccupation of democratic Athenian men, as Nancy Sorkin Rabinowitz discusses in her chapter. Rabinowitz maintains that 'the feminine' is used as a cultural tool to reinforce social ideals and inscribe boundaries. Therefore, the mere existence of women and the thought of their potential power presents a threat in the minds of Athenian men. This threat is manifested like a warning through the Attic playwrights' representations of powerful women on stage. As a result, women can be seen to have had an indirect influence on democratic policy and ideals. While the behaviour of Clytemnestra and Medea would have seemed inappropriate to an ancient Athenian man, feminist scholars can find inspiration and gain insight into the modern world by examining these portrayals.

In this case, women are deliberately portrayed as acting inappropriately in order to provide a cultural lesson, but elsewhere the sources intentionally portray women acting only according to the ideals of *appropriate* behaviour and, thereby, obscure what women's actual behaviour was. As Suzanne Dixon discusses in her chapter, women's active role in commerce is sometimes obscured by ancient writers for various reasons (especially because of the moral implications) and incorrect assumptions have, therefore, been drawn by modern scholars. In her article, Dixon shows that women did make active contributions to commercial enterprises in ancient Rome, not just to domestic labour. In particular, Dixon shows that women played an active role in the production of cloth which was an important part of the Roman economy. Dixon, therefore, demonstrates that women were integral to the Roman economy which is normally identified as a male-dominated arena.

Likewise, Roman women took an active role as architectural patrons introducing a female voice into a predominantly male culture, as Margaret L. Woodhull discusses in her chapter on female architectural patrons. Woodhull argues that, while scholars have long been aware of the role imperial women played as *euergetes*, they have focused on male benefactors. Yet, as Woodhull shows, imperial women transformed Rome's urban environment and, in doing so, wove women into the heart of Rome's urban fabric. Woodhull focuses on an arch built by Salvia Postuma in Pola and shows that women not only contributed to the fabric of provincial cities but did so in their own way. By becoming involved in architectural patronage, women had the opportunity to introduce their own concerns, especially matters regarding their own family, into the public arena, as well as to contribute to the artistic culture of Rome.

Women's artistic contributions to ancient Athens are discussed by Fiona McHardy in her chapter. In reality, Athenian women were the authors of artistic oral compositions, especially laments, and it was these compositions that influenced male-composed tragedies. The plots of the plays also appear to have been inspired by popular beliefs about women's role in inciting revenge acts. However, the real activities of women are totally distorted in the literary plots in order to present a warning to Athenian men about the dangers of influential women. In tragedy, women are no longer represented as contributing positively to a traditional aspect of culture, but are instead portrayed as fearsome figures who act inappropriately and excessively.

Similarly, Rebecca Langlands notes that women, as readers, could influence the composition of Roman texts even when they were written by a man. She focuses on Seneca's *Ad Marciam* and discusses Seneca's need to deal with complex philosophical issues, regarding gender and ethics because Marcia is a woman. In this instance, women indirectly influenced literary culture because male authors needed to tailor their works in order to accommodate a female audience. In addition, she shows how courageous Roman women could serve as *exempla* for degenerate youths, although this in itself could be problematic.

Women could also bring influence to bear through marriage. Eireann Marshall argues that Libyan women were an important means by which Libyan culture was transmitted to Cyrene. As the mothers and wives of

Cyrenaean citizens, Libyan women appeared not only to have influenced cultural spheres normally associated with women but also those traditionally seen as masculine. Libyan women seemed to have influenced Cyrene's religious cults, both those which were quintessentially feminine and those which were important to the city as a whole. Furthermore, Libyan women may have indirectly transmitted Libyan culture to Cyrene as they were an important means by which Cyrenaean men developed contacts with their Libyan counterparts.

The ability of a woman to influence the behaviour of her husband is also at the heart of Mary Harlow's chapter which shows how Galla Placidia was thought to have influenced her husbands' behaviour. In her first marriage, she is shown to have a positive effect on her Gothic husband by educating him in Roman laws and appropriate Roman behaviour. However, in her second marriage, Placidia's control of her Roman husband shows him to be a weak man. As Galla Placidia was a central figure in late antique politics, the influence she had over her husbands had political implications. As a result, she can be seen to have contributed to political culture.

Finally, Jane Rowlandson's chapter shows how different attitudes to gender occurred in different parts of the ancient world. In the cultural mix which existed in Roman Egypt, women were able to take advantage of more lenient Egyptian laws in order to achieve their ends. Women could go to court, manage property, and sometimes they performed their own business transactions through their knowledge of reading and writing. It is possible that women were also influential in choosing the artistic design of funerary art for their families. Rowlandson's chapter demonstrates that it is not possible to pigeon-hole women, saying that they belong exclusively to an Egyptian/private category. Instead, she argues, women united with men to create a unique shared culture.

As will have been understood, the chapters in this volume cover a wide spectrum of different approaches to the topic of women and culture in antiquity. While some focus on the activities of individual women, others attempt to interpret the activities of the unnamed masses. Some examine the behaviour of the elite, while others investigate the lives of ordinary women. In addition, some contributions discuss the ways in which women exert indirect influence on culture through the reaction they provoke in male writers, while others show how women acted in their own right.

Three key lessons spring from a consideration of the chapters. First, as scholars we must attempt to look past our own cultural expectations when interpreting the behaviour of women in antiquity. Second, we must attempt to read past the idealization and problematization of women by classical male writers. Third, by opening our minds to new approaches, such as feminist methodology or the use of comparative evidence, it is possible to make deductions and speculations about the manifold contributions of ancient women to classical culture.

Notes

1 Acknowledgements to Tamar Hodos for some of the contents of this introduction.
2 Sarah Pomeroy's seminal *Goddesses, Whores, Wives, and Slaves* (1975) is frequently cited as the first women's history. This has been followed by a large body of works on women in antiquity including: Archer, Fischler and Wyke (1994); Blundell (1998); Cameron and Kuhrt (1983); Clark (1993); Fant and Lefkowitz (1977); Fantham *et al.* (1994); Foley (1981); Gilchrist (1999); Hawley and Levick (1995); McAuslan and Walcot (1996); Peradotto and Sullivan (1984); Reeder (1995); Rowlandson (1998).
3 This has also been a fruitful area of research for anthropologists who have found that women are frequently more powerful than we think, especially in the area of the household (see esp. Dubisch 1986; Friedl 1967; Rosaldo and Lamphere 1974).

1

THE LOGISTICS OF GENDER FROM CLASSICAL PHILOSOPHY

Gráinne McLaughlin

In this chapter I argue that, in the context of an examination of women's influence on culture in antiquity, it is impossible not to 'look outside the box' and consider not just their contribution to the world of ancient Greece and Rome but also the influence of Graeco-Roman ideas about women and their role on later Western European culture. After all, study of the ancient world is simultaneously a meditation on our own; and as we shall see, given the esteem in which the perceived wisdom of the Greeks and Romans was held in the Middle Ages and thereafter, the classical philosophical legacy is particularly prominent. In the ancient world a key dichotomy was that between *nomos* (man-made law or custom: masculine noun) and *physis* (nature: feminine noun), a dichotomy which has persisted to the present day and which can be shown to be, literally and metaphorically, a gendered dichotomy. In what follows I look at a particular aspect of this dichotomy, namely the equivalence of the male rather than the female with reason and the ability to do mathematics and science.[1] The discussion includes a survey of the biographical treatment of women involved in the development of mathematics and science, particularly physics. This survey highlights a parallelism in the biographical treatment of women philosophers from antiquity and later female figures in science and mathematics: to a significant degree both ancient female philosophers and later female scientists were often either prevented from participating fully in their chosen fields or else accommodated only through their association with a distinguished male relative or family associate. The reasons for the social acceptability of the exclusion of women from philosophico-scientific endeavour from antiquity to the modern era are of course complex and beyond the scope of a single contribution to a volume such as this. However, it is worth emphasizing that what was believed to be the wisdom of the ancients was a powerful force in philosophical and scientific communities down through the centuries. The misogyny of ancient

Greek philosophy was transmitted as part of the cultural heritage of European society.[2] The fact that ancient philosophy included mathematics and what would now be regarded as the natural sciences meant that later mathematicians and physicists who privileged ancient philosophy as source material for their own work saw the enduring misogyny of their own society bolstered and validated in the writings of the ancients, as will be seen in the discussion of passages from Plato and Aristotle below. The impetus for this chapter is primarily the research of the physicist Margaret Wertheim (1997), who has emphasized the enduring influence of, in particular, Pythagoreanism on the agenda and subject matter of modern high-energy physicists. Following on from Wertheim, I focus on the influence of purported Pythagorean elements on the thinking of key scientific figures. Because of the intractable misogyny of this philosophical and scientific tradition, we must at the outset note that the recovery and assessment of ancient and later women's contribution to it is no easy task;[3] and also that, given this environment, the achievement of the women who did manage to engage in philosophical and scientific discourse is, therefore, all the more remarkable.

I begin with some general comments on the approach adopted. Like Wertheim (1997: xvii), I have treated astronomy as a branch of physics, rather than as a separate discipline; and I do not distinguish systematically physics from maths–physics or mathematics. However, I differ from Wertheim in the following respect. She, arguably correctly, stresses the religious aspect of physics and traces this back to classical times (Wertheim 1997: xi–xvi; Keller 1985: 6–7). She also attributes the relative exclusion of women from science, in part, to their corresponding exclusion from the priesthood in Western societies. Rather than supplementing her work on the pervasive and enduring religious aspect of physics, I complement her thesis by examining the influence of ancient Greek perceptions of gender on modern science and mathematics. Furthermore, whereas Wertheim views the male–female dichotomy in terms of the history of religion and science, I believe there are interesting parallels which can be drawn with classical Greek views on the male–female dichotomy articulated as part of the philosophical discourse on *nomos* and *physis*.[4]

Pythagoreanism

These views are reflected in some of the same Greek philosophical texts on science and metaphysics which directly and significantly influenced the development of modern science and mathematics. I concentrate on two elements of the so-called Pythagorean tradition which, for the purposes of this chapter, need to be taken together: specifically the dictum or sound-bite 'All is Numbers' and the Pythagorean Table of Opposites.[5] I show that the importance of the sound-bite 'All is Numbers' as a statement of the goal of Western physics and mathematics is difficult to overestimate. This can be seen from the influence ascribed to Pythagoreanism in standard works on the history of mathematics. For example, as Kline says of the intellectual revival of ancient Greek culture in the Renaissance:[6]

> Almost as a corollary to the revival of Greek knowledge and values came the revival of interest in mathematics. From the works of Plato especially, which had become known in the fifteenth century, the Europeans learned that nature is mathematically designed and that this design is harmonious, aesthetically pleasing, and the inner truth . . . Platonic and Pythagorean works also emphasized number as the essence of reality, a doctrine that had already received some attention from the deviating Scholastics of the thirteenth and fourteenth centuries. The revival of Platonism clarified and crystallized the ideas and methods with which these men had been struggling. The Pythagorean–Platonic emphasis on quantitative relations as the essence of reality gradually became dominant. Copernicus, Kepler, Galileo, Descartes, Hugyens, and Newton were in this respect essentially Pythagoreans and by their work established the principle that the goal of scientific activity should be quantitative mathematical laws.
>
> (Kline 1972: 218–19)

It should be noted, of course, that any Pythagorean influence ascribed to key figures such as those mentioned above must be defined carefully: Pythagoras (b. *c.*570 BC), Pythagoreanism, and traditional perceptions about Pythagoreanism, must be distinguished. Pythagoras and his personal contribution to the philosophy of mathematics are elusive creatures.[7] There is also no concise definition of Pythagoreanism, which has been shown to contain elements of ancient and diverse origins. Burkert, for example, has noted that certain numerical correspondences which were regarded as Pythagorean as early as Aristotle, in fact pre-date Pythagoras and may also be, like the famous Theorem, of oriental origin (Burkert 1972: 476; Laroche 1995 and cf. Lloyd 1991: 27–48). In addition, Lloyd (1987: 275–8) has observed that the attribution to Pythagoreanism of the dictum 'All is Numbers', in the sense that the universe is composed of, and is explicable in terms of, numbers, is an inference from what Aristotle says about Pythagoreans in the fifth chapter of the first book of the *Metaphysics*, as opposed to a direct statement of attribution. Zhmud (1989) has gone much further and argued that a survey of ancient sources does not support the widely held belief that 'All is Numbers' was a key tenet of Pythagoreanism. Similarly, O'Meara (1989: 5) has emphasized the danger of confusing the Pythagoreanizing Neoplatonism of the opening centuries of the Christian era with ancient Pythagoreanism.

However, while these are of course legitimate areas of interest and concern for modern scholars, they must not be allowed to overshadow the following

9

basic point. For the purpose of my argument, what is significant is the medieval and humanist *perception* of Pythagoreanism. The fact that this was based on such indirect and diverse sources as, for example, Plato, Aristotle, Cicero, Ovid, Plutarch, Iamblichus, Proclus, Macrobius and Simplicius, sources which were themselves subject to the vagaries of translation and transmission,[8] is undeniable but not directly relevant. The ideological influence of the dictum 'All is Numbers' is illustrated by the quotation from Kline above. This dictum was consistently regarded by tradition as a central belief in Pythagoreanism. I believe that ideological influence has also been exerted by the misogyny of the so-called Pythagorean Table of Opposites. The Table in effect has provided generations of scientists and philosophers with a pseudo-scientific rationale for their exclusion of women from mathematical, scientific, and philosophical discourse. I believe this to be so partly because a key source for the dictum and Table throughout history has been Aristotle's *Metaphysics*, where they appear in close proximity to one another (1.5.985b–986a).[9] The significance and influence of the proximity has not received comment but in my opinion this proximity has served to valorize and compound the misogyny of the Table.

Before I highlight the Pythagorean elements in the thought of key figures in the development of Western mathematics and physics, it will be helpful to emphasize the perceived Platonic–Pythagorean inheritance. I will then quote the relevant section of Aristotle's *Metaphysics* and explicate its transmission to medieval and renaissance scholars. In so doing I will emphasize that the misogyny in Plato and Aristotle's own works interacts with Platonic mathematical Pythagoreanism and Aristotle's authority as a metaphysicist and critic of his precursors. The Pythagorean Table of Opposites has, therefore, exerted a powerful influence because of both its physical position in Aristotle's work and Plato's apparent espousal of Pythagoreanism: the two most important figures in ancient Greek philosophy were accordingly perceived by subsequent generations to espouse its tenets.

Plato: *Timaeus*

Plato has conventionally been regarded as a physicist's or mathematician's philosopher and continues to be so (Brisson and Meyerstein 1995). Similarities between the Platonic theory of forms and harmony of the spheres and, indeed, concepts relating to the soul, and Pythagoreanism have been noted since antiquity.[10] From the fifteenth century onwards, when translations of his dialogues preserved in the Islamic world became much more widely available, Plato started to eclipse Aristotle. However, it is noteworthy that one of the few Greek works known throughout antiquity and the Middle Ages, and therefore in less need of rediscovery in the Renaissance, was the *Timaeus* (Lindberg 1992: 148–9). It is one of the works where Plato's Pythagoreanism has appeared most obvious to scholars, as can be seen from

Crombie's comment that: 'Plato himself, in his Pythagorean allegory, the *Timaeus*, conceived of substance as mathematical form which gave order to the disorderly movements of chaos' (Crombie 1953: 4).

This is significant for our purposes, since this dialogue has been of particular interest to scientists throughout history; and, as Annas (1996: 11) has noted, it is somewhat strident in its misogyny: the man who did his best in this life, first time around, gets to live a blessed life in his native star, second time around; whereas the man who did not lead a good life would be reborn a woman (Plato *Tim.* 42b: see also 42e, 90e–91a and 563b7–9; cf. Bluestone 1987: 13). Like Chapter Five of Book One of the *Metaphysics*, therefore, science and the female are not presented as concordant concepts[11] in the Platonic text arguably of most interest to scientists and mathematicians.

Aristotle: *Metaphysics*

... the so-called Pythagoreans ... thought that the principles of mathematical entities were the principles of all entities ... Since, then, all other things seemed to be assimilable to numbers in their nature, and the numbers were primary of the whole of nature, [986a] they assumed that the elements of the numbers were the elements of things as a whole, and they thought that the whole heaven was a harmony and a number ... Well, even these thinkers seem to hold that number is a principle both as matter for the things that are and as affections and dispositions, and that the elements of number are the odd and the even, and that of these the one is limited and the other unlimited, and that one is from both these (since it is both even and odd), and that number comes from the one, and that, as we have said, the whole heaven is numbers. Now other members of this same group say that the principles in the sense of elements are ten:

limited	unlimited
even	odd
one	many
right	left
male	female
still	moving
straight	bent
light	darkness
good	bad
square	oblong

(Aristotle, *Metaphysics* 986a; trans.
Lawson-Tancred 1998: 19–20)

As Lovibond has observed of the Table:

> ... the fact that the Table of Opposites is composed of a 'good' and a 'bad' column confirms the point that despite its mathematical orientation, this [Pythagorean] philosophy was permeated by moral concerns and made no claim to be 'value-free'.
>
> (Lovibond 1994: 89)

It has been assumed that the text known as the *Metaphysics* was given its title by Andronicus of Rhodes (fl. 30 BC), when he put together his edition of Aristotle's works (Ross 1924: xxxii). Having been taught in Greek schools, its content was preserved in the Greek world in subsequent periods by scholars such as Alexander of Aphrodisias (fl. AD 198), who wrote a commentary on the first four books of the *Metaphysics* (Dooley 1989: 62–76), and the sixth-century neo-Platonist Simplicius (Sorabji 1990: 29–30, 275–304, 475–80). Two of the three important medieval translations of the *Metaphysics* into Latin[12] contain the part of Book One which concerns us: the *Metaphysica vetus* and a translation from the Greek dated 1260–70 by William of Moerbeke, who also worked on Proclus and commented on parts of Plato's *Timaeus*.[13] As Ross notes (1924: clxiii–clxiv), Moerbeke's translation can be seen for our purposes either to follow the *vetus* or to be more literal.[14] The *vetus* was in common currency in England and France by 1235, as is indicated by the fact that there are nearly a hundred copies of it extant from the thirteenth and fourteenth centuries which are based on manuscripts which pre-date 1235. Although certain works of Aristotle, including the *Metaphysics*, were for some time proscribed, records show that by 1250, if not before, the *Metaphysics* was being taught in European universities, including Oxford (Callus 1944; cf. Haskins 1924).[15] The key figures discussed below, specifically Robert Grosseteste, Nicolas of Cusa, Johannes Kepler and Isaac Newton, therefore had access to it in the form of Latin translations.

Pythagorean elements in the thought of key figures in the history of physics and mathematics

I will now consider the extent to which our scientific and mathematical culture is a male construct, through a selective examination of key figures in the conventional canon.[16] In approaching such a canon the following questions may be asked, among others: what have been the selection criteria involved; who decides who joins such an exclusive 'club'; and how have the judges been selected?[17] As Berubé has noted: 'Canons are at once the location, the index, and the record of the struggle for cultural representation; like any other hegemonic formation, they must be continually reproduced anew and are continually contested' (Berubé 1992: 4–5).

Waithe (1987: i–xxi) has emphasized the significance of this statement for women philosophers, given their enduring marginalization. For our purposes it will be instructive to see how often the male scientific tradition, bolstered as it has been by a Pythagorean agenda and mentality, and the perceived validation of their misogyny by Plato and Aristotle, has excluded women from its conventional canon and marginalized any contributions they did make. In so doing, it is not my intention to assert that the influence of the misogyny of the classical philosophical tradition was the sole cause of the hostility of the subsequent scientific community to the alien influence of the feminine: Roger Bacon, for example, was strident in his distaste of the feminine, as he was in his severe criticism of Plato, Aristotle, Hippocrates and Galen, whose own misogyny he complemented (Keller 1985: 33–42).

One of the 'founding-fathers' of Oxford University, Robert Grosseteste (b. 1168) was a towering intellect in the thirteenth century (McEvoy 1982, 2000). He played a significant role in the expansion of Aristotelian learning at Oxford (Callus 1944: 22) and was familiar with Aristotle's *Metaphysics* (Crombie 1953: 35 and 91 n.1). He wrote a comparative critique of the *Timaeus* and Aristotle's views of the constituent elements in the heavens (Crombie 1994: 330–5). He is described by Wertheim (1997: 48) as a Pythagorean Christian, who saw God in the image of himself, i.e. as a mathematician who 'disposes everything in number, weight and measure'.[18] It is notable, however, that Grosseteste's Pythagoreanism was an exclusively male preserve. As Wertheim summarizes:

> Grosseteste also championed an ideal of life from which women and families were entirely absent; his image of the perfect learned community was an exclusively male world. And so while he created a glorious Pythagorean–Platonic metaphysics, as far as women were concerned Grosseteste sided with Aristotle – who had insisted that women were mentally defective and less than fully human. Women's supposed mental inadequacy was yet another ruse used in subsequent centuries to bar them from access to academe – the crucial locus of mathematical training.
>
> (Wertheim 1997: 49)

Like Grosseteste before him, Nicolas of Cusa (b. *c.*1401) is another example of science and Church working hand-in-hand. He was a cardinal and represents the pinnacle of Pythagorean Christianity. He believed that to study mathematics was to study the mind of God. Numbers were the 'image' of God's mind. He appears to have adhered quite strictly to the polarities in the Pythagorean Table of Opposites, as can be seen from the following summary of his work:

> He paid special attention to the relation of oneness and otherness, which he represented as two opposed quadratic pyramids, conjoined

so that each had its vertex at the center point of the other's base plane. One pyramid stood for the light, the other for darkness, one for the male principle, the other for the female, and so on.

(*DSB*: vol. 3, 514; cf. Izbicki and Christianson 2000)

His belief in a world soul is regarded by Pedersen (1993: 254) as evidence of how the 'wilder speculations' of ancient Greek Platonists and neo-Pythagoreans were embraced by fifteenth-century scholars, while his Platonism is discernible in Crombie's account (1994: 1096) of his reference to Plato's use of the analogy of painting in expounding the levels of perception of his Forms or Ideas.

Johannes Kepler (b. 1571) was also a Christian Pythagorean who specifically stated that he followed in the footsteps of 'our teachers, Plato and Pythagoras' (Caspar 1938: 9). He searched for cosmic harmony, and was thoroughly familiar with what Caspar (1959: 44) describes as the 'geometrical mysticism' of Nicolas of Cusa. Furthermore, although Caspar distinguishes Kepler's vision from what he calls the 'conjured . . . mysticism' of Pythagoras (1959: 93), he acknowledges that the main stimulus for Kepler's work was the ideas ascribed to Pythagoreanism, Platonism and neo-Platonism, particularly Proclus (1959: 85–96). Kepler's knowledge of the biographical tradition concerning Pythagoras and the Pythagoreans is certainly revealed in the following anecdote. He was anxious not to attract controversy by open espousal of Copernican views; accordingly, he decided not to make all his opinions known to the public and informed a friend that in keeping his beliefs secret 'we shall imitate the Pythagoreans' (Caspar 1959: 68–9).

The legacy of Isaac Newton (b. 1642) is said to be testament to the power of the equation.[19] Until Einstein, his three laws of motion were the mathematical equivalent of the ten commandments. However, it is important to note that the groundwork for his equations was laid by Kepler, who provided certain clues about the workings of gravity. Although outwardly pro-establishment, particularly towards the end of his life, and an advocate of science as the handmaid of God, Newton held beliefs which now seem strange and counter to conventional religious belief. He was very interested in alchemy, which had ceased in his own time to be a respectable occupation. He believed Christian knowledge had passed from Noah to Moses, then to the Egyptians, and then to the Greeks, especially Pythagoras and Plato. He also thought that his work was one of rediscovery and believed that Pythagoras had known the universal law of gravity.

It has been noted that Newton does not appear to have spent much time in the company of women (Wertheim 1997: 115). The relevance of this personal proclivity must be considered in the context of the lifestyle of his contemporaries. For example, Robert Boyle (b. 1627) is regarded as the father of modern chemistry. He took a vow of chastity, as did his assistant Robert Hooke. Hooke was one of the greatest physicists of the seventeenth century.

He became secretary of the Royal Society, which did not have a woman member until 1945. It is notable that a founding member of the Society described women as 'traitors to wisdom' and that the first secretary said that the purpose of the Society was to raise a 'Masculine Philosophy . . . whereby the Mind of Man may be ennobled with the knowledge of Solid Truths' (Wertheim 1997: 100). The lifestyles of Newton, Boyle, and Hooke recall that of Grosseteste; and the irony in the exclusion by Christian Pythagoreans of women from philosophical and scientific activity should not go unnoticed, given the apparent involvement of women in ancient Pythagoreanism (Lambropoulou 1995: n.1; cf. Hawley 1994: n.2 and n.21).

A common fate: earlier female philosophers and later female mathematicians and scientists

I now turn to women's role in helping to create the scientific culture we have inherited, and would like to draw attention to the fact that, in the hostile environment described in the previous sections, any contributions made by women seem often to have been dependent on the legitimizing presence of a male relative or social connection. In this there is an apparent similarity in the circumstances of ancient female philosophers and some more recent female mathematicians and physicists.[20]

Hawley (1994) has noted that the presence of a supportive male relative, generally a father or husband, is a significant feature in the lives of the few women who appear to have practised philosophy in ancient Greece. Theano (late sixth century BC), for example, is defined in terms of her male relatives. While he lived she was first and foremost the wife, apparently, of Pythagoras. After his death, she may have been her husband's successor, but the succession was shared with her two sons. Hipparchia (third century BC) survives as philosophical foil to her husband Crates and was probably introduced to philosophy by her brother Metrocles. Arete of Cyrene (fifth century BC), daughter of the philosopher Aristippus, survives only through the fame attaching to her son Aristippus: in order to minimize confusion with his grandfather, the younger Aristippus is distinguished by the epithet *metrodidaktos* (taught by his mother). There is no trace of the several dozen books she is said to have written or information concerning her teaching of philosophy and natural science. Hawley concludes his review of the sources for information on ancient women philosophers as follows:

> Two significant patterns can be observed in these texts. Firstly, the continued importance of male connections. As in other spheres of the Arts, women did not study philosophy alone. Often they entered the world through male relations . . . Secondly, the women philosophers are still treated primarily as women. Interest is expressed in their beauty, their sexual passions. They represent

physical temptation . . . Moreover, it is ultimately ironic that just as the male connections and relatives were allowing women to become philosophers, the male sources that recorded various aspects of their lives were driving them back into the dangerous shadows of anecdotal sources.

(Hawley 1994: 84)

Hawley's observation is particularly pertinent in the context of the earlier quotation from Berubé. This is because, in being driven into the shadows of anecdote, women were simultaneously not only driven out of the canon but even out of the possibility of consideration for inclusion therein. Indeed, so little from antiquity is known about the women referred to above that the only way to provide dates for general guidance is to assume that they were younger contemporaries of their husbands; likewise, the reader will for the most part search in vain for separate entries in standard reference works such as the *Oxford Classical Dictionary*: the best place to look is under any entry for the women's husbands, fathers, or sons; and even then we must note that basic details such as dates are not always reliable or available.

A brief and undeniably selective chronological survey of women scientists and mathematicians from late antiquity onwards will show that what Hawley said of women philosophers in ancient Greece could be said of certain key female figures who, despite an unconducive climate, managed to make a contribution to the fields of science and mathematics. The way in which female intellectual activity is subsumed by the male, in a sense, is an enactment of the hierarchical polarity of the Pythagorean Table of Opposites which, in effect, dictates that the product of philosophical or scientific discourse belongs to the male side of the Table. In those cases where women appear to have made a contribution to such discourse, they have in fact been converted into 'midwives' for the intellectual output of their male relatives. The anxiety caused to the ancient Greek male by the female's role in reproduction and creativity has been explicated by Carson (1990), Halperin (1990) and Sissa (1990). The writing out of the female contribution can be regarded as a reflection of this anxiety.

For example, Hypatia, the prominent Alexandrian neo-Platonist and mathematician, was the daughter of the mathematician Theon (Dzielska 1995). She died in AD 415, when she is said to have been stripped naked and torn to pieces by Christians. As with Arete of Cyrene, tradition decided she must be beautiful (Dzielska 1995: 102; Hawley 1994: 82). Although with a considerable reputation in antiquity as a philosopher and mathematician, later authorities minimized her contribution and placed her in the role of scribe to her father. However, in recent years mathematical research has shown that her own original work can be identified because she used an idiosyncratic method of division in the hexagesimal system. So although Hypatia's work has been incorporated into texts attributed to other people, it can be discerned.[21] Tradition, however, has preferred to wallow in almost pornographic accounts of her death.[22] In so doing, the contribution of the work she did with her father and independently of him has been obscured for centuries; and she has rarely received the recognition accorded her in, for example, Taub's recent discussion of the question of graduation in Alexandrian astronomical instrumentation, where she refers to a 'jointly produced commentary' of Theon and Hypatia (Taub 2002: 133–4; cf. Rome 1926).

For the purposes of the issues under discussion in this chapter, Hypatia may also exemplify the agonistic process involved in the creation of a canon, as described above by Berubé. Some scholars believe that she was originally included among the famous classical philosophers in Raphael's iconic *School of Athens* (1508–10), but that she was morphed into Pope Julius II's nephew, Francesco Maria della Rovere, in the final version of the fresco. The argument that her exclusion is explicable on the grounds that her beliefs ran contrary to the Church cannot carry any serious weight in discussion of a work littered with polytheistic pagan philosophers. It would appear that Hypatia was considered the only female philosopher worthy of inclusion: as it is, her ultimate exclusion means that not a single female philosopher appears in the fresco (Hall 1997: 1–47; Joost-Gaugier 2002: 94–6).

Hypatia may not have been the first or only female Alexandrian mathematician-philosopher of note. Netz is certain that she had a predecessor. Having referred to Hypatia in the course of his discussion of ancient Greek mathematicians, he goes on to state that:

> But, about a century earlier in the same city, we hear from Pappus about another female mathematician, Pandrosion. Pappus is very critical towards her, but then he is just as critical towards Apollonius and indeed towards almost everyone except (to a large extent) Euclid and Archimedes. So there are two *well-documented* [my italics] women in our group, which is not a little given the obvious obstacles in the way of women in antiquity.
>
> (Netz 2002: 197)

I would quibble over the use of 'well-documented' to describe Hypatia, in the light of the difficulties in separating her work from that of her father and given the extent to which her work has been underappreciated and unrecognized in the past: the process of uncovering Hypatia's intellectual identity has been seen to be complex and, as yet, incomplete. The documentation on Pandrosion, if anything, illustrates how difficult it may have been for women's work to be recorded at all: her identity is disputed. Pandrosion may have been a mathematician of sufficient standing to have attracted pupils and be the addressee of a work by Pappus.[23] Let us therefore look more closely at the sources of information about Pandrosion to see how she has been edited out of existence as part and parcel of the editorial decision-making process. I will argue that in this particular case a key tenet of textual criticism may have been passed over for no good reason: gender bias.

The prime source quoted by Netz is Pappus of Alexandria (*Collection* 3.1).[24] The reader who consults this passage is at the mercy of the particular version of the text available. The Greek words which give the name of the person being addressed at the beginning of Book Three have been considered problematic by textual critics editing the text and scholars translating it. The result of this is that the gender of Pandrosion fluctuates depending on which edition or translation the reader consults; and the reader must be fairly fluent in Greek, Latin, and French in order to compare the standard versions available. For example, according to Ver Eecke's French translation (1982: 21), Pandrosion is '*excellent Pandrosius*' and therefore male. Likewise in Hultsch's edition, where the Greek original has a Latin translation opposite it as was the norm, Pandrosion is male: κράτιστε Πανδροσίον / *clarissime Pandrosio*. Thus far there is no 'problem' apparent. It is only if the persistent reader of Hultsch looks up the name Pandrosion in his Greek index that the possibility, on textual, i.e. prime-source grounds, that Pandrosion was a woman becomes apparent (Hultsch 1878: vol. III, tom. II, 82). Hultsch explicated the Greek in Latin which I translate as follows: 'Pandrosion, the name of a man, a mathematician apparently, to whom Pappus dedicated the third book of his work'. Here ends the definitive statement on Pandrosion. However, the entry continues in brackets and it is in the brackets that Hultsch refers to the manuscript reading 'κράτιστη Πανδροσίων', which has the support of some scholars (e.g. Lambeck (1665–79: 433), who says 'in fact I think that Πανδροσίων is a woman's name and refers to a woman, skilled in the mathematical sciences and very like Hypatia, the daughter of Theon, who lived in the fifth century'). For our purposes, what is significant is that this manuscript reading, which is not retained by Hultsch in the production of his text, gives the feminine vocative form, rather than the masculine form κράτιστε, which Hultsch introduces into his text. Hultsch justifies his decision to ignore what is in the manuscript on the grounds that he restored the similarly formed masculine name Megethion elsewhere in the text: his logic is that if there is a name Megethion and it is masculine, it follows that if there is a name Pandrosion, it must be masculine; or, as Hultsch puts it, 'with the result that we have preferred Pandrosion to be masculine' (my translation). Cuomo (2000: 7–8) has noted that Hultsch was not slow to bracket entire paragraphs of the text if he felt that they were redundant or lacking in inner consistency; and it was presumably on the latter ground, by linguistic analogy with the Megethion form of his own restoration, that the feminine form relating to Pandrosion was ejected from his version of the text.

The gender of the name in ancient Greek, however, can be divined only by its accompanying adjective, which in the manuscript is in its feminine form. On what grounds did Hultsch therefore alter the feminine form in the manuscript tradition to what appears in his printed text? After all, despite the plea to analogy advocated by Hultsch in his index, a principle in editing ancient Greek and Latin texts is that a more difficult or less likely reading (*lectio difficilior*) is to be preferred by editors to an easier or more obvious one (*lectio facilior*), given that scribes are inclined to simplify what is in front of them, thereby moving further away from the original form of the text. I would argue that in the case of Pandrosion, the fact that a masculine form Megethion may elsewhere have been restored in the text, does not nullify the presence of κράτιστη in the manuscript. In terms of the practice of textual criticism there is arguably a substitution at the editorial level of a *lectio facilior* for a *lectio difficilior* in the alteration of κράτιστη to κράτιστε. We must also consider whether criteria other than palaeographical, critical, or linguistic were in operation to justify the apparent breach of the *lectio difficilior* principle. In this context it is interesting to observe that in a recent statement of the basic principle at issue here, Huygens simultaneously gave the following critique of it:

> The basic idea behind this term [*lectio facilior*] is, that a *lectio difficilior* is more likely to be simplified into a *lectio facilior* than the opposite . . . Generally speaking this may be true, but one should be aware of the trap hidden underneath this apparently sensible principle: much nonsense has been printed simply because some word or construction was less common or correct than the alternative.
>
> (Huygens 2000: 49)

Huygens is of course talking about 'nonsense' in the sense of readings which are gibberish or rubbish in linguistic terms, the end result of the principle being applied blindly. However, if we accept the point being made, we should then ask the following question: in the case of Pandrosion, is the editorial substitution of the masculine form in place of the feminine explicable, if not justifiable, even partly on the grounds that it is 'nonsensical' to imagine that Pandrosion was actually a scholar of substance, and female? Is this a case of gender-related assumptions and biases operating under the guise of the objectivity attributed to textual criticism? Hultsch's imposition of a masculine gender through the substitution of the masculine form of an adjective in his text for the feminine form in the manuscript is not the only way editors and translators have coped with the Pandrosion problem, i.e. the possibility that Pandrosion was a woman. Jones pulls no punches in his summation of the lengths to which editors have gone rather than accept the feminine reading of the manuscript:

> Pappus's Pandrosion has suffered strange indignities from Pappus's editors: in Commandino's Latin translation her name vanishes, leaving the absurdity of the polite epithet κράτιστη being treated

as a name, 'Cratiste'; while for no good reason Hultsch alters the
text to make the name masculine.

(Jones 1986: 4, n.8)[25]

In considering women's role in creating philosophico-scientific culture
from antiquity onwards, we cannot assess their contribution outside the traditional and almost exclusively male canon. Rather, we must be aware of the
social factors which hindered not only women's actual participation in
discourse but also even the acknowledgement of their participation in it.
The case of Pandrosion is an example of the very tenuous thread by which
any awareness of a woman's contribution may hang: her existence falls or
stands on the length of a single vowel. In short, to return to the phrase with
which this discussion of her opened, she is therefore nowhere near as well-
documented as we would like. Her successor in the line of notable female
figures in philosophico-scientific culture, Hypatia, is by comparison well-
documented, although as has already been noted, prime source materials are
at a premium. We have to wait half a millennium before a climate arose in
which some women could leave their own words.

The most famous of these is Hildegard of Bingen (b. 1098), who, as an
abbess in the Middle Ages, had more autonomy than other women: she also
had the support of the ultimate male relative, God. She developed a
Pythagorean cosmology as the basis for natural science and she also practised
medicine. She had the good sense to attribute much of her work to Divine
revelation, a 'coping strategy' per level three of Helen King's categorization
of the changing focus of research on women in ancient societies.[26] For our
purposes, what is interesting is the way Hildegard appears to have been very
aware, as one also might say of King's ancient Greek woman patient, of the
need for an acceptable form of self-representation. Rapp has summarized
the stance adopted by Hildegard as follows: 'Keenly cognizant of her status
as a 'mere' woman in a man's world, she nevertheless used language to exploit
her unique visionary gifts to procure for herself the power and influence she
could not otherwise hope to have' (Rapp 1998: 3).

Another half a millennium later and masculine support of a more worldly
kind facilitated a woman's contribution to scientific discourse. Sophie Brahe
(b. c.1556), astronomer and alchemist, had the support of her brother Tycho
(Christianson 2003: 255–61). Not only did Sophie have her brother's active
encouragement but it would appear that the presence of another woman,
Elisabeth Paulsdatter, was tolerated if not actually encouraged (Christianson
2003: 288–9).[27] The astronomer Maria Cunitz (b. 1610), who corrected some
of the mistakes in Kepler's astronomical tables, had an enlightened father
and married an astronomer. Likewise, Elisabetha Koopman (b. 1647), who
compiled the largest star catalogue of her time, had a supportive father and
married an astronomer. Both the father and husband of Maria Winkelmann
(b. 1670) were astronomers. It was she who discovered the comet of 1702,

but credit was given to her husband as court astronomer, even though he stated that it was his wife who had observed it first. On her husband's death, the job passed to her son. She was eventually barred from entry to the observatory. In effect, she was edited out of her field of research in a manner that recalls the fate of Arete of Cyrene.

Margaret Cavendish (b. 1623) had a wealthy husband who moved in scientific circles. When exiled in France, Descartes and Hobbes (a fellow Royalist in exile) were dinner guests. Cavendish wrote on natural philosophy and had her own version of the atomic theory. However, despite the fact that minor royalty routinely became members of scientific societies, regardless of intelligence, she was not allowed to become a member of the Royal Society. Even though she donated considerable sums to the Society, she was only ever allowed to watch Boyle as he carried out one experiment. Like Cavendish, a wealthy spouse was instrumental in providing intellectual opportunities for Emilie du Chatelet (b. 1706), who married an elderly marquis for convenience and then had a relationship with Voltaire. It was she who provided the mathematical expertise for his writings and she who translated Newton's *Principia Mathematica* into French; indeed, her translation remains the standard one. Her credibility suffered because of her relationship with Voltaire: in this respect her situation perhaps resembles that of the female Epicureans whom tradition has preserved as courtesans rather than philosophers (Hawley 1994: 79–81).

Laura Bassi (b. 1711), who was educated by the family doctor and married a scientist, has the distinction of being the world's first woman professor of physics and the second to gain an academic qualification. Although she was awarded the Chair in Bologna her subsequent career to an extent recalls the biographical tradition surrounding Hipparchia. Just as tradition has preserved the latter for biographical colour in the life of Crates, she was kept as a curiosity by the university and not allowed either to pursue her research or to teach in the same way as her peers. Although she had the support of the pope, among others, and did her best to integrate herself into the system, rather like one of King's Hippocratic patients, she nonetheless remained a source of anxiety for it. This has been shown in Findlen's analysis of the actions of the university authorities at Bassi's graduation ceremony, which in some respects resembled a wedding:

> Recalling both the religious tradition of women in orders as brides of Christ and the civic tradition of virgins whose chastity cemented the foundations of republican government, Bassi, as a 'most learned virgin', found herself fulfilling these ancient topoi.
>
> (Findlen 1993: 454)

She was also depicted as a Minerva-like figure: in short, imagery of this pagan goddess of wisdom, and of the Vestal virgins, and of the established precedent of Christian virgin, 'celibate' marriage to Christ was deemed necessary to accommodate and neutralize the reality of Bassi's interest in, for example, electricity. We may also note in passing that the political, religious and mythologico-philosophical culture of the ancient Romans, not just the Greeks, could be called on to legitimize the position of a woman such as Bassi.

Finally, Marie Curie (b. 1867) had the support of her husband Pierre. She is famous for work on radioactivity. She proved it was an atomic property and was awarded a Nobel Prize in Physics in 1903. The only other woman to get a Nobel in Physics was Maria Goeppert-Mayer in 1963, who was also married to a supportive husband. With respect to Curie, what is much less well-known is that she was denied admission to the French Academy, not considered for positions given to her husband or other males, was believed as recently as 1971 not to have done the work for which she was awarded her Nobels (even though Pierre died in 1906 and she won her Nobel in Chemistry in 1911), and was denied funding despite the prestige of her Nobels. Her husband provided her with opportunities during his lifetime, but after his death the extent to which she was regarded as merely his wife became all too apparent; and we are perhaps tempted to recall the way Hypatia's role came to be regarded as that of amanuensis to her father.

Conclusion

Mathematicians and physicists, encouraged by their Pythagorean inheritance, are still trying to explain the world in as small a set of equations as possible. Hence the use in their literature of the abbreviation ToE for 'Theory of Everything', also referred to as the Unified Theory of Forces. In essence this is the modern equivalent of 'All is Numbers'. Wertheim concludes her book (1997: 223–52) with provocative observations on this agenda. She emphasizes that recent and increasingly expensive research in the field of high-energy physics has absolutely no practical application whatsoever. By contrast, in 'soft' sciences such as anthropology, astrophysics, physiology, genetics and other areas of biology, where women are less under-represented, useful advances of medical and economic applications have been made. As an example, Wertheim discusses the case of the Nobel Prize Winner Barbara McClintock's revolutionary work on 'jumping genes' (1997: 244). In contrast to her predecessors and colleagues, McClintock operated on the basis that an organism's genetic code is dynamic, i.e. it responds to its environment. The medical and agricultural implications are obvious. However, Wertheim's point is not just that outsiders such as women and members of ethnic minorities can bring a fresh perspective to old problems, or that the intellectual resources of all of the population are greater than those of half of it. Rather, it is that it is healthier for the individual member of society and society as a whole if that society does not perpetuate a policy of exclusive acculturation:

the legacy of ancient philosophy, which included mathematics and science, whether Pythagorean, Platonic or Aristotelian, can be put to better use. The earliest philosophers asked the question: how does the world work? This is a question still in need of an answer, for as Wertheim had observed at the beginning of her work:

> A clear understanding of your culture's world picture is a basic human need . . . Knowledge of a society's world picture is essential for psychological integrity within that society. Without such under-standing an individual becomes, in a profound way, an outsider.
>
> (Wertheim 1997: xi)

To a significant extent women were regarded as intellectual aliens or outsiders in classical Greece. We may now regard the years prior to adulthood as an important period of acculturation when social values and skills are trans-mitted. For the ancient Greeks the process of acculturation was man's work: women may have taught the baby how to talk, but men taught the male how to think. The discussion in this chapter of the history of women's involvement in ancient philosophy and later science shows that the prevailing societal dynamics militated against the full participation of ancient and later women in the philosophico-scientific culture of their respective soci-eties, where the agenda has been a male construct bolstered and justified in part by the misogyny of the unceasingly privileged classical philosoph-ical tradition. Given this predominantly hostile climate, it is perhaps surprising that women succeeded in playing any active part in philosophical and scientific discourse as opposed to being, as living instantiations of the feminine, merely a construct within those discourses. The vagaries and biases of tradition and transmission mean that we cannot either recover or appraise fully their contribution, or indeed know what these ancient women in particular thought about their lot. But, as the examples of Hypatia and Pandrosion show, the operation of the conventional and ideologically loaded canon is likely to have ensured that women's contribution from the ancient world onwards has been understated. Yet the survival against the odds of even just their names serves as a reminder that there is a female con-tribution to be taken into account: the presence of the 'female' on the 'wrong' side of the Pythagorean Table of Opposites is just the start of a very complicated story.

Notes

1 Classical Greek philosophy is substituted for science in the above statement in the discussion by Lloyd (1996); cf. Keller (1985: 21–32, 1992: 1–12); Lloyd (1993: 1–9); Longino and Lennon (1997). For an overview of feminist scholarship on gender and science see Longino and Hammonds (1990). For the connection between a clerical culture and the exclusion of women from science see Noble (1992).

2 See, for example, Richard de Fournival's use of material from the opening book of Aristotle's *Metaphysics* (discussed below) in his thirteenth-century misogynist *Le Bestiare d'amour*, as discussed by Beer (1995).

3 Despite the difficulties, women's contribution to culture can be extracted from problematic historical sources: see, for example, the approach taken in van Houts (1999).

4 For a multidisciplinary approach to the history of women in science see Keller and Longino (1996) and cf. McGrayne (1993).

5 For an analysis of the Table see Lovibond (1994); cf. Lambropoulou (1995).

6 Cf. Kline (1972: 147–54), where Philolaus is cited in connection with the dictum 'All is Numbers'. See also, for example, Pedersen (1993: 254) and Lindberg (1992: 31–2, 294, 371 n.15).

7 The various idiocies in his biographical tradition are covered in the fragments selected in Barnes (1987: 81–8); cf. Kingsley (1995) and Riedweg (1997).

8 The Scriptural authority with which Pythagoras and other Greek and Roman sources are cited is illustrated by quotations in Murdoch (1987); cf. Eastwood (1987).

9 The standard edition is Ross (1924). For translations and select bibliography see Barnes (1984); a recent translation is Lawson-Tancred (1998).

10 Current research on the Pythagorean strata in Plato is illustrated by Kingsley (1995: 71–132), with respect to the *Phaedo* in particular. The influence of Archytas on Plato is discussed in Lloyd (1990).

11 *Pace* Dillon (1986). The epistemological barrier of the female in Plato and Aristotle is discussed in Lloyd (1996) who analyses the classical underpinnings of Francis Bacon's misogynist epistemology; cf. Tuana (1994) and Tong (1989).

12 Aristotle was read mainly in Latin until the middle of the seventeenth century. Cf. Schmitt (1983: 64). Schmitt (1973) has also emphasized the enduring influence of scholastic Aristotelian philosophy until the seventeenth century.

13 For details of the twelfth-century translation by James of Venice see d'Alverny (1982). Aquinas' commentary to a degree follows from Moerbeke's work on the *Metaphysics*: Rowan (1981). For the preservation of the *Metaphysics* in the Islamic tradition see Walzer (1962: 60–113 and 114–28): the Arabic versions, which were based on more than one Greek manuscript (1962: 121), are to be found principally in the lemmata of the *Great Commentary* by Ibn Rushd (Averroës: b. 1126). It should be noted, however, that in twelfth-century Spain 985b–986a was missing from Ibn Rushd's text of the *Metaphysics* (1962: 119).

14 For a detailed discussion of the basis of Moerbeke's translation see Vuillemin-Diem (1987): there is a useful table on page 463.

15 Haskins (1924: 373) quotes from a twelfth-century manuscript belonging to Caius College. This states that a student must 'also study Aristotle's *Metaphysics, de Generacione et de Corrupcione,* and *de Anima*'. The manuscript pre-dates the first Oxford statute of 1267. For further information on the curriculum at Oxford in the thirteenth century see Catto (1984).

16 Biographical and bibliographical information on the figures discussed below can be found in the *Dictionary of Scientific Biography* (*DSB*) and the *Dictionary of the Middle Ages* (*DMA*); cf. Lindberg (1992), Pedersen (1993), and Wertheim (1997).

17 For an example of the very palpable effect of the structure of authority on the entry requirements for inclusion into the canon of French science at a particular point in its history, see Shinn (1980). Wertheim's work is, in part, an attempt to rewrite the canon to include the contribution of women, both ancient and modern.

18 The quotation is from a summary of Grosseteste's work made by the fourteenth-century scholar and cleric William of Alnwick which is quoted in Crombie (1953: 102).

19 For a general overview of Newton's life and works see Fauvel *et al.* (1988). Cf. also Rattansi (1988) and Casini (1984) on Newton and classics.

24

20 In addition to *DMA*, *DSB*, and Wertheim (1997) see Yont and Brown (1999) and
    Kohlstedt (1999). Further biographical information on the women mentioned below
    is to be found in Alic (1986). It should be noted, however, that the interpretation
    of detail therein must be viewed in the context of the arguably debatable statement
    on the first page of the book: 'Science is that body of knowledge that describes,
    defines and, where possible, explains the universe . . . Women have *always* played an
    essential role in this process [my italics]': it might be more accurate to say that,
    though of course not intrinsically incapable of contributing, women were, with rela-
    tively few exceptions, until very recently usually prevented from making a consistent
    and significant contribution, due to complex and inter-related societal, political, and
    religious reasons.

21 Cameron (1990: 126) says: 'Hypatia and Isidore did more than proofread somebody
    else's text. They constituted their own'. Dzielska (1995: 102–3) notes that it is
    possible Hypatia edited and commented on Diophantus' books, in addition to
    working on Ptolemy's *Almagest* and *Handy Tables*, as Cameron has noted: other work
    has, unfortunately, perished.

22 Dzielska (1995: 102) notes that Hypatia was actually sixty years old when she was
    murdered but that posterity prefers the dismemberment of a nubile young girl to
    that of an old woman.

23 For Pandrosion as a mathematician and teacher with followers, see Cuomo (2000:
    73 and 127).

24 For Pappus' life and works, see Cuomo (2000) and Jones (1986). The basic history
    of the text is in Cuomo (2000: 6–8): the first printed edition of a Latin translation
    of the text was published in 1588 and was based on the work of Federico
    Commandino. The standard edition is that of Hultsch (1876–8). I am grateful to
    Dr Anna Chahoud for her help in locating the various versions of Pappus.

25 Cuomo (2000) cites Jones on 127–8, and refers to Pandrosion as female on 127, yet
    prints the masculine form of the epithet on 170 in the Greek text in n.4.

26 'It seems to me that we have moved on from "weren't women treated abysmally?",
    to "finding women's voices in otherwise unpromising sources", and on to "strategies
    women used within the system"' (King 1995: 136).

27 The slow pace of the change in cultural attitudes to women's participation in the
    'hard' sciences particularly is seen in the fact that centuries later in the 1950s the
    nuclear physicist Fay Ajzenberg-Selove was told she was not eligible for an instruc-
    torship at Harvard because she was a woman and, like Paulsdatter, was able to work
    in a lab at Princeton only at night, because of the chairman of the department's rule
    that women were not allowed in the building (Wertheim 1997: 222–3).

2

MATRIOT GAMES? CORNELIA, MOTHER OF THE GRACCHI, AND THE FORGING OF FAMILY-ORIENTED POLITICAL VALUES

Judith P. Hallett

Politics, and the values that inform them, rank high among the contributions of classical Greece and Rome to later culture. And specifically to 'male culture', the nexus of socially transmitted practices generally regarded as the creation and domain of men. Relationships among powerful families in republican Rome, moreover, characteristically attract close scrutiny as central to its distinctive brand of elite politics and culture. Nevertheless, relationships within such families merit careful attention too, since the interactions among family members afforded women as well as men the opportunity to influence both politics and political values. This discussion will focus on Roman republican political 'intrafamiliarity', by comparing some paternal and patriotic with maternal and, 'matriotic' values, and by considering how and why the latter were represented by the Romans themselves as putting family first.

In its entry on *patria potestas*, the supreme power invested in a Roman father, the latest edition of the *Oxford Classical Dictionary* states the following:

> Legends and some accounts from the historic period show *patres-familiae* executing, banishing or disowning adult children. Private judicial action, normally on the advice of a council, shows the exercise of *patria potestas*; execution of traitorous or insubordinate sons by public officials, such as the famous execution of the Bruti (509 BC) or Torquatus (340) by consular fathers . . . exemplify paternal severity in a public role. Sons are portrayed as liable to punishment chiefly for offences against the state.
>
> (Nicholas and Treggiari 1996: 1122–3, s.v. '*patria potestas*')

26

Historically speaking, we cannot place much credence in legends or even in accounts from the historic period that depict republican Roman fathers resorting to extreme measures when dealing with traitorous or insubordinate sons, even those *patres* portrayed as having done so in a public role. After all, these accounts do not come from the fathers themselves. Nor do they come from eye witnesses, or even from historical contemporaries. Indeed, the historians who provide our earliest surviving narratives about the public exercise of *patria potestas* by Lucius Junius Brutus in 509 BC, and by Titus Manlius Torquatus one hundred and fifty years later, date from the latter part of the first century BC: nearly half a millennium after the consulship of Brutus, and over three centuries after that of Torquatus.

Still, these accounts, however anachronistic and fictionalized, do have a valuable, cultural if not historical, purpose. For they vividly reminded their Roman readers that Roman fathers, especially those holding high public office, were legally entitled to punish, and were justified by hallowed precedents in choosing to punish, adult sons for insubordination, chiefly in the form of offences against the state. Furthermore, the authors of these anachronistic and fictionalized accounts, at times, attempt to explain why it was that these fathers felt obligated to opt for such extreme measures. In this way, they furnished their Roman readers with an acceptable rationale for such paternal severity.

At 8.7.15 of his *Ab Urbe Condita*, for instance, Livy scripts for Torquatus a stern speech accounting for his decision to put his own son to death, and thereby set 'a painful but healthy example for the youth of the future'. Livy's Torquatus begins by faulting his son for having revered neither *imperium consulare*, consular power, nor *maiestatem patriam*, a father's higher authority. He claims that he has been placed in the position of 'having to forget either the Roman state or myself.'

And in between these neither/nor and either/or clauses (and again a few lines later), Torquatus emphasizes that his son has broken military discipline, *disciplina militaris*, by which the Roman state has stood firm to this day (*qua stetit ad hanc diem Romana res*). To be sure, Livy does have Torquatus admit that he is emotionally stirred by an inborn affection for children, as well as by his son's display of individual *virtus* (manly excellence), before Torquatus orders his son bound to the stake and hacked to death with an axe. Nevertheless, Livy's Torquatus assigns greater importance to upholding, rigidly and inflexibly, a single, abstractly defined, principle of civic conduct – the necessity of adhering to military discipline – than to the affective pull of family ties on him personally.[1]

The overwhelming majority of Roman fathers, however, did not opt to use their *patria potestas* to kill (or exile or repudiate) their politically insubordinate sons, presumably because they reared and treated their sons in such a way as to render these extreme measures unnecessary. But what strategies did Roman fathers deploy to motivate, urge, even browbeat their sons to behave 'subordinately', in a patriotic and hence familially desirable fashion, when performing public duties – so that drastic punishments might be avoided? As it happens, Livy does not tell us if Torquatus and, for that matter, Lucius Brutus, had previously communicated to their sons how they were expected to behave, and bring credit to their respective families, as Roman citizens. However, even if Livy had depicted these two fathers as having long extolled adherence to abstractly defined principles of civic conduct, on the grounds that such behaviour was patriotically and hence familially desirable, Livy's account would be at best an imaginative as well as an anachronistic effort.

Yet we do have some earlier, and first-hand, evidence of how actual elite republican Romans themselves deployed such motivational strategies, at least with their grown sons. For there survive two excerpts of a letter – dated to approximately 124 BC – from a parent seeking to motivate, urge and, indeed, browbeat an adult male child to behave in both a patriotic and familially desirable fashion when performing his public duties. These excerpts are found in the manuscripts of Livy's fellow Transpadane Cornelius Nepos (who died in 24 BC, a few years after Livy launched his Roman history).[2] The first excerpt reads:

> You will say that it is a beautiful thing to take vengeance on enemies. To no one does this seem either greater or more beautiful than it does to me, but only if it is possible to pursue these aims without harming our country. But seeing as that cannot be done, our enemies will not perish for a long time and for many reasons, and they will be as they are now rather than have our country be destroyed and perish.

And the second excerpt, from the same letter in a different passage, says:

> I would dare to take an oath solemnly, swearing that, except for those who have murdered Tiberius Gracchus, no enemy has foisted so much difficulty and so much distress upon me as you have because of all these matters. You should have shouldered the responsibilities of all of those children whom I had in the past. You should have shown concern that I might have the least anxiety possible in my old age; that, whatever you did, you would wish to please me most greatly; and that you would consider it sacrilege to do anything of rather serious significance contrary to my feelings, especially as I am someone with only a short portion of my life left. Cannot even that time span, as brief as it is, be of help in keeping you from opposing me and destroying our country?
>
> What end will there finally be? When will our family stop behaving insanely? When will we cease insisting on troubles, both suffering and causing them? When will we begin to feel shame about

disrupting and disturbing our country? But if this simply cannot take place, seek the office of tribune when I will be dead; as far as I am concerned, do what will please you, when I shall not perceive what you are doing. When I have died, you will sacrifice to me as a parent and call upon the god of your parent. At that time will it not shame you to seek prayers of those gods, whom when they were alive and on hand you considered abandoned and deserted? May Jupiter not for a single instant allow you to continue in these actions nor permit such madness to come into your mind. And if you persist, I fear that, by your fault, you may incur such trouble for your entire life that at no time would you be able to make yourself happy.

Now who is this man getting 'parentally motivated' here? Since our manuscripts identify the letter-writer and give the name of the letter-writer's two illustrious sons, and since the letter refers to the murderers of Tiberius Gracchus, we are able to identify the 'motivatee' here as one of these sons, Tiberius' brother Gaius Gracchus. And what is this son being motivated (and arguably urged and browbeaten) to do by this parent? In the first excerpt, the letter-writing parent seems to voice agreement with Gaius in endorsing an abstractly defined mode of civic conduct: the principle of taking vengeance on personal enemies, *inimici*, in the political arena. But, at the same time, the letter-writer refuses to adhere to this principle rigidly and inflexibly, in all instances and at any cost. Rather, the parent states that such vengeance should not be pursued if it harms one's own country.

And in the second excerpt, the parent first likens the behaviour of Gaius to that of a personal enemy. Other than those who murdered Tiberius Gracchus, says the letter-writer, no personal enemy has made my life as difficult as you have. The letter-writing parent proceeds to fault Gaius for failing to shoulder the responsibilities of his dead siblings, to minimize the anxieties of his parent in old age, and to make an adequate effort to please and obey his parent. In other words, the letter-writer voices feelings of unhappiness over the son's dereliction of family duty and, in turn, seeks to exploit the son's own family feelings. Then, by associating the son's opposition to parental wishes with 'destroying our country', the letter-writer briefly returns to the earlier theme of limiting revenge on personal enemies to activities that do not harm one's nation.

But the letter-writer immediately resumes the topic of family feelings: by accusing their entire family of acting in an emotionally inappropriate way, insanely, and by using a series of rhetorical questions to arouse the son's own emotions of shame and guilt. Only at this point does the letter indicate precisely what the son has done to cause the parent such distress – deciding to run for tribune of the people – by asking him to postpone his campaign for this office until the parent is dead and can no longer feel. And the letter-writer closes by again attempting to elicit feelings of shame from the son for his dereliction of family duty, and by predicting emotional distress and personal difficulties for him if he persists in acting insanely.

The motivational strategy, the patriot game as it were, adopted by this letter-writing parent to deal with this politically insubordinate son is hardly subtle. After all, the words and tone of this parent are angry, confrontational, demanding, egotistical, intimidating, explicitly shame- (and implicitly guilt-) inducing. But, as the reference to the murderers of Tiberius Gracchus as personal enemies alone makes clear, both the political and personal stakes for this particular parent and son were extremely high. Tiberius Gracchus had been killed by political foes after he had won the office of tribune, and when he was pushing similar agrarian reforms; Gaius was this parent's sole surviving son.

What is more, unlike Livy's Torquatus, who hard-heartedly privileges political principle – in the form of an uncompromising adherence to military discipline – over personal and familial feeling in organizing his moral priorities, this parent views what matters politically, familially and morally as inseparable from personal and familial feeling. Yes, an abstractly defined, civic-oriented mode of conduct is endorsed. But at the same time this parent recognizes such conduct as of restricted value. Preventing harm to one's country is more important. Furthermore, this parent does not view keeping the Roman state strong and harm-free as inimical to and incompatible with family loyalties, or as in conflict with the affective pull of family ties. Rather, a family-oriented, emotionally grounded ethos underlies this parent's definition of appropriate, moral, civic and patriotic conduct.

Yet, if we are to utilize this letter to Gaius Gracchus as an example of how actual republican Roman parents voiced motivational (as opposed to punitive) remarks to their sons, we must not overlook its most striking feature. The manuscripts in which this text survives also specify that the letter-writer was not a father with the weapon of *patria potestas* held in reserve, but Cornelia, the mother of Tiberius and Gaius Gracchus. And the attribution of this motivational text to a mother rather than a father immediately raises questions about the link between the gender of its author, and the tone and the content (and for that matter the motivational purpose) of its words.

Of special relevance to these questions is *In a Different Voice*, Carol Gilligan's 1982 study of psychological theory and women's moral development. Gilligan has based this study, we should acknowledge, on responses from a very small sampling of individuals, and pointedly makes no claims to generalize about a wider population, across cultures or through time. In it, Gilligan contrasts the self that is defined through separation with the self that is delineated through connection, and an ethic based on rights with one based on relationships and responsibilities. She contends that women are more likely than men to think about themselves in connection with others. She also maintains that when women make moral judgements and decisions, they tend to give greater weight to their relationships with, and responsibilities to, the other individuals involved than to abstract rights and principles (1982: 24–63).

Can Gilligan's contentions about how women make decisions help illuminate what is distinctive about Cornelia's letter? Absolutely, especially if we compare the values that Cornelia espouses and the rhetorical strategies Cornelia uses in the course of motivating (and urging, and browbeating) her insubordinate adult son with the values and strategies that Livy ascribes to Torquatus in the course of condemning his son to death. Livy's Torquatus gives pride of place to his right (as both father and consul) to treat his son as he sees fit, as well as to the principle of military discipline. At the same time Torquatus sets up a sharp contrast between his own welfare and that of the Roman state. But Cornelia invokes Gaius' (and her own) family ties; emphasizes her own feelings and those of Gaius toward her; and insists that attending to personal and familial relationships and responsibilities is ultimately more beneficial to the Roman state than disregarding them.

Can Cornelia's motivational arguments also be interpreted as linked with her female (in contrast to Torquatus' male) gender identity? Quite possibly, as can the mere fact that she is arguing as she motivates rather than rationalizing as she pronounces final judgement. After all, Cornelia cannot punish her son in the same way that Torquatus allegedly did. She wields no *patria potestas*, and is ineligible to hold consular (or any public) office. Nor is it in her self-interest for her son to leave Rome or even distance himself from their family. As a woman she depends on her male kin for her social identity and personal validation far more than would a man like Torquatus.

Then can we judge Cornelia's way of dealing with her politically insubordinate son a typically Roman female strategy, or at least a typically maternal one? Well, not just yet. For the matter of what we might label Cornelia's self-fashioning in terms of gender identity is rather complicated. Significantly, there are no grammatical details (such as a feminine adjective or pronomial form) in the first excerpt of Cornelia's letter, and only two details in the second excerpt, that even identify the author as a woman, i.e. the repeated use of the feminine adjectival form *mortua*. Indeed, at one point Cornelia uses the masculine phrase *deum parentem*, 'parent-god, parent who has become a god' in speaking of herself.[3] She acts in what might be regarded as a 'male-identified' Roman fashion, too: by 'one-upping' Gaius in the area of patriotism to disparage his defence of vengeance against enemies, and by portraying the future without her guidance as a time of unrelieved misery for him.

To be sure, Cornelia was both a privileged and (by 124 BC) a mature woman. Widowed when her sons were still young, she may have had to adopt both a paternal and maternal role towards them. But her self-assertive stance and outspoken criticisms of an adult male child – whose formal rights and authority in a patriarchal society far surpass her own – do not accord well with conventional Roman notions of respectable female behaviour. It might well be argued, in fact, that Cornelia, here, engages in what Barbara McManus has termed 'transgendered' conduct. For she has assumed the positively valued masculine function of political adviser and admonisher to an insubordinate son, and done so despite the fact that she was barred by her gender from participating in Roman politics in any office-holding capacity.[4]

It should be noted that Cornelia failed to exert any political influence on her son in this instance, as these motivational strategies proved completely ineffectual with Gaius. He ran for, and was elected, tribune anyhow, and suffered the same fate as his brother (see, e.g. Plut. *Gaius Gracchus* 17). Both Cicero and Quintilian, moreover, may maintain that Cornelia wrote letters proving that she influenced the eloquence of her two sons, but neither authority says anything about her influence on their other actions.

Cicero makes this assertion about Cornelia's influence on Gaius' speech when he has his interlocutor Atticus observe the following:

> But it is of great significance what kind of individuals each one hears each day at home, with whom he speaks from the time he is a boy, and how fathers, instructors and mothers also speak. We read the letters of Cornelia, mother of the Gracchi; they show that her sons were not so much reared in their mother's bosom as in her speech.
>
> (Cic. *Brutus* 211)

Quintilian similarly remarks on Cornelia's influence on her sons' eloquence:

> I would wish that there be as much learning as possible in a future orator's parents, nor am I only speaking about fathers. For we have learned that Cornelia, mother of the Gracchi – whose most erudite speech has also been handed down to future generations through her letters – had contributed a great deal of eloquence to them.
>
> (Quintilian *Institutiones Oratoriae* 1.1.6)

These statements by Cicero in the first century BC and Quintilian in the first century AD are important for a further reason. Both furnish evidence that Cornelia wrote letters which these men themselves were able to consult in their own day. They therefore allow the possibility that the letter excerpted in Nepos' manuscripts was among those consulted. Even so, Cornelia's authorship of this letter has long been challenged by a variety of modern scholars, in part because it is not quoted anywhere else.[5] And if Cornelia is not the author, who do these scholars think is? Apparently they assume it is a man.

I myself would take issue with those who would deny that Cornelia (or any Roman woman) wrote this letter, and have offered various arguments in support of my contention elsewhere. But what I would like to argue here is that, regardless of who actually wrote this letter, ancient Roman readers assumed that the author was a woman. For there are apparent echoes of this letter in various Augustan literary texts, best explained if we ourselves assume that their authors viewed Cornelia as having written this letter. More important, though, these echoes also suggest that these authors who echo her letter viewed her mode of dealing with an insubordinate adult male son as characteristic of a well-born Roman woman operating from a maternal position. And these echoes, this evidence for a perception of female authorship (if not proof of Cornelia's actual authorship) occur in a group of speeches, ascribed to elite women who also seek to motivate politically insubordinate or not-yet-subordinate sons, by Livy, Virgil and Propertius.

Cornelia's letter, for example, seems to have strongly influenced Livy in the angry words delivered by the aged Veturia to motivate, as it were, her traitorous son Coriolanus to abandon his plans for invading Rome:

> When Coriolanus, confused in his mind as if he were on the verge of insanity, rose from his seat, and held out his arms in embrace for his mother as she came to meet him, the woman, turned from her entreaties into anger. 'Allow me', she said, 'before I receive an embrace, to know whether I have come to an enemy of the state or to a son, whether I am a captive or a mother in your camp. Have a long life and a wretched old age dragged me into this situation, that I looked upon you as an exile, and then as an enemy of the state? Have you been able to devastate this land, which bore and nurtured you? Didn't anger vanish from you – even though you had come with a hateful and threatening attitude – as you entered the boundaries of your country? Didn't the thought come into your mind, when Rome was in your sight, 'Within these walls are my house and household gods, my mother, wife and children?' Thus if I had not given birth, Rome would not be under siege, if I did not have a son, I would have died a free woman in a free country. But I am able to endure nothing either more shameful for you or more miserable for myself. Nor, as I am extremely miserable, am I about to be for so long. You will see about these people for whom – if you proceed on your course – either an untimely death or a long slavery remains.' . . . In the works of Fabius Pictor, by far the most ancient authority, I find that this man lived to old age . . . Roman men did not begrudge women their own praise – to such an extent did people live without disparaging glory earned by another – and it was as a commemoration of this event that a temple was built and dedicated to the Fortune of women.
>
> (Livy 2.40)

Like Cornelia in her letter, Livy's Veturia confronts her son through a series of rhetorical questions. She, too, refers to her own wretched old age with the noun *senecta* (rather than with the more ordinary *senectus*, which Livy employs later in the passage).[6] By using the conjunctions *nec . . . nec* to negate a pair of comparative adjectives that govern personal pronouns in the dative case (*sed ego nihil iam pati nec tibi turpius nec mihi miserius possum*), Livy has Veturia recall Cornelia's phrase *neque maius neque pulchrius cuiquam atque mihi esse videtur* (To no one does this seem either greater or more beautiful than it does to me). She further resembles Cornelia in likening her son to an enemy (albeit a *hostis*, enemy of the state, rather than an *inimicus*, personal political foe). Most importantly, Livy has Veturia link what is politically consequential with what is best for a family and its feelings. For Veturia's speech not only emphasizes the emotional pain her son's conduct has caused her personally but also underscores her son's emotional ties and obligations to herself and other family members (mentioning, as Cornelia does not, her son's wife and sons).[7]

By characterizing Rome itself as having given birth to and nurtured Coriolanus, Livy even has Veturia equate her son's native land with herself, thereby representing it as his *matria*. To be sure, Livy's Veturia, whose guilt- and shame-evoking tactics include blaming Rome's woes on herself (because she gave birth to her son), comes across as angrier and more confrontational than Cornelia. But her son's more outrageous political conduct warrants as much – and Veturia, unlike Cornelia, proves successful in getting her son to do what she wants.[8]

Scholars generally date Livy's first five books to 27–25 BC, around the time of Nepos' death. It is thus the earliest of the Augustan literary texts containing echoes of Cornelia's letter.[9] Virgil's *Aeneid* – which was nearly, but not entirely, completed at the time of its author's death in 19 BC – comes next chronologically.[10] In it we find speeches that recall Cornelia's words to Gaius assigned to three different female characters: Dido, queen of Carthage; the mother of the fallen Trojan warrior Euryalus; and the Latin queen Amata. All of these women resemble Cornelia (and, for that matter, Livy's Veturia) in their noble birth, maturity of years and emotionally distraught state.[11]

Amata's two speeches that call to mind Cornelia's letter warrant our special attention. One, at *Aeneid* 7.359–372, is addressed to her husband, king Latinus. Protesting his political decision to betroth their daughter Lavinia to Aeneas rather than their kinsman Turnus, it demands that family ties and family feeling be given pride of place in forging political alliances. Virgil has Amata begin her speech by firing off a series of rhetorical questions much like those that Cornelia directs at Gaius. She further recalls Cornelia's appeal to Gaius by begging her addressee to consider her own emotional needs, by stressing his responsibilities to others, and by invoking divine authority.

For Amata asks:

> Is Lavinia to be given as a bride to Trojan exiles, o man who begot her? Do you feel no pity for your daughter and yourself? Do you

feel no pity for her mother, whom a treacherous pirate, seizing the maiden and heading for the high seas, will with the first favourable wind, leave forlorn? And isn't it the case that Paris, the Trojan shepherd, insinuated himself into Sparta in just this way, and carried off Leda's daughter Helen to the Trojan cities? What about your hallowed pledge? What about your longstanding concern (*cura*) for your family members, and for your right hand so often given in promise to Turnus, who shares our blood? If a son-in-law is being sought from a people foreign to the Latins, and that is surely resolved, and if the commands of your father Faunus weigh upon you, indeed I think every country which is free from our sovereignty is foreign, and that this is what the gods mean. And, if the primal origin of his home is in fact going to be traced, the Argive Greeks Inachus and Acrisius were ancestors to Turnus, and the heart of Mycenae was his homeland.

(Virgil *Aeneid* 7.359–372)

Amata's other speech, at 12.56–63, is addressed to Turnus – her nephew and surrogate son – himself, and urges him not to engage in single combat with Aeneas for Lavinia's hand. Immediately prior to addressing him, she is described as *moritura*, about to perish, thereby evoking Cornelia's two references to 'when I will be dead' (*mortua*). Virgil then has Amata recall Cornelia by lamenting her wretched old age (with the word *senecta*), claiming that the fate of their entire household rests with Turnus, and raising the prospect of her own imminent death. Amata further resembles Cornelia in that her advice goes unheeded: Turnus proceeds to fight Aeneas in a duel to the death anyway. Strikingly, at 7.357, Virgil characterizes Amata's indignant expression of family-first sentiments as speaking *solito matrum de more* 'in the manner customary for mothers'. He thus implies that her fierce display of emotion, insistence on sensitivity to family members' feelings, and privileging of blood family ties over other political goals are typical features of maternal motivational speaking.

Propertius' final elegy, (4.11), takes the form of a speech by a historical rather than a fictitious figure – a newly dead noblewoman, also named Cornelia – to the family members who survive her. It is set in, and appears to have been written shortly after, 16 BC, the year in which Cornelia's brother held the consulship. This Cornelia issues two sets of orders to her two young sons, who would grow up to be consuls in AD 1 and AD 6, sixteen and twenty-three years respectively after their mother's death.[12]

A number of textual details in this poem call the letter of Cornelia, mother of the Gracchi, to mind. Propertius has his Cornelia allude twice, at 29–32 and 37–38, to the military achievements of the Scipionic ancestors that both Corneliae shared. So, too, he portrays her in 75–76 as ordering her husband to assume her maternal duties, and as telling her sons in 93–94 to console their father as old age (*senecta*) approaches. He thus has her emphasize the obligations of survivors to replace the dead for those still living, and of sons to minimize the anxieties of aging parents: both themes figure prominently in Cornelia's letter to Gaius. Cornelia's use in this context of the noun *senecta*, and of several verbs in the imperative mood, also recalls the language of her earlier namesake.

To be sure, the commands that Propertius' Cornelia issues to her sons in 87–94 merely concern the way she would like them to treat their father's next wife or – if their father does not remarry – their father himself. Still, it merits notice that she defines her sons' major obligations to their father as emotional in nature. Although she mentions her husband's and brother's high public offices and demands that her daughter imitate her own mon-ogamous, moral life style in 65–68, she wants her male children to lift their father's spirits, not follow his political example.

These Roman literary portrayals of motivational speeches by elite women – speeches that resemble Cornelia's letter in striking regards – therefore suggest that this style of political, motivational speech was closely asso-ciated, at least in Augustan culture, with the female gender. This association, moreover, may well have occurred because this style of speech was itself connected with a much-scrutinized and admired woman like Cornelia. As we have seen, such efforts at dealing with an actually or even potentially insubordinate son certainly contrast with those attributed by Livy to Torquatus. Not only are these efforts motivational rather than punitive, but, in defining what is best for the Roman state, they also accord priority to family ties and family members' feelings over abstract political rights and principles.

It merits emphasis, however, that these Augustan authors who seem to echo Cornelia's letter do not limit such motivational speech and family-oriented, emotionally grounded political values to their female characters. For we find this same nexus of values being articulated to, and inculcated in, an adult male child by a father – Anchises – in Book 6 of Virgil's *Aeneid*. Encountering his son Aeneas in the underworld, Anchises instructs him in a basic political right and responsibility: to rule the nations under empire, imposing the custom of peace, sparing the conquered, and waging war against the arrogant:

> *tu regere imperio populos, Romane, memento*
> *(hae tibi erunt artes), pacis imponere morem,*
> *parcere subiectis et debellare superbos.*

But you, Roman, must remember that you have to guide the nations by your authority, for this is to be your skill, to graft tradition onto peace, to show mercy to the conquered, and to wage war until the haughty are brought low.

(Aeneid 6.851–853; trans. Jackson Knight 1958)

In so doing, he addresses Aeneas, generically and anticipatorily, as *Romane*, and commands him, archaically, with *memento*.

First, however, Virgil has Anchises parade before his son a host of men, as yet unborn, who provide both positive and negative examples of Roman civic and military leadership. In addition to the male kinfolk of Cornelia – both Scipiones and Gracchi – at 842–843, this group includes several Roman leaders who endured, and caused suffering, as a result of paying insufficient heed to family ties and feeling. Among them are the son-slayers Lucius Junius Brutus and Torquatus. The latter is mentioned briefly in 824–825, as *saevum securi*, 'cruel with his axe'. But Brutus receives a seven-line description, one that blends praise with criticism, at 817–823.

Virgil has Anchises label Brutus *ultor* (avenger), and hence respectfully allude to Brutus' avenging the rape of Lucretia by overthrowing the Tarquin kings. Yet he also calls Brutus' attitude haughty (*superba*), thereby calling to mind the Tarquin kings Brutus overthrew as well as Rome's military foes, the *superbos* whom Anchises will soon instruct his son to overthrow. And, after acknowledging that 'as a father Brutus will call his sons to punishment for [the principle of] fair liberty', and before observing that, however future generations regard Brutus' deeds, Brutus' 'love of country and passion for praises will prevail', Virgil has Anchises refer to Brutus as *infelix* (unfortunate). Brutus is thereby associated with Dido, who suffered and caused profound emotional pain by placing personal and political revenge ahead of her country's welfare.[13]

After imparting political advice to his own son, moreover, Anchises tearfully describes the unfulfilled promise and sorrowful funeral rites of Augustus' adopted son (and son-in-law) Marcellus, addressing Marcellus at 882 as *miserande puer* (pitied son). We should note, too, that Anchises earlier presents Augustus' adopted father Julius Caesar and his foe Pompey as father-in-law and son-in-law (*socer . . . gener*) on 830–831, and addresses them, too, as *pueri* (sons) in 832, when vainly attempting to motivate them against civil strife. Barbara McManus (1997: 110–14) has persuasively argued that Virgil has 'transgendered' the character of Aeneas by assigning him traits conventionally associated in contemporary Roman culture with positively valued female conduct, such as *pietas*, devotion to family. If Anchises' motivational efforts to inculcate family-oriented, emotionally grounded political values belong to a tradition conventionally associated in contemporary Roman culture with women like Cornelia, Virgil has 'transgendered' him as well.

This 'matriotic' tradition, of course, still thrives in our contemporary and male-dominated political landscape. Admittedly, Richard Bauman (1992: 43–4) characterizes Cornelia as a 'moderate conservative', although he acknowledges that her mind 'was not closed to liberal ideas as long as they did not subvert the existing order' and that she 'shared her father's relatively progressive views about popular sovereignty'. I, however, would prefer to regard her championing of family-oriented, emotionally grounded political values as a radical political stance. After all, such values have been most conspicuously voiced (though by no means exclusively voiced) by politically progressive, and at times radical, male leaders over the past century.

Those observing the thirtieth anniversary of Robert F. Kennedy's passing in June 1998, for example, extolled the family-oriented, emotionally grounded political values which RFK embodied, transmitted to his own children, and derived from his reading of Edith Hamilton and her vision of the ancient Greeks.[14] Strikingly, a recent biography by Michael Beran (1998: 177–8) claims that RFK spent much time with his sisters as a child (so much so that he was thought to be headed for sissyhood), and thereafter viewed women as 'an indispensable bulwark of character'. Cornelia, *mater Gracchorum*, may have lost her match with the renegade Gaius. But she has influenced later Roman, and modern Western, culture through a succession of males whose political visions have given due regard to family and feelings.

Notes

1 Cf. also Livy (2.5.5 ff.) on the death of Brutus' sons.
2 For the dates of Cornelius Nepos, see Hornblower and Spawforth (1996: 396) and Horsfall (1989: xv–xvi, 104). For the date of this letter, see Horsfall (1989: 42, 125), Bauman (1992: 42–5) and Courtney (1999: 136). I follow the text given by Courtney (1999: 135–6). The translation is my own.
3 On this phrase, see now Farrell (2001: 62–5).
4 On 'transgendering', see McManus (1997: 94–5).
5 For challenges to the authenticity of Cornelia's letter, see, for example, von Mercklin (1844: 27 ff.), Meyer (1894: 4.6), Herrmann (1964: 87–9), Astin (1970: 291, s.v. 'Cornelia'), Pomeroy (1975: 172–3), Dixon (1988: 179), Horsfall (1989: 41–2, 125), Bauman (1992: 43, 228–9), Badian (1996: 392, s.v. 'Cornelia'). Both Horsfall and Bauman posit – in the words of the latter – that 'even if Nepos [or an earlier editor] has not given us the letter as Cornelia wrote it, he has adapted his material without destroying its essential veracity'; still, they view the work as having undergone substantial modification at the hands of a man. Similarly, Courtney, following Instinsky (1971: 189), maintains that 'Nepos had occasion to quote this letter from the text of some historian . . . in which case it is a free composition by that historian'.
6 For (the more poetic) *senecta* and *senectus*, see Glare (1982: 1734).
7 For Gaius Gracchus' wife and son, see Plutarch (*Tiberius Gracchus* 21.1–2; *Gaius Gracchus* 15, 17.5).
8 On Veturia's speech, see also Ogilvie (1965: 334–6).
9 See, for example, the article on Livy by John Briscoe in the *Oxford Classical Dictionary*, third edition, 877–9.
10 See, for example, the article on Virgil by Don Fowler and Peta Fowler (1996: 1602–7).
11 For echoes of Cornelia's letter in speeches by Dido and Euryalus' mother, see Hallett (2002: 159–67).
12 For the date of this poem, and the later careers of this Cornelia's sons, see Hallett (1985: 73–88).

13 For Dido as *infelix* (at, e.g. 1.712 and 4.68, 450, 529 and 596 as well as 6.456), see Hallett (2002).

14 On Robert Kennedy, Edith Hamilton and the classics, see, for example, Hallett (1996–97) and Kennedy (1998).

3

POLITICS OF INCLUSION/EXCLUSION IN ATTIC TRAGEDY[1]

Nancy Sorkin Rabinowitz

What kind of influence could women wield in fifth-century Athens, given that they were, in some ways, defined as outside the *polis*? In this essay, I discuss that question, with specific reference to Greek tragedy; the female characters of tragedy are omnipresent, even dominant, in contrast to the situation of actual historical women (cf. Gagarin 2001: 161–2). Although in theory, and perhaps in practice, Athenian women were relegated to the home or private sphere, that boundary was unstable and required cultural work to reinscribe it. The tragic festival was one place where that work went on. In this essay I explore two potential sites of female influence – one the ancient production of tragedy, and the other feminist re-readings in the present. I will argue that though tragedy was consistent with the other institutions of democracy in excluding women, it also produced women as characters who were central and who wielded considerable political power. In the cases of Clytemnestra and Medea, their influence is construed as dangerous to the city and in need of control, in order to reaffirm the public/private dichotomy that their power undermines. Thus, I see female excursions into the public in Attic tragedy as signs of the dangerous strength of women. If we define women's influence as political, then, we have to see it as negative. As I will show, contemporary feminists can, however, make use of that influence in other ways by reading against the grain.

As should be clear, I see the question of women's influence as directly related to the so-called public/private dichotomy, which has organized much feminist thought over the last thirty years. At an early stage of second wave feminism, much US writing was devoted to finding universal causes of women's oppression, itself taken to be universal. The nature/culture dichotomy implied in the call for papers for the conference that led to this volume ('An Alien Influence') made up part of that discourse as the new women's studies scholarship took on the question of how biological male and

40

female in nature are turned into men and women in culture; this body of theory built on the basic insight of Simone de Beauvoir (and reframed by Monique Wittig) that one is not born a woman (de Beauvoir 1953: 301; Wittig 1992: 9–20). Two major early anthropological collections, *Toward an Anthropology of Women* and *Woman, Culture, and Society*, stimulated thinking along these lines. Michelle Rosaldo and Louise Lamphere introduce their volume with a statement of its concern for the sources of sexual asymmetry, which they maintain are not determined by biological factors. They ask 'how is it that social groups, which change radically through time, continue to produce and reproduce a social order dominated by men?' (Rosaldo and Lamphere 1974: 6, 7). This question dominates the first three papers in the collection, including Michelle Rosaldo's own essay, 'Woman, Culture, and Society: A Theoretical Overview', which offers the public/private dichotomy as a universal cause of women's oppression, and Sherry Ortner's 'Is Female to Male as Nature Is to Culture?', which suggests that it was because of women's perceived closeness to nature that they were taken to be less worthy than men.[2] Feminist historians were engaged in a similar investigation, although they developed the terminology of separate spheres, based on the language of the nineteenth-century ideologues.[3]

In a structuralist division of the world into binary pairs, culture and nature lines up with the public/private dichotomy or doctrine of separate spheres; and as Carole Pateman (1989: 281) argues, 'The dichotomy between the private and the public is central to almost two centuries of feminist writing and political struggle; it is, ultimately, what the feminist movement is about.' Pateman is talking about the relationship of feminism and liberalism: as she goes on to say,

> Feminism is often seen as nothing more than the completion of the liberal or bourgeois revolution. . . . Liberal feminism has radical implications, not least in challenging the separation and opposition between the private and public spheres that is fundamental to liberal theory and practice.

At least two paths underlay and then branched off from this discussion, one the Marxist critique, which saw the goal of the feminist movement as the entry of women into the work force, so that they would no longer be financially dependent on men. The other, radical feminism, took oppression based on sex as the root problem;[4] in time, its analysis of patriarchy gave way to what Alice Echols and others dubbed cultural feminism, which turned the tables and positively evaluated the world of women, seeing women's spirituality as a source of empowerment. Redefining power was part of this project, and particularly revisiting matriarchy (Echols 1989; cf. Eisenstein 1983; Hartmann 1981). The kinds of influence that women could have differed in these two perspectives. The former stressed the need for women to enter the paid labour force in order to be effective, the latter stressed the separate sphere as a locus of women's agency and power.

Like the assumptions imbedded in the slogan 'The personal is political', the conversation about public and private, to some extent, avoided thinking about race and other differences that divided women (Kerber 1988: 17).[5] Working-class women and African–American women were not, in fact, limited to the home, if by that we mean their home; but that did not mean that they were immune to sex discrimination, only that the discrimination they were subject to was racialized. I mention this here because the criticism of the racism of early feminist theory is closely related to the challenges to the traditional curriculum from 'multiculturalism', and that critique certainly affects classics. Until recently, access to high culture via the classics was, for the most part, limited to white men though there were some notable exceptions, including the African–American women who attended Oberlin in the nineteenth and early twentieth centuries. Thus, these early critiques of feminism apply to the academy as a whole, and to classics in particular. Not only were women excluded from influential roles, but feminism's own analysis marginalized the experiences of subordinate groups.

The racial critique points out the fact that belief in the salience of the binaries is an artefact of culture; they are discursively constructed and maintained. As Claude Lévi-Strauss (1969) makes explicit, the culture/nature binary is closely tied (even wedded) to marriage and the family through the incest taboo (which it both constitutes and is constituted by). The culture/nature and public/private binaries seem very applicable to ancient Athens and Mediterranean societies in general. Specifically, the greater humanity of Greek men was based on their being able to move from an involuntary form of association in the *oikos* to the higher freely chosen association of the city; women did not make that move, and thus did not appear to exercise choice. Remaining in the private sphere, they were less powerful, especially since men had authority over both city and household (Sourvinou-Inwood 1995; Woods and Woods 1978: 227).[6] The geographical city of Athens was inhabited by men and women, free and slave, Greek and foreigner, but it was also the ideological democratic *polis* of free, Athenian citizen men. Athens was a culture based on democracy, but it was also an elite men's club. We cannot minimize the novelty of the democracy that gave unprecedented direct power to the common man, nor can we forget that it also excluded women and foreigners from citizenship and was a slave-holding culture. By reciting these obvious points, but not usually mentioned together, I hope to show that though women were acknowledged to be part of the culture in one definition, they were also excluded from its public forms.[7] This ambiguity precipitated a tension between the elements on which the city-state depended for its stability, and which we can perhaps exploit to our advantage as feminist thinkers.[8] In the city women could only exert indirect influence.

The cultural work of the democratic city of Athens is, then, taken to be uniquely men's work. Xenophon's Ischomachus is proud that he is free to spend his time outside, because his wife is 'more than capable of managing everything inside the house by herself' (*Oeconomicus* 7.3). He believes that the division limiting women to the inside was made by a god on the basis of nature (*physin* 7.22); he then treats it as if it were not a hierarchy (7.13–19). Aristotle does not see the sexes as occupying complementary spheres, but rather subordinates woman to man in the family as a fact of nature, comparing their relationship to master/slave and father/children relations (*Politics* 1252a 24b–27, 1253b–11, 1254b 13–16). Thus, for the Greek thinkers, like later philosophers, nature supports the gendered division of labour, and a public/private dichotomy; culture/nature seems parallel and analogous to city/household, *polis*/*oikos*, masculine/feminine, although in fact the division itself is a feature of culture.

Thus, and I will develop this more fully later, ancient configurations of nature and culture, the public and private, were not static and clear cut, but that very lack of clarity may be useful as we try to figure out a better relationship between the two realms ourselves.[9] There is no doubt that current concerns about gender and sexuality demand a better thinking through of the relationship of marriage and family to the state, and the invention of new forms of relationality.

What is the relation of tragedy to the culture/nature or public/private binaries? On one level, tragedy was part of Athens' creation of a civic culture and shared in the ideological contradictions of democracy (see Sommerstein *et al.* 1993: 19); the theatre like the Pnyx and the agora was a distinctive location of Athenian democracy (Wiles 1997: 14). Christian Meier (1993: 3) hypothesizes that the citizens 'sought in the plays, in the festival of the Great Dionysia, renewed confirmation of their order and its principles, and of the justice of the world', On a more mundane level, the city controlled the production of tragedy: the eponymous archon of Athens granted three poets the right to produce plays, assigned the actors and appointed the choral leaders. Men who took on the expense of training the chorus were fulfilling a civic duty comparable to outfitting a ship for the navy. In the events surrounding the performance, tribute from the empire was displayed, male orphans of those who had died in battle marched in armour, and honours were conferred upon those (whether citizen or metic) who had served the city. This problematically democratic city then was crucial to tragedy. Others have put it eloquently. Oddone Longo (1990: 16) argues convincingly that 'These rituals were understood to be celebrations of the *polis* and of its ideology, and they constituted the immediate framework of the plays.' Simon Goldhill (1990) maintains that the Great Dionysia was fundamentally a festival of the democratic *polis*, basing his analysis on the ceremonies before the competition proper. More recently David Rosenbloom (1995: 104) has asserted that 'We can understand the City Dionysia and the genre of tragedy as a function of Athenian institutions regulating relations between the inside and outside of the *polis* – slavery, *metoikia*, the family, citizenship, warfare and hegemony, the agora and economy, cult and festival.' He points out that 'The festival and the genre projected an ideal image of Athens and disseminated the principles of Athenian identity' (1995: 105).

That ideal identity of Athenian culture was class and gender based: women were excluded from the cultural production of tragedy as they were from the assembly and juries. Although my teachers, emphasizing the mass cultural aspect of tragedy, used to say that 'everybody went to the theatre', that fact is debated, and at the very least, they went in different capacities. In his recent book on theatre production, David Wiles (1997: 26) asserts that 'The procession which came down this sacred way was a huge event in which the *polis* put its identity and structure comprehensively on display. . . . The council who sat as a collective probably walked as a collective, as did the ephebes on military service.' He notes in passing that 'Women were present, and their role as bearers of new life was symbolized by the maiden who walked in front with unripened spring fruit.'

While there is good reason to believe that women did attend the tragic festival, as with so much else about women in antiquity, it is striking that we cannot really know. Simon Goldhill (1994: 368) concludes a recent consideration of the problem by saying 'What I hope to have shown in this chapter is *not* whether women were present or not at the Great Dionysia. The evidence on either side simply will not allow such a firm conclusion.'[10] The fact that we cannot know does not mean that the gender of the audience would not have been a significant influence, for instance in the creation of the atmosphere of the event. If you take the view that women were members of the audience, then the playwright must have written for a mixed audience. Another view is that they may have been seated in the back of the audience in lesser numbers than men; the seating still arguably distinguished them from the men who were seated in tribal order, which reaffirmed their status as citizens.[11] Taking this view we are forced to recognize that the festival was not intended for women. That is, civic culture as constituted by the plays, the watching of the plays, was male. Women were eavesdropping. Thus, whether you take the extreme view – that women were not in the audience at all – or not, the end result is the same: tragedy was not meant for women's viewing.

The ambuiguity about audience is consistent with the rest of the performance practice: women were neither the authors, nor the judges of the plays. Furthermore, it is commonly accepted that the actors were male. This aspect of performance comports well with traditional assumptions about Greek culture, in particular with the public/private binary.[12] It was neither obvious nor necessary that men had to represent women in tragedy. There was no absolute rule for drama as a whole (see, e.g. Walton 1980: 146; Webster 1970: 32–3). Why shouldn't there have been women in the tragic festival, itself a celebration of Dionysos, when maenads accompany the god, and women are so important in ritual practice? Women did participate in the dithyramb, often taken to be the origin of tragic performance (Alkiphron 4. 18.16, Plut. *Mor.* 299ab), and did sing in public choruses (Calame 1977: 152–3; Seaford 1994: 262–75; Stehle 1997: 4).[13]

Displacing women from the theatre necessitated putting men in women's place (or using only stories about men, animals, or objects from nature) and, particularly given notions of gender construction, it was not without certain risks. Gender is a fact of culture, not nature. Maud Gleason (1995), Jack Winkler (1990), and Thomas Laqueur (1990) argue that the Greeks saw gender on a continuum; that masculinity was carefully constructed as the hard opposite of a soft feminine, but there was the possibility that the normative male could end up a woman. If they are right, then the male actor of female roles might be a dangerous figure.[14] Acting in general, and enacting women in particular, was problematic for Plato:

> We will not allow our charges, whom we expect to prove good men, being men, to play the parts of women and imitate a woman, young or old, wrangling with her husband, defying heaven, loudly boasting, fortunate in her own conceit, or involved in misfortune and possessed by grief and lamentation – still less a woman that is sick, in love, or in labour.
>
> (*Republic* 3.395d–e)

Under what circumstances was it worth running the risks to masculinity and the city? It has to have been important. Margarete Bieber's answer (1961: 9) is straightforward: 'Attic morality banished women from public life. Thus the parts of the maenads and of other women were always played by men.' Were women simply banished from public life? The very terms of the discourse (culture vs. nature, public vs. private) predispose us to see clarity where there is ambiguity and to take as a premise what is, in fact, being established. For instance, the association with birth and death, by which women are taken to be closer to the body and thus to nature, are culturally determined sets of practices. In any event, even if women of the citizen class were separated from men at home, and even if they did not freely leave the home, there were many occasions on which they did go out, for ritual observances, to attend at births and deaths, to visit, to draw water, perhaps more frequently than we know. The point then is that the festival was not just public, outside, but political, civic, one of the ways in which the city represented itself to itself. My hypothesis is that it was too dangerous to have actual speaking female bodies on stage because of the political aspect of tragedy; the city *wanted* to represent itself as a male culture. At the same time, however, that masculinity is bolstered by taking on feminine roles, because tragedy is to some extent a form of initiation, albeit civic more than cultic (Rabinowitz 1998; Seaford 1994: 273; Zeitlin 1985).

In this cultural artefact through which Athens represented itself to itself, then, real women were abjected, alienated, excluded, as they were excluded from the ideological construction of the democratic city, even though they inhabited the physical city. The plays themselves, however, repeatedly return to women and the family; thus we may see the female characters most definitely as an influence, albeit alien; though women were cast out from the political realm, representations of women nonetheless dominate the plots of tragedy. As is frequently pointed out, only the *Philoctetes* of extant tragedy has no woman character.[15] Moreover, considerations of gender have been very influential in contemporary studies of tragedy (e.g. Foley 2001; McClure 1999; Wohl 1998). Though an earlier humanist tradition focused on Greek tragedy because of its articulation of timeless verities, coming to them as a feminist in the postmodern era, I still find the plays stimulating not because they have the answers, but because they raise interesting and relevant questions and because they show the power dynamics in such stark and raw forms.[16]

What does the predominance of 'women' signify? If tragedy is a civic discourse of a society that normatively relegates women to the inner realms and then denigrates the private as closer to nature, why *are* women so influential in tragedy? What is the relationship of tragic discourse to civic and gender ideology? There might be a tension between the festival of tragedy, which celebrated the male civic order of Athens, and the plots of the plays. The playwrights might well have contested the ideology. Simon Goldhill (1990: 127) points to 'a questioning of the basis of those norms', and John Winkler (1985: 58) notes that 'Tragedy is the city's nurturance of that precious youth by a public ritual of discipline, enacting tales (more often than not) of its blight.' Might this not be true on the level of gender, as well? The staging of the plays clearly supports the view of the civic culture as a male space, while the plots make women prominent in that space. The plays show the interrelationship of culture and nature, city and family, rather than separating them, in part because of their focus on myth and the family. After all, in royal families, the private is the public, the natural ties of blood form the rulership. As a result, tragedy is a place where we can see the centrality of 'women' to civic order; constructions of public and private are deployed to control them.

The plays return to women and the biological family, in part, because the relationship of culture and nature is not stable but needs to be reinscribed; some of the tragedies do that by enacting the danger of a certain kind of female influence, marking her eruption from the private sphere into the public. Framing the issue as dichotomous, culture/nature or public/private leads us to turn our attention away from the relations between the elements, as well as the mechanisms by which the binary is constructed and maintained. Looking at the plays, we can understand those mechanisms better.

How do women in tragedy make their presence felt? The fact that women are prominent is not necessarily cause for feminists to feel optimistic. They are not restricted to the house, but to what end? I argue that they are not normalized as a power in the public realm; rather, their physical desires (often those associated with nature) lead them to be represented as the transgressors of a boundary that must be maintained. In the rest of this essay, I will focus on two famous transgressive characters, Clytemnestra and Medea; in each case I will ask first what we see when we look at them as outsiders to the *polis* culture. The plays represent mature women with active sexual desire as attacking men and, through them, the city. Then, following the lead of theorists of separate spheres who found a source of women's power in their occupation of separate space, I will turn to women's relations to women as a possible site of women's autonomy and agency. These texts have been exhaustively studied; I return to them in a somewhat schematic fashion because they present in particularly clear and interesting ways the complex relations of culture and nature.

As Athenian women were removed from political power, so when a character asserts her right to control, she may be punished for it. Her influence is resented, and the public/private line is re-established. In one reading of the *Oresteia* we see that Clytemnestra is made an active opponent of the civic/cultural order and is punished for it. In my early work on the trilogy, I argued that Aeschylus uses the framework of cosmogonic myth and represents Clytemnestra as a monster to be conquered in order to give Orestes the status of a culture hero (Rabinowitz 1976, 1981; cf. Foley 2001; Wohl 1998; Zeitlin 1978). She is made the dragon, and Orestes plays Perseus to her Gorgon and slays her. On the psychological level, the boy rejects his mother and becomes free and independent; on the mythic level, the hero conquers the dragon and establishes his lineage. Athena completes the creation of the city in the *Eumenides* both by freeing Orestes and by establishing the court of the Areopagus.

The political culture of the city cannot tolerate Clytemnestra; it has to get rid of her. The conflict between Chorus and Clytemnestra is framed in terms of the public as well as gender: she will be cursed by the people (*demos* 1409) and cast from the city (*apopolis* 1410), an object of hatred to the townspeople (*misos astois* 1411). Clytemnestra objects that the chorus did not mention the people before (1412); we know that they were aware of the grumblings of the people, did talk of complaints against the king, but they squelch them when Agamemnon arrives on his chariot with Cassandra; the victorious sacker of another city throws his glamour over them, leading them to forget their bitterness about the war. Clytemnestra, however, does not forget her bitterness about her daughter slain to make that war possible.

It would seem that French feminists like Hélène Cixous and Catherine Clément (1986: 67) were right when they analysed myth and said: 'There is no place for you in our affairs of state.'[17] Except, of course, that the affairs of state are put together by the traffic in women; the outsider is within. In Aeschylus' presentation of the myth, culture, as constituted by the language-based ties of city, marriage and the law, wins out over nature, the blood ties of family. Further, to the extent that Clytemnestra represents them, these values are eroticized by her speech of exultation to the chorus: she feels fertilized by the blood, and is titillated by having killed Cassandra, who adds a fillip to her bed (1447). Her physicality and energy are problematic for the culture of the city.

The move of the trilogy to Athens and the staging of a version of the Panathenaia make the contest for power over the female, positioned as elements of nature, more apparent. The Erinyes are transformed; the female-dominated blood relations they stand for are subordinated to the city's norms. The Erinyes serve Clytemnestra; they ooze blood and poisonous fluid; they are made disgusting, like the messy female Greek culture would keep in check. Later they are sanitized; through Athena's persuasion, the Furies don red robes and, like the non-citizen metics of historical Athens they resemble, become useful to the city. From the city's point of view, this is a happy ending. The house of blood ruled by 'two women' has been purged; we could say that nature has been brought back under control, as the woman who crossed the boundary is brought under control, and her negative influence is transformed into the positive influence of the Eumenides.

Aeschylus manages to make the sacrifice of Iphigenia and the murder of Clytemnestra count for less than the revenge killing of Agamemnon; he must do so in order to make Orestes and Athena the victors. To create order out of chaos, he used the conquest of 'a woman'. As a young woman and young scholar, I accepted the dominant reading about the great creation of democracy in the *Oresteia*. Coming back to the *Oresteia* and re-reading it after teaching courses in feminist theory, and in the wake of the critique of feminism's universalizing gestures from the perspectives of identity politics and postmodern theory, culture and creation still seem vital to the play. What can a feminist reading accomplish?

First, on a large-scale political level, by resisting the powerful pull to see the culture and nature binary as essential, we can see the construction of the place of women in culture and in the public realm. The trilogy lays bare some of the many ways in which power works and becomes stabilized (for the time being) in institutions. Clytemnestra's temporary power is controlled by making her an enemy of culture.

Second, Aeschylus makes it possible to question Agamemnon's decision to sacrifice Iphigenia, though I would argue that ultimately the trilogy ignores his mistakes and more than forgives him.[18] We can use the play to understand the construction of civic culture in our own day. Agamemnon's choice between his daughter and his army still haunts us: family must still be destroyed to make war possible, for instance, and the political institutions are still gendered male even though women now serve in the US army. Aeschylus questions Agamemnon's choice, though ultimately he rehabilitates Agamemnon. Can this process help us to understand politics today?

Indeed it can. Heroes are still created out of men, like John F. Kennedy, Jr, who take unconscionable risks with their own families. Second, we can interrogate the positive valuation that Aeschylus puts on the culture he lovingly creates. As a resisting reader, I question the public institutions of democracy that are established at the expense not only of the woman, but (because of the way Clytemnestra and the Erinyes are represented) of the body and the erotic. This abjection of the feminine from politics continues into the present. The power that Clytemnestra asserts is rejected in part because it is eroticized.

Third, once we have seen how the founding of the city-state overvalues marriage through its privileging of language and culture, we can look for new models. We can insist on not subordinating the bond of mother and child to that of husband and wife. That might lead us into new ways of thinking about 'single mothers'. This critique would also entail questioning the relation of state and family, the privileges handed out to married persons, and might indeed lead to questioning certain current political campaigns. How much would gay marriage, if permitted by the state, change the institution of marriage? How much would it work to normalize some gay relationships at the expense of other? (cf. Warner 1999)? In the context of current redefinitions of the family and kinship, Athena's preference for the legal bonds of marriage over blood ties can be taken as evidence that blood ties might be a site of possible resistance to the state. Is that a significant warning?

Fourth, on the level of the character, one can reject Aeschylus' vilification of Clytemnestra and valorize her strength. Indeed, Clytemnestra has enormous political power in *Agamemnon*; that is precisely the problem with her.[19] The public/private and culture/nature dichotomies do not limit the queen; she comes and goes freely. And the beacon speech attests her power. That speech goes on for 85 lines and leads the Chorus to reply that she speaks sense like a man; they believe her. It shows her power to command and gives the impression of great expanses of territory under her control. As in the Watchman's famous description of her *androboulon kear* (man-counselling heart), the text underlines Clytemnestra's masculinity and her related desire for authority or rule (see Foley 2001: 202–34; Wohl 1998: 103–10). Chorus and Cassandra find her masculinity terrifying, but the modern reader can find in her masculinity the creativity, the artistic bisexuality, so desired by writers like Cixous (Cixous and Clément 1986: 84–5), Woolf (1957: 102), Duras (1985). Biology is not destiny. It remains a question, though, of how much resistance we can find in that assertion, or how effective that resistance is, given the recuperation of the queen's power by Orestes' vengeance. Her imitation of the male and her assertion of her power in the quintessentially male realms do not unsettle male power.

The resistance offered by the Erinyes and their incorporation into the city is another place for feminists to focus. Froma Zeitlin (1996: 113) tracks a transition from the political power of Clytemnestra to the ritual power of Erinyes, but they too have status in the public culture. Although Apollo would simply cast them out, Athena knows that their female influence is essential and that she must integrate them into the life of the city. There can be no culture without nature. Thus, Clytemnestra's blood thirst and sexual desire are transformed into their concern for fertility. Even from Aeschylus' point of view, the power and violence remain, repressed but ready to return. The resistance offered by the Erinyes and their incorporation into the city is one place for feminists to focus. While Aeschylus does clean them up, the female principle is essential to civic success. As in the treatment of Clytemnestra, the structural emphasis seems to be on the civic and symbolic power asserted by Athena, but the goddesses emblematize a countervailing power beneath the conscious level; it remains to be seen how unsettling that remainder is, but at least we must realize that Athena's city is not simple and single.

Finally, feminists have to deal with Athena, for Clytemnestra is transformed into Athena as well as the avenging Erinyes; indeed the same actor would have played both. It is easy to make fun of Athena as any kind of female at all, or to put too much stock in her as female.[20] Nonetheless Clytemnestra/Athena still have a great deal of contemporary relevance: success in the public sphere may require wearing a business suit, if not an aegis. In the *Oresteia* in order for a female principal to have civic authority, she must be asexual; is it still true? The trilogy associates women with blood and liquid, and that is interpreted as problematic in Athenian culture. Can we change that evaluation? I have rejected readings which celebrate the vilified feminine, thinking that they focus too much on the silver lining and ignore the cloud. Reading deliberately anachronistically, salvaging what Aeschylus discarded, can have its merits for getting us to think differently. If we fail in the effort, that may be because we are stuck in the terms of an old dualism, or that though feminists now demand both the public and the private, we cannot imagine a synthesis of the terms we have been given.

So far I have been working to reveal the ways in which the powerful female is represented as a threat to culture, her destruction made essential to the creation of order; I have then read against that representation. As I said earlier, an emphasis on women's sphere and motherhood also came out of feminist discussions of the public/private. Does that have anything to offer us as a way of reading the *Oresteia*? In the myth, when deprived of her daughter, Clytemnestra takes civic power; in the trilogy, Aeschylus refuses to let the daughter predominate so that Clytemnestra's motives are undercut and she loses audience sympathy. In his presentation, the woman who is not a proper woman rejects the physical ties to her children, and to her male child in particular. Clytemnestra is made a bad mother in the *Choephoroi*, willing to kill Orestes if necessary; she did not even nurse him, as the Nurse makes clear. When Clytemnestra tries to revert to nature, by showing Orestes the breast that supposedly fed him, we know it is a false image. This woman who claims devotion to one child is represented as a traitor to two others; she claims the ties of blood, but is shown to be not closer to nature, but unnatural.

Clytemnestra resists the patriarchal order, moves from the private sphere and the world of women. In order to succeed, Clytemnestra must act like a man. In this and other ways, Aeschylus discredits the mother–daughter tie, the blood tie, in other words the matriliny, but we might be able to excavate it if we take our eyes from Aeschylus' presentation and look behind it.[21] If, as various scholars note, the light imagery in the play recalls the mysteries of Eleusis, perhaps we can excavate a buried image of Clytemnestra as Demeter (Headlam 1906; Stanford 1942; Thomson 1950). The goddess deprived of her daughter can make her displeasure felt globally, but the mortal mother can only turn against her husband. Interestingly enough, the *Agamemnon* has a chorus of old men; the Queen is denied any contact with the world of women. This staging isolates her, and then the dialogue associates her isolation with her aggression and masculinity. Not only is she divorced from other women, but she is shown in rivalry with Cassandra. There *is* a community of women made up of Electra, the Chorus and Nurse in *Choephoroi*. The commonality of these women is stressed by Orestes' initial view of them as a group – he cannot distinguish between one and the other (*Cho*. 10–21). They share a common sense of purpose, even though they have vastly different statuses (101–3). Orestes treats both Chorus and Electra in the same way: both should be silent in the house (579–82). Whereas Clytemnestra defies the category woman, these others conform. These are the women who are close to nature: the Nurse is associated with the physical in her speech about caring for Orestes, and Electra's unchecked emotionalism marks her femininity. Thus, it is 'women as victims' that Aeschylus represents connecting with other women and with nature; Clytemnestra's desires are rendered masculine and thus unnatural.

If we put this characterization of women within the play in the context of the performance practices and, in particular, the fact that these are not biological women, we realize that whatever Clytemnestra's resistance, whatever Electra's complicity/resistance, these characters are being used by the culture to think through issues of concern to it. We can similarly use them to ask questions of concern to us. What are the exclusions that found our democracies? How has the liberal ideology of the divorce of public and private blinded us and forced us to separate culture and nature? What kind of influence do women have in affairs of state? Feminists need to ask ourselves whether, like the Erinyes, we have to tame ourselves to be acceptable in the 'city'.

In Euripides' *Medea*, we once again see excessive female sexual desire and passion overrunning their borders, leading to revenge and destruction of the culture of the city. As Clytemnestra kills two in revenge for one, Medea's revenge spreads out around her direct target; like Clytemnestra, she is compared to the monster Skylla; like Clytemnestra, she is a threat to the city (Boedeker 1997: 127–48). Medea cannot be contained within the *polis*. A literally alien influence, she moves from city to city, from land to land; she is unwelcome and in exile.[22] Although Medea originally acted as culture hero and conquered the mythical beasts for Jason in his quest for the Golden Fleece and his quest for rule, her subsequent actions precipitated their flight from civilization in Iolcos. Thus her desire has rendered her cityless. Medea's speech to the Corinthian women of the Chorus highlights her tenuous relationship to civic culture. She first says that foreigners should go along with the norms of the city and not be wilful (222); later she points out that she must be more careful than these other women because she is the outsider; she does not have a city, nor her father's house (252–5).

In her case, as in Clytemnestra's, the intimate or familial and the cultural are inseparable (the family in question is ruling): because she threatened to attack Creon's family, she is exiled from the city; because she was attacked by a close relation, a *philos*, she attacks the ruler of Corinth (cf. Foley 2001: 81–2, 126, 212). Her exclusion from the city does not mean relegation to the household, however, for she also has no *oikos*; she has destroyed her natal family in the interests of love. As structuralist analysis makes clear, any woman is an outsider in exogamous marriage; depending on the extent of the exogamy, any woman might be cityless. Since, as Medea argues, each woman has to buy a husband (233), her situation merely exaggerates women's legitimate fears about marriage.

Unlike Clytemnestra, Medea is represented as speaking to other women as a woman. In that role she critiques the public/private split and the sexual double standard based on it. Once married, she says, men have many potential liaisons, but 'necessity gives women only one soul to look to' (247) because, she continues, 'They say that we live a life free of danger in the house, while they do battle with the spear' (248–9). As a reward for their bravery, men have multiple sexual options. But women are brave too. Medea goes on to establish that female claim, with her famous boast that she would rather stand behind a shield three times than give birth once (250–1). Thus, the work of the mother is more difficult than the work of the hoplite/warrior.

At the same time that Medea tries to get sympathy for herself from other women as a woman, like Clytemnestra she is anomalous and ultimately loses the Chorus' support. From the beginning, she is feared for her intransigence, like a rock or the sea (28), and she behaves like a male hero, Ajax or Achilles, in her attention to her honour, her fear of being a laughing stock. In her speech to the chorus, she draws attention to her emergence from the inner, private, space,[23] but gives it a masculine twist. We might expect her to apologize for a failure of *sophrosyne*, but instead she says that if she did not come out, they would have the right to think of her as haughty (*semnos* 216); in this passage (214–18), she sounds more like the male Athenian afraid of being accused of excessive devotion to private concerns.

There are other contradictions that blur the public/private divide. She concludes her speech by accepting the stereotype of women she has just undercut: 'Woman is full of fear in all things and a coward both as far as strength goes and in looking on steel; but whenever she meets injustice with respect to the couch of marriage, there is no mind more bloodstained' (263–6). It seems now that Euripides' Medea is not claiming a public status equal to that of men, only that women will defend the marriage bed (not even the entire house) as men defend the city. However, with these words in the air, Medea confronts Kreon who fears that very bloodiness and exiles her from the land. She gains the right to stay in the city by playing on gender and donning a mask of feminine incompetence. As in the speech to the Chorus, Medea shows her acute awareness of the power of public appearance; here she talks about the danger of raising your child to be *sophos*, and the danger of leading a private life. Her speech suggests complaints that would not be made about an Athenian woman of the citizen class, who was not supposed to be busy in the public realm because not a citizen herself. Most women did not have to worry about a reputation for *sophia*, but if they had one, they would be considered witches like Medea. Rhetoric in the law courts and the assembly were quintessentially male practices in Athens. Thus, although Medea plays on the stereotypes of femininity, her use of rhetoric masculinizes her (see Burnett 1973; cf. Foley 1989; Knox 1977).

Clearly *Medea* has a great deal to do with women and culture. Medea's effort to get sympathy for herself from women as a woman is followed by the Chorus' reflections on the masculinity of culture: men make up the songs leading to women's reputation for duplicity (421–2). Jason articulates very strongly what he feels that he has given Medea, and it is culture: fame and the power of law (536–40). She owes her reputation to him, and this is more valuable than gold (540–4). Civilization must eject Medea because it cannot control her, the sexual and aggressive woman. Like Clytemnestra then, Medea is active in *polis* life, leaves the *oikos* freely, and is masculine but plays the feminine. And she is constructed as lethal. The influence is negative, though powerful.

I have adopted a dual perspective of then and now – seeing women's influence as dangerous because it erodes the boundary of public and private. The plays I have looked at show women's power in the civic arena, but they make it threatening. As a feminist I can try to recuperate the influence wielded by Clytemnestra and Medea, but a wholehearted acceptance is made difficult because of the ways in which they are portrayed. Have Aeschylus and Euripides put their finger on something that we still need to take into account, or are they guilty of special pleading, stacking the deck? For instance, the *Oresteia* makes us ask what counts as a woman's success, or whether when women succeed it is any different from men's succeeding: is Athena a model any more than Margaret Thatcher was? These plays make feminists ask how far outside male institutions of culture we are willing to go, while they reveal the costs of inhabiting that culture. Doesn't our public/political culture still reject the wisdom that comes from outside by characterizing it as unruly?

In the end, it is not just by looking at the characters that we learn from tragedy. Rather, the very contradictions between prominence within the plays and exclusion from the dramatic festival can suggest ways to interpret the construction of our own reality. In these centrepieces of tragedy, it does seem that woman was to nature as man was to culture. The rewriting of those stories from another point of view will have to come in our own day, in other forms like French feminist theory or novels such as Christa Wolf's *Cassandra*. Our task as scholars and educators is to pull at the threads to show what influences have been alienated in order to make tragedy/democracy/culture possible.

Notes

1 Versions of this paper were presented at the symposium on 'Tragedy and the City' (University of Florida 1997) and at the University of Chicago (May 1998). I am grateful to the questions and comments of my colleagues on those occasions, as well as at the Exeter conference on 'An Alien Influence: Women's Role in Creating Culture'.

2 Rosaldo rethought that position a few years later (1980).

3 See the epigraphs to Kerber (1988).

4 See Gayle Rubin's classic essay, 'The Traffic in Women' (Rubin 1975), for a clear statement of these positions and their consequences.

5 For women's studies' exclusion of race as a factor, see for instance, Anzaldúa and Moraga (1981, 1983); Smith (1983); Smith, Hull and Bell Scott (1982); Lorde (1984); hooks (1989).

6 Cf. Hegel (1977) and his treatment of Antigone in 'The *True* Spirit: The Ethical Order'. I am indebted to Judith Butler's seminar on Antigone for this reading of Hegel.

7 On the name of Athens and Athenians, as it relates to the question of women's place in Athens, see Loraux (1981), Patterson (1981) and (1986).

8 So Hegel calls women the 'internal Enemy' to the state; see Rabinowitz (1993) for the outsider status as it affects Euripides' *Alcestis*.

9 Humphreys (1993: x, xi, xiv) remarks that our own distress about these subjects influences and is influenced by our reading of antiquity.

10 For a publication of the testimonia, see Podlecki (1990) who ultimately answers the question in the affirmative, but only on the basis of an assumption: 'Although the scales for and against women attending the theatre are about equally balanced, what seems to me to tip them in favour of women's inclusion is the central place held by drama in the educational program which Athens offered her citizens' (42). In contrast, scholars of the English Renaissance have evidence not only of women's attendance but also of a moralizing debate about it (cf. Howard 1988; Orgel 1996; Traub 1992).

11 Longo (1990: 16) makes the connection between city and the spectators: 'The community of the plays' *spectators*, arranged in the auditorium according to tribal order (no different from what happened on the field of battle or in the burial of the war dead), was not distinct from the community of *citizens*.'

12 For a fuller working out of the significance of the male actor, see Rabinowitz (1998). On another form of this bias, see Haigh (1898: 324).

13 On other forms of female public speech, see Blok (2001).

14 On the power of female acts in tragedy, see Foley (2001: 13).

15 Griffith (2001: 117) points out that 'over one-third of all speaking roles (including choruses) are female, and in several plays more than half the lines are delivered by women.'

16 Burnett (1998: xiv) emphasizes the distance between Attic culture and our own, arguing that the plays are 'categorically unlike what has been seen in the Western theatre.' I am not arguing here that Greek tragedy shared our values, but that by virtue of the plays' extremity (cf. Burnett's 'outsized and essentially impossible deeds', xiv) they show conflicts that continue into the present day. We can look to them for examples of what not to do. See also Meier (1993: 204–16). On reclaiming Greek literature from conservative ownership, see duBois (2001).

17 Cf. Irigaray 1985a, especially 'Blind Spot of Symmetry'; 1985b: 81–4, 127–8, 161. Irigaray (1985a: 75) makes what might be an allusion to the *Oresteia*: 'In this economy, woman's job is to tend the seed man "gives" her, to watch over the interests of this "gift" deposited with her and to return it to its owner in due course.'

18 Early readings focused on the justice issue, in particular the justice of Zeus, e.g. Lloyd-Jones (1971), Kuhns (1962). When I delivered this paper, Richard Seaford argued that feminist reading has so won out that these theories no longer have any power. That is only partially true, however (see Meier 1993, for example). If we do not accept Aeschylus' resolution, what resolution is possible?

19 The cities of Troy and Argos are destroyed in part by women who resist domestication: Helen as well as Clytemnestra ('destroyer of cities' *Ag.* 688, the Chorus calls her as they try to name her appropriately).

20 Sue-Ellen Case (1988: 15) calls her 'male-identified'; Kate Millett (1970: 114) says that 'Athena marches on spoiling to betray her kind.' Froma Zeitlin (1996: 114) sees Athena as the displacement upward of the androgynous female.

21 As Fritz Graf (1997: 4) points out about *Medea*, 'we tend to forget that, in reality, each of these works is just a single link in a chain of narrative transmission: on either side of the version that is authoritative for us, there stands a long line of other versions'.

22 McDermott (1989: 109) 'every city which has offered her nurture is ravaged or polluted by her presence'; cf. Friedrich (1993: 219–39), on her destruction of the city.

23 See Sourvinou-Inwood (1997) for a recent treatment of Medea's negotiation of good/bad woman. On the masculinity of Medea, see Knox 1977; Bongie 1977; Foley 1989; Boedeker 1991. Foley (2001: 258–9) discusses Medea's relationship of similarity and dissimilarity to the Chorus.

4

EXEMPLARY HOUSEWIFE OR LUXURIOUS SLUT?

Cultural representations of women in the Roman economy

Suzanne Dixon

The wool was never out of her hands without cause.
(*Carmina Romana Epigraphica* 1988: 14)[1]

For this reason, since that ancestral custom of Sabine and Roman housewives has not only totally declined but actually disappeared, the essential responsibility of the female bailiff (*vilica*) has grown to encompass the duties of the lady of the house.
(Columella, *Praef.* 10, book 12, *On Agriculture*)

Women have always worked and have always played significant roles in what we now call 'the economy' – for which there was no Greek or Latin word. Yet, in the modern West, popular and academic media continually address, and thereby problematize, women's place in corporate cultures and ways of assessing their unpaid contributions to subsistence economies or the voluntary sector. If women are still so alien to our dominant economic categories, how do we determine their impact on the classical equivalents? In this chapter, which is necessarily restricted to a narrow selection of sample activities and institutions, I suggest some possibilities but they involve a re-think of our own presumptions, both about what we can expect from the surviving sources and how we might define the economy and women's influence on it.[2]

In my 1988 book *The Roman Mother*, I noted that one of the crucial roles attributed to the ideal mother was the transmission of traditional moral values and Latin speech to the children of both sexes and the training of the daughter in specifically female skills and virtues. These included chastity and domestic industry, particularly spinning and weaving. Such praise accorded

56

Roman women in biographies, funeral eulogies (*laudationes*) and epitaphs proclaims their importance to Roman culture, but scholarship has defined culture narrowly and the presumptive female sphere even more narrowly. The diverse topics of this volume attest the revolution in this traditional concept of culture(s) and feminist classical scholarship of the last generation has made us wary of simplistic source readings.[3] Women and their activities appear in ancient media as symbols of virtue or vice. In Roman discourse, virtuous women are chaste and industrious, bad women are lascivious and lazy. In both cases, women are consigned to the private sphere and characterized first and foremost as wives and mothers, even when their roles as workers and breadwinners might be evident from incidental features of the same account.

There are, in addition, specific difficulties in reconstructing the economic cultures of Roman society, which are obscured by the strongly moral tone of many of the surviving source categories. The men of the senatorial class, the group which dominates our literary sources, represented themselves to the community and posterity in their political and military roles and, to a lesser extent, as patrons and benefactors. That they also engaged in some sense in profit-oriented activities is apparent, but their self-image (and their own laws) required some rationalization of this aspect of life, which was in any case excluded from the *genre* of history.

It is even more difficult to retrieve the attitudes of the mercantile and lower classes to their own commercial activity. In Roman sources, work of any kind is typically presented, if at all, in romantic settings, the Italian peasantry is invoked for rhetorical purposes and commerce is largely excluded from elite narratives as sordid. Historians today have to live with these built-in impediments to reconstructing Roman economic life. They are serious limitations, but pursuit of the clues they do throw out and the judicious use of 'controlled inference' can help us retrieve some trace of women's contribution to the Roman economy and to the culture of which it was an essential ingredient. Scholars have established that the senatorial contempt for most jobs was not shared by those who carried them out and that trades and commerce had their own culture.[4]

The task is not made any easier by the theme of moral degeneration beloved of Roman authors of diverse epochs and genres. Like their modern equivalents, they employed standard, favoured targets when venting their disapproval of contemporary morality. From time to time, they combined their anxieties about women with stock laments about the change (necessarily a decline) from the old ways. Such laments rely on a very hazy historical sense of traditional practices but sometimes purport to supply specific information about contemporary (particularly elite) practice. On scrutiny, the information often proves illusory or misleading, as reliable as modern tabloid claims about youth illiteracy.

Both work and wealth figured, as moral categories, in Roman constructions of contemporary decadence, but they are not addressed directly, in a
concrete way of use to a modern-day historian of Rome. Yet we must work
out some way of interpreting Roman laments about wealth. The moral
emphasis on its softening effect should not blind us to the fact that a new
kind of upper-class wealth did indeed accompany and fuel the cultural transformation of Roman Italy from the time of Hannibal's defeat and the
subsequent territorial expansion. Land capitalism and urban investment
surely became as much part of elite Roman culture after 196 BC as basilicas
or rhetorical schools, but – like the morally problematic issue of upper-class
involvement in commerce, let alone the livelihoods of the great mass of the
population – they were not fit topics for most literary forms, with the result
that circumstantial accounts of women's (or men's) pursuit of profit are few
and far between in the surviving *corpus* and we are sometimes reduced to
arguing about how to interpret literary stereotypes like Juvenal's contrast
(*Sat.* 6.287–90) of decadent modern Roman women with their ancestresses,
who had been too exhausted from their industrious woolwork to have energy
left for adultery. It was not only satire which resorted to such clichés: consider
Columella's claim, in the quote above from his agricultural manual, about
the changing role of the elite woman who delegated her traditional hands-
on role to a slave or freed subordinate. Yet children and husbands continued
to praise the women of their families for their devotion to household production, as in the tombstone quote above this text. The sources are replete
with such contradictions.

Roman women participated, as slaves and free citizens, in the world of
work and the market-place. Indeed, the domestic sphere itself was not demar-
cated clearly from the commercial in the Roman world. In this overview of
economic roles taken by Roman women, especially those performed in
conscious pursuit of profit, I take 'Roman culture' to include work and other
aspects of economic production which are poorly served by our surviving
sources, with a focus on business and exploitation of surplus produce rather
than subsistence activity.[5]

Although I have suggested that the references to women – particularly
those of the upper classes – as symbols of moral decline are of little use as
hard-core historical information, they may attest the cultural significance of
areas poorly served by the literary sources in general: work, wealth and
women. Commerce, as we shall see, seldom attracts even this kind of mention. When we do find references in Roman sources to commerce and profit,
the role of women is often excluded or obscured. It is almost a commonplace
now that women are typically the 'marked' category in dominant discourses.
Just as references in modern media (e.g. to factory workers) are taken to be
male unless specifically marked as female ('a woman doctor'), so ancient genres – literary and otherwise – regularly submerge Roman women in general

classes like 'slaves', 'Romans' or 'peasants'. They single women out from time to time to illustrate a moral point (e.g. the decline of traditional simplicity) or to address a 'problem' posed by women as a group. References to women's economic activities and legal standing tend to fall into the 'problem' category ('Should women stand surety for male debtors?'). Notwithstanding such inbuilt distortions, I maintain that careful reading of the texts and recourse to what Marilyn Skinner has termed 'controlled inference' can yield insights into the more mundane economic roles which Roman women performed.[6] I believe, moreover, that we can profitably (!) explore the interaction of cultural representations and economic 'realities', particularly in relation to the ideal of the virtuous *matrona* and the production of cloth.

In the ancient world, hereditary succession was, for the freeborn, a primary mode of acquiring wealth or transferring substantial property (Duncan-Jones 1974: 27; Hopkins 1978: 48).[7] Freeborn Roman citizen women always had the capacity to inherit a share of their patrimony on equal terms with their brothers, when the death of their *paterfamilias* father rendered them all legally autonomous (*sui iuris*). But a female heir lost free access to her own fortune if she passed into her husband's *manus* (literally, 'hand') and everything she owned merged with his (or his family's) fortune.[8] The property of a woman *not* in her husband's 'hand' was strictly separated by law from his. Both types of marriage existed for centuries, but the sources imply that women typically transferred to the husband's *manus* in the early and mid-Republic, while the separate regime became the norm by the early principate. One consequence of this was that women had to make wills to ensure that their own children succeeded to their estates.[9]

Indeed, all adult Roman women *sui iuris* – single or married – were subject to an institution, *tutela* (conventionally translated by the misleading term 'guardianship'), which compelled them to seek the endorsement of male *tutores* – traditionally, though not always in practice, their own heirs (brothers or cousins) – before carrying out certain legal acts which reduced their fortune or put it out of the reach of these heirs: making a will, freeing slaves, entering into the *manus* of a husband or father-in-law, selling land.[10] In describing an incident of 195 BC, Livy (34.2.11) has Cato the elder state that 'our ancestors did not even want women to conduct their private business without a *tutor*, but wanted them to be under the authority of their fathers, brothers or husbands',[11] representing a loose rhetorical summary of the legal position. This institutionalization of female legal incapacity in Roman law (and rhetoric) is a classic example of a cultural construct which misrepresented the active reality of property access. In the 1980s I explored this paradox and the complexity of historic adjustments to the institutions in numerous writings.[12] In this chapter, I am focusing on its cultural implications, particularly the repetition by male authors and speakers of this (increasingly anachronistic) principle.

Profit and the seriously rich

> Women of full age, after all, conduct their own business affairs and
> in certain transactions the *tutor* gives his permission as a matter of
> form. Indeed, the *tutor* is often compelled by the praetor to give
> permission against his will.
>
> (Gaius 1.190–191, 2nd century AD)[13]

By the late Republic, both *manus* and the 'guardianship of women' (*tutela
mulierum*) appear to have weakened considerably. This is generally acknowledged by scholars, although contemporary authors made few allusions to
the process of decline.[14] We must, therefore, make do with observations
from the jurist Gaius, supplemented with scattered references to specific
transactions which are of interest to the male letter-writer or orator in the
texts of the late Republic and early empire. These references make it clear
that the women of Cicero's and Pliny's circles acquired, exploited and transmitted their wealth on much the same basis as the men of their social
level, without any obvious limitation by male *tutores*. In a forensic speech
of 63 BC, Cicero half-seriously blamed legal experts for coming up with a
category of *tutores* bound to obey the women they were traditionally intended
to monitor (*Mur.* 27).[15] Given this conservative public stance, it is telling
that he himself was unable, some five years later, to prevent his wife Terentia
from selling an urban property (*vicus*) to further the campaign to restore
him from exile (*Fam.* 14.1.5; cf. 14.2.3). Clearly, Terentia was not in his
manus and not in the power of a living father. The property – probably
a block of apartments and shops – would have been a source of income,
like the rural holdings she exploited in diverse ways (*Att.* 2.4.5; 2.15.4).[16]
It is significant that Cicero mentions these transactions and properties in
his letters, but never makes any reference to Terentia's *tutor*, who might
well have been a former slave or a socially subordinate freeborn expert,
which seems to be the burden of Cicero's comment in the law-court in 63
BC. Even if the *tutor* (or *tutores*) was a relative, Terentia clearly made her own
decisions on the assumption that she was effectively independent of his
(or their) advice.

Like Pliny the younger more than a century later, Cicero sometimes shared
inheritances with female fellow-heirs (*coheredes*).[17] In addition to their inheritances from family, elite Romans often benefited from the estates of non-kin
– friends – of both sexes (Verboven 2002: 189–96). While professional usury
was beneath the dignity of the upper classes, loans at interest were a common
feature of upper-class exchange (Dixon 1993a; Verboven 2002: 116–182).
Cicero himself – who had invited a jury to draw sexual inferences from
Clodia's loan to his client Caelius Rufus – accepted a substantial loan from
his friend Caerellia, in spite of Atticus' warning that it might cause gossip
(*Att.* 12.51.3–45 BC).[18] Similar examples can be produced from

Cicero's speeches and from the letters of Pliny the younger, who shared inheritances with women such as Corellia and benefited from the wills of women such as Pomponia Galla. The wealth of Pliny's mother-in-law Pompeia Celerina was notable even within the fabulously rich senatorial order.[19]

It is frustrating that the letters are so skewed: we learn only of incidents and transactions which directly concern Cicero or Pliny or were subjects of general gossip or legal speculation. Even so, these examples amply demonstrate that many women of the elite were wealthy in their own right and treated their properties in the same way that their male peers treated theirs (Setälä 1998). The implications are interesting, for their involvement in borrowing, lending and inheritance attests the participation of women in the socially embedded exchanges of the upper class. These were sources of material enrichment but also expressions of friendship (*amicitia*) and all that that entailed (see Dixon 1993a, 1993b; Saller 1982; Verboven 2002). It is an economic corroboration of the literary impression that women of this group participated in the social life of their class on terms which, if not gender-neutral, strike a familiar chord with moderns: they attended mixed dinner parties where they joined in conversation on a range of topics, they wrote and received letters, they counted men as 'friends'. As one might expect, the implications of financial arrangements could differ for the two sexes. Cicero had, himself, demonstrated – and Atticus reminded him – that material exchanges between a man and a woman could be open to sexual interpretation. Vertical social relations were, on the whole, less likely to give rise to gossip. It was expected that upper-class women, like their male counterparts, held audiences of petitioning *clientes* and accepted the social and economic obligations (and benefits) of patronage to their former slaves (Dixon 2001a: 100–12).

Inscriptions sometimes throw light on these institutions. Pliny's account (*Ep.* 7.24) of the will and lifestyle of Ummidia Quadratilla, grandmother of his friend Ummidius, paints a vivid portrait of this grand old lady gambling and being entertained by the pantomime actors she retained for the amusement of her circle. An inscription recording her gift to her native Casinum of an amphitheatre confirms her wealth and her role as a regional patron, akin to the role Pliny played in his native Comum.[20] Another inscription from Puteoli commemorating a *libertus* pantomime artist is a likely corroboration of her interest in pantomime (*ILS* 5183). Nero's *libertina* (freed slave) mistress Claudia Acte appears in Tacitus's narrative of court intrigue and family conflict, then surfaces in inscriptions and papyri attesting her considerable landed wealth, particularly in north Africa.[21]

In the essentially agrarian Roman economy, land was generally perceived as the most desirable, respectable and stable means of support. All classes aspired to possess it: men toiled in the Roman army for decades in the hope of a small plot on retirement and those who made their fortune through commerce converted most of it to land.[22] Elite literary sources repeatedly express the view that mercantile activities are incompatible with the highest status and from 218 BC a law limiting the cargo of senatorials effectively forbade them to engage in maritime commerce – always regarded as the riskiest and least respectable of investments.[23] Since the legal prohibitions applied to 'senators and their sons' senatorial women should – like equestrian men of the upper classes – have been capable of engaging in such enterprises, but the convention might have extended beyond the technical limit. We are hampered by the ultimate impenetrability (to us) of social and practical distinctions which were apparently clear to the ancient actors. In spite of explicit denunciations of such activity, there are indications that by the late Republic, senatorial men were involved in maritime loans and export, either directly or through freed slave agents and debtors. Scholars have been divided on how to interpret the evidence. In the last analysis, we cannot tell how serious the moral sanctions were, how far they extended down the social scale and whether they changed over time.[24]

Stamped amphora remains, retrieved from dumps and shipwrecks, have yielded the names of women like Calvia Crispinilla or Caedicia, apparently engaged in viticulture and wine export.[25] Extensive cultivation of vines was considered highly respectable and profitable but required substantial capital investment.[26] It is not surprising, therefore, to find names from court circles in these records. We would class the production of amphorae as a form of manufacture, but to the Roman mind it was a natural extension of agriculture, like Varro's aunt (*RR* 3.2.14–15) running a profitable specialist farm just outside Rome to provide fowl for festive occasions in the capital. All such ventures were free of the taint of commerce.[27] The same principle applied to the manufacture of bricks, which were stamped from early imperial times with the name of the owner – *dominus/a* – of the factory and, therefore, of the land.[28] Of 149 such owners, 49 were women, some from the imperial family itself, such as the two Domitiae Lucillae (mother-in-law and mother of the emperor Marcus Aurelius).[29]

It is not difficult, then, to demonstrate that there were many wealthy women in the Roman elite and that they made profitable uses of their resources. Like their male peers, they utilized expert slaves and freed slaves to get the best result from their holdings (Aubert 1994). Such experts would continue to serve their former owners even after manumission with advice on investment and could be trusted to collect their debts and facilitate other deals. Terentia's freedman Philotimus performed all these services.[30] Other slaves could be trained in specialist jobs and set up in small businesses which would themselves yield a material and social return in the form of rents, gifts and loyal support (Cic. *Clu.* 178).[31] There is little trace of deference by these women to their husbands or *tutores*, nor – interestingly – do the moralizing sources complain of the women's independence as they do of their luxuriousness and acquisitiveness – a negative but rather telling lack.[32]

Businesswomen

The explicit contempt for commerce readily demonstrated in elite literary sources obscures the fact that the Roman economy accommodated a broad spectrum of businesses and that the scale of an enterprise largely determined its social status and moral acceptability. Or, as Cicero put it:

> Trade (*mercatura*) should be deemed sordid if it is petty but if it is on a grand, lavish scale, conveying many goods from all over the world and imparting them to many recipients without hype, it is not quite deserving of condemnation.
>
> (Cic. *Off.* 1.151)

Businesswomen, accordingly, ranged from shopfront artisans to high-powered merchants (*negotiatrices*) engaged in commerce and shipping on the grand scale, or great landed ladies funding the ventures of their social inferiors as gracious patrons. We have already seen that women of the highest social order were involved in the manufacture of bricks and amphorae for the market.

While it is possible to collect examples of specific Roman women with commercial interests, or to cite passages assuming their existence as a group, serious social and economic analysis is bedevilled by the usual vagueness of our sources on such subjects and exacerbated by the general tendency to exclude or obscure female involvement. Spanish inscriptions record women ship-owners engaged in the export of wine (*CIL* 15.3691, 3729, 3845–7). Claudius's legislation granting special benefits to freedwomen importers of grain to Italy makes it clear that women could not only engage in such high-level commerce but that some exceptional women could attain such prosperity in spite of servile origins.[33] The matter-of-fact reference by the jurist Paulus to the estate of a *negotiatrix* demonstrates the social acceptability of enterprises on this scale and – by implication – that it was not surprising for women to engage in them (*Dig.* 34.2.32.4).[34] In the late Republic and early empire, the term *negotiator* implied greater social elevation than the more mundane *mercator*.[35]

Such references, however, are relatively unusual – even more so than general references to commerce or to male *mercatores* and *negotiatores*. We are reminded that women are the marked sex, mentioned specifically only for some special cause. Ulpian's ruling in the second century AD that a masculine expression in the praetor's edict covered women as well as men, 'for there is no question that women can conduct business and be involved in litigation about it', makes it clear, on the contrary, that there *was* such a question in some minds (*Dig.* 3.5.3.1).[36]

It is difficult, though, to know when these male terms *do* include actual women. Unlike *negotiator*, the word *mercator* has no obvious feminine form, so the plural *mercatores* might sometimes imply women. The general term *tabernarii* and its singular *tabernarius* denoted the shopkeeper/artisan class, but the female *tabernaria* referred only to a woman who kept a wine-shop and whose respectability was therefore equivocal, although as landlady she was respectable enough (unlike her slave or free barmaids) to be subject to the sexual prohibitions of the Augustan *Lex Iulia*.[37]

Other problems of economic interpretation present themselves. The eternal question about the extent of upper-class – particularly senatorial – participation in commerce is complicated by high-minded ideological statements (e.g. Liv. 21.63, Cic. *Off.* 1.151, Tac. *Ann.* 4.13. Cf. Wiseman 1971: 77–89). The wealthy patron – male or female – who lent a substantial capital sum to an artisan or shipping entrepreneur might be perceived as a benefactor rather than an investor. For the upper-class creditor, this had the advantage of limiting the risk of financial loss and of social opprobrium (although our impression of the latter could well be exaggerated by the literary sources). Literary references to such transactions usually specify that the inferior party is a freed slave, but that might reflect the general literary (and legal) skewing towards relations between the upper classes and their slaves or former slaves, rather than the free poor.[38]

We have seen that upper-class women participated in the social-financial networks within their own stratum. They also extended patronage to lower social groups, notably to their own freed slaves.[39] The wealthy municipal Italian widow Sassia provided her freedman doctor with a shop from which to practise his profession – for a sinister aim, according to Cicero, but such an arrangement between patron and client was probably common. The capital loan or investment would constitute a *beneficium* in the terms of Roman patronage, and yield the patron a small income (*officium*) as well as the usual social return of *gratia*, a public acknowledgement of the relationship.[40]

Inscriptions commemorating the artisan-shopkeeper stratum show a high incidence of freed slaves, particularly in the district around Rome, where the greatest number of such references is found.[41] The typical workshop is a small family affair, with a married (or cohabiting) freed slave couple at its core and a small number of slaves or freed slaves of their own involved in the enterprise. Studies of 'occupational inscriptions' have focused on the subjects as workers rather than on the workshops as businesses.[42] Women often appear in such inscriptions, but seldom with a job title, particularly within *tabernarii* inscriptions, for reasons which are not clear.[43] They do, however, feature as owners – of slaves and, by implication, of the business in which the slaves have been trained. The names of manumitted slaves in small businesses reveal both joint and separate husband–wife ownership and sometimes show that the wife purchased and manumitted the husband himself (e.g. Cameria Iarine, *CIL* 6.37826).[44] Other women appear as single operatives, an example being the Ostian shoemaker Septimia Stratonice, commemorated by a male friend, M. Acilius, for her favour (*beneficium*) to him.[45]

In considering the operations of small businesses, we encounter the usual source difficulties over details. We cannot even be certain that artisan specialities were transmitted (as one would expect) through family traditions and whether particular workshops were operated by the free occupants in their own right or on behalf of their former owners. All the evidence is ambiguous. The shops at Puteoli which Cicero (and perhaps Ovia) both inherited from Cluvius were expected to yield a significant income (*Att.* 14.10.3; 16.2.1; 16.6.3).[46] Iunia Libertas of Ostia bequeathed the income of an apartment block, including shops and gardens, to her former *familia* and their descendants (Dixon 1992). But we do not know if the lessees of such lucrative properties rented in their own right or in their capacity as slaves or agents for owners and patrons.

Legal references to women owning or managing businesses confirm that they were not viewed as an oddity.[47] Gender divisions were expressed in different ways, notably in the public representation of work categories and the apparent exclusion of women from guilds.[48] Their roles are also obscured by generic and social skewing, as in the general tendency to describe groups – whether *tabernarii* (shopkeepers), *servi* (slaves) or *negotiatores* (merchants) – in the masculine or to embed them in collective nouns like *familia* (slaves of a particular owner) or *plebs* (the free, non-lite citizenry). Diverse references to women in business are nonetheless sufficient to make it clear that they fostered the international exchange of goods which characterized the complex economy of the Roman empire. They also contributed to the commercial culture of Roman towns and to the patronage networks which underpinned small businesses, established by freed slaves who had been trained in prosperous households. Sometimes funded by their former owners and retaining social and financial links with them, such freed slaves then trained and manumitted slaves in their turn, thus maintaining and widening the specialist base of the *tabernarii* class of artisan-shopkeepers in successive generations.

Women and cloth production

The role of the Roman *matrona* in producing clothing for the free and slave members of her household came to symbolize feminine virtue in particular and traditional Roman virtues in general. The practical components of the task were passed from mother to daughter (or from other older generation women to little girls) in a chain of cultural transmission which involved women of all status groups. The task itself became synonymous with efficient management of the household or estate and care of its members. The role is associated with famous icons like Lucretia (Liv. 1.57) or 'Turia' (*CIL* 6.15271 = 37053) and invested with moral meanings. Augustus boasted publicly, as part of his own moral image-making, that it was performed by the women of his family (Suet. *Aug.* 64, 73). But it was also associated with many of those women, nameless and otherwise, of little interest to the traditional historian but valued by their families for their domestic contribution. Consider this example from the vicinity of Rome in the 2nd century AD:

> Here lies Amymone, wife of Marcus, an excellent and very beautiful woman, who worked at wool, was dutiful, virtuous, thrifty, chaste and kept to the house.
>
> (*CIL* 6.11602 = *CE* 237)

which echoes the oft-quoted tribute to one Claudia, dating to the late 2nd century AD (*ILS* 8403 = *CIL* 6.15346).[49]

All ancient sources assume widespread female involvement in the process of turning fleeces into cloth. The women concerned ranged across the social spectrum, from contract weavers to slave spinners and freeborn women of high social station. Representations of their work and of the women themselves vary greatly, according to the *genre* and to the status of the woman designated. Consider Arnobius' reference to slave weavers telling each other folktales, 'weaving-girls passing the time in their tedious work' (5.14; cf. Petronius *Sat.* 33.3; Ovid *Met.* 4.39).

For wives, participation in the process – including the supervision of female slaves – symbolized the female virtues of industry and devotion to the household which (along with thrift) were publicly proclaimed in funeral *laudationes* and epitaphs.[50] There have been attempts to argue away the role of the free elite *materfamilias* in the process on the grounds that tombstone praise of the *lanifica* must have been emblematic in the case of 'busy women of affairs like Turia' and amount to little more by the late Republic than a generalized accolade for being a 'good wife'.[51] Such readings rely heavily on modern assumptions about appropriate status roles (i.e. rich women do not make clothes) and economic distinctions, notably between domestic and commercial production, which are not necessarily applicable to the ancient context. A few Roman authors imply that contemporary society women disdain wool-work and leave it to their slaves, but such comments fall into the general category of laments for the past which would have us believe that young noblemen had abandoned all military pursuits by the 2nd century BC.[52] The bulk of references support the contention that slave and free women continued to be crucially involved in the provision of cloth for domestic and commercial needs, both as workers and owners. Those who write about the Roman economy pay little attention to women, but when they do, they associate women's work with the domestic sector and lean to the view that more specialized and 'industrial' production for the market was undertaken by men, especially slaves, with some slave and freed women playing a minor and subordinate role (e.g. Moeller 1969).[53]

But, in the ancient world, even shopfront businesses involved in the cloth 'trade' spanned the domestic and commercial sectors. Archaeological finds, notably in Pompeii, confirm that relatively large-scale cloth production and processing could take place in residential settings, even in residences of some social consequence.[54] The fact that other types of production were also sited in residences strengthens the impression that the modern separation of the home and workplace is not applicable to the Roman context.[55] The inclusion in the funeral monument of the Statilii Tauri of slaves with job titles denoting specialist aspects of cloth treatment implies the involvement of this noble family in the textile business. The designation of eight slave-women as spinners – a low-status category, rarely commemorated in epitaphs without reference to their owners – has been taken as indicating a 'factory atmosphere' (Treggiari 1975: 99).[56]

Several freed slaves who appear in epitaphs sharing the *gentilicium* Veturia/Veturius and a role in the provision of dyed cloth suggest a different relationship between shopfront operations and their likely origin (*CIL* 6.37820, *NS* 1922, 144; *CIL* 14.2433; 6.9489). The examples do not appear on a single *monumentum* and the precise relation of the different Veturii to each other is conjectural, but the recurrent association with textiles, particularly dyeing, is suggestive. Each inscription appears to commemorate members of a small workshop, probably a husband–wife business. It has been inferred that there must, at some time in the Republican period, have been a prosperous family which trained slaves in this specialist aspect of the luxury cloth trade and that the groups commemorated in epitaphs possibly represent small off-shoots of that original business, run by freed slaves either as managers or independent owners.[57] The households of the Statilii and of the (original) Veturii might therefore have served both as domestic residences and as workshops producing at least in part for a market. The smaller businesses generated by the Veturii, begun probably after the manumission of the key parties, all seem to have been family-based concerns, with a free couple at the core, like the shops (*tabernae*) discussed above. It is clear that women were involved as slave-owners and – as far as one can see – as shop-owners throughout the process of transmission, whereby slaves would be trained in a more prosperous household and, if manumitted, eventually train and manumit a successor in their own small business. Examples include the *purpuraria* (merchant or producer of purple/scarlet cloth) Veturia Fedra, who commissioned *CIL* 6.37820 'with her own money' (*sua pecunia*) and Veturia Tryphera, who dedicated *NS* 1922, 144 to her *purpurarius* husband Atticus (a fellow-freed slave of Decimus Veturius) 'in accordance with her judgement' (*arbitratu*).

It is not really surprising that interpretation of Roman epitaphs, typically terse and formulaic, involves 'controlled inference'. This applies to reading family, commercial and patronal relations. Joshel (1992) has argued that family and patronal links are sometimes subordinated to work in inscriptions of this type, which typically commemorate a mixed-status group from a small shop. It is noteworthy that business-owners' children are not mentioned in these apparently work-based commemorative groups, except by implication, although the general presumption is that they were also trained by their parents in the family trade and would inherit the business in the normal course. The only reference to children in this block of inscriptions is *CIL* 6.9489, in which Veturia Deutera states that she has erected the monument 'for herself/themselves and hers/theirs'.[58]

There seems little doubt that, as part of her wifely duties as *materfamilias*, a Roman matron of any social level accepted responsibility, as supervisor and participant, for supplying the clothing needs of family members and the wider slave household (*familia*). In her absence, a *vilica* (farm bailiff's wife) or *lanipenda* (in an urban household) stood in for her and allocated the work to the slave women of the establishment (e.g. Pomponius, *Dig.* 24.1.31.*pr*.). Production for a market – including specialist tasks such as fulling and colour dyeing – could also be encompassed in larger, prosperous households run on the usual lines with a free *materfamilias* presiding over the largely female workforce, but delegating some powers to a slave forewoman. This was apparently the case with the Statilii Tauri. Smaller shops, specializing in fine tailoring, mending or dyeing, like those of the Veturii cited above would be run as family businesses, often by freed slaves who had been trained in the larger establishments or in similar small family businesses.

The various stages of cloth production and its sale or provision to households seem therefore to have been spread between the domestic and commercial sector as they would now be defined. Some prosperous households would have been in a position to market surplus cloth in the same way that surplus agricultural produce was marketed after the retention of the necessary goods for the producing unit. Other shops would have operated as largely commercial concerns, from shopfronts or *textrinae* positioned in residences. Women seem to have been involved in most of these processes, with the acknowledgement of their roles varying according to their social status.[59] The work considered low-grade if done by a slave in a factory context or by a contract-weaver to support her family was elevated to a cultural emblem if performed by a housewife or mistress of her own establishment and celebrated by her family on her epitaph or in her funeral eulogy. While the role of slave (or freed slave) men in weaving is still debated, spinning is always assumed to be a female task, so the strong implication is that women were the teachers of both essential skills, whether as mothers teaching daughters, as slave-women teaching female charges and subordinates or mistresses teaching slave-girls in their own households. Whatever the finer points of job allocation and market orientation throughout the empire, women surely had an impact on the economically and culturally crucial activity of cloth production.[60] Far from demonstrating its emptiness, the elevation of this particular aspect of female productivity to a moral category and its durability underscores its material and cultural importance.

Conclusion

It will be evident from this brief overview that generic conventions frequently obscure the economic roles of women in the Roman world, not least by excluding or allegorizing them. Representations of women's work, wealth and commerce suffered particular distortions and omissions. Exclusions and skewings in a range of sources – shop-signs, epitaphs and funerary iconography among them – attest a dominant preference for consigning virtuous women to the private realm. But this vague cultural bias is not backed up with systematic exclusion of women from acquiring or using wealth on a basis comparable with that of their male peers. The examples cited here confirm that artisan women seem to have exercised their crafts freely even if they were excluded from *collegia* and perhaps from formal apprenticeships.[61] We have seen, too, that women managed or owned small shop-front businesses and elite women exploited the vast agricultural holdings they inherited on much the same basis as their brothers, with the assistance of expert advisers and freed slave agents.

By Cicero's day, children regularly inherited from their mothers, in spite of inbuilt limitations on women's testamentary capacity. Institutions such as the 'perpetual guardianship of women' and the husband's potential power, under *manus*-marriage, to control his wife's estate had eroded significantly by the late Republic. Their continued invocation and exaggeration in masculine discourse – including that of the imperial jurists – suggests a male need at some level to construct women as dependants, while collaborating in the effective economic independence of the women in their lives. If the Roman patriarchy seriously wanted to lock women out of business and wealth, it did a poor job of it. But the relative silence about senatorial wealth creation and enhancement makes it difficult for us to analyse elite methods of training the younger generation in estate management. This applies equally to male and female proponents of the mindset behind the frankly commercial activities which emerge from the ideological haze of the literary references to property sales, rentals and loans for profit.[62]

Today, it has become commonplace to refer to a 'business culture' or 'corporate culture', but the conventions of ancient (mostly elite, masculine) public discourse make it difficult for us to discern the classical equivalents. Above all, scholars wanting to reconstruct the factual basis of ancient attitudes and their preservation have to contend with the overwhelmingly moral preoccupations of their sources. As always, we must base our assessment of the female contribution to Roman culture on our readings of male-dominated sources and decide where we wish to place the emphasis. While misogynist and paternalistic references to women exist in Roman literature and law, they are never stigmatized as 'other' in the consistent style of Aristotle's political and biological taxonomies. Against the tendency to play down or denigrate female commercial activity we must set the elevation of the Roman woman as mother and hardworking mistress of the household. In these recurrent images, we find a contrast with the Greek equivalent.[63] The mother is cast as a vital transmitter of traditional Roman culture and wives are valued for their work in running the household and, in particular, for their responsibility for cloth production. This high-minded emphasis of the commemorative genres translates in practice into women, as mothers, training their daughters in the work of the household and, as mistresses of the household, in passing on to their slave-girls the standard and specialized skills which might eventually earn them their manumission and then their own ability to transmit these skills in their turn to their own daughters and slaves of either sex. Artisans and shopkeepers had their own cultures, distinct from those of the upper classes who patronized them (in every sense of the word), and we are very slowly learning to discern that hidden culture, obscured by pompous ruling-class pronouncements about the status of paid work and commerce. We have seen that Roman women feature in all these groups. That they – and their children and menfolk – chose primarily to represent them to the community and posterity in their roles as exemplary wives and mothers might suggest that it was in those 'private' functions that they exercised their primary influence and from which they derived their social power. Bereaved husbands celebrated their wives' industry, orators praised the stern mothers who passed on Roman values and language – perhaps all of these are coded references to the ways in which Roman businesswomen and workers wielded influence and transmitted the economic skills appropriate to their class.

Notes

1 From an epitaph in the vicinity of Rome, 1st century AD.
2 I have discussed these issues in greater detail in Dixon (2001a: chs 6–8), and in my article on female occupations (2001b).
3 For a review of feminist scholarship, see the introductory chapter of this volume and the first chapter of Dixon (2001a).
4 Cic. *Off.* 1.150–1 is the classic upper-class statement of the moral value of different trades. Cf. Aristotle *Pols* 1256–1328. See Kampen (1981a), Joshel (1992), Dixon (2001a: 113–16; 2001c) for attitudes of the Roman lower classes to their work.
5 This is a demarcation of convenience. As I argue here and elsewhere, the domestic and commercial economy were not distinct in the ancient world, and a lot of economically significant labour was domestically based and oriented. See especially Dixon (2001b: 1–20).
6 'Real women, like other muted groups, are not to be found so much in the explicit text of the historical record as in its gaps and silences – a circumstance that requires the application of research methods based largely upon controlled inference' Skinner (1987: 3).
7 Cf. Shatzman (1975: ch. 2) on the difficulties of tracking the origins of specific fortunes. As always, the fictional example of Trimalchio's inheritance from his master is suggestive (Petronius *Sat.* 75–6). Dowry was another major means of property transfer. Gifts, technically limited at law, were in reality entrenched in the social realities of Roman patronage, as in the case of the small farm Pliny the younger gave

to his former nurse (*Ep.* 6.3.1). On patronage generally, see Saller (1982); Wallace-Hadrill (1989); Verboven (2002).

8 See Crook (1986) and the relevant chapters of Gardner (1986), Arjava (1996) and Grubbs (2002) for elaborations of the hereditary position of women in Roman law. Crook (1967: ch. 6) and Dixon (1992: ch. 3) and Champlin (1991) deal with Roman inheritance generally. Many of my articles elaborate the principles discussed here e.g. Dixon (1984a; 1985a). And see the references in n.12 below.

9 See Dixon (1988: 44–60) for details of this historical development.

10 The details are specified by Gaius (1.190); Ulpian (*Tit.* xi.27). The connection between inheritance and *tutela* is summed up in *Dig.* 50.17.73, based on a Republican statement by the first Q. Mucius Scaevola. See Dixon (1984b) for historical changes.

11 Cato's character as a colourful conservative was established by the time Livy composed his history in late Republican and early Augustan Rome. The statement is not necessarily to be taken more seriously than Cato's warning that allowing women to wear gold jewelry (and therefore to benefit from the public demonstration they had staged) amounted to letting them run the state political system.

12 Most notably, in the case of *tutela mulierum perpetua* (the 'guardianship' of women). Dixon (1984b) discusses in some detail the legal ramifications and theoretical significance of the institution. The reality of women's access to property (as against the notional limitations) has also been explored in some detail in Dixon (1984a) and (1985a). See Dixon (1988: ch. 3) for the role of mothers in Roman inheritance, and Dixon (1985b) on daughters and succession. For those with little Latin but an interest in pursuing issues of Roman law, Grubbs (2002) with its extensive collection of translated sources, should prove invaluable.

13 Cf. Paul, *Dig.* 34.2.32.4 on the will of a *testatrix negotiatrix* and the status of her merchandise following her death; or *Dig.* 3.5.3.1 (Ulpian), affirming that a masculine term in the praetorian edict included women, 'for there is no question that women can conduct business and be involved in litigation about it'. Inscriptions concerning *negotiatrices* include *CIL* 12.4496 (Narbo), *AE* 1973, 71 (Rome), but see Treggiari (1979: 84) for possible qualification.

14 On the shift in marriage preference, see Treggiari (1991: 442–6); Dixon (1985c: 357–361). On the change in *tutela mulierum*, see Dixon (1984b); Crook (1967: 113–115).

15 He refers to *genera tutorum quae potestate mulierum continerentur* – presumably, dependent *liberti*, former slaves freed by the women in question.

16 She owned woodlands and leased public land, probably for pasturage. On the income from the *vicus*, compare the annual return from the properties on the Argiletum and Aventine hills which Cicero retained from her dowry for the support of their son Marcus, following the divorce settlement March 45 BC, see 12.7 and compare *Att.* 15.17; 15.20.4.

17 Ovia was probably a *coheres* with Cicero in the estate of Cluvius (*Att.* 16.2; cf. 16.6.3). *Att.* 14.10.3 seems to concern Cicero's attempt to buy out her share of the estate. Alternatively, he owed her money.

18 Cf. Cicero (*Cael.* 31, 33) on Clodia's alleged loans to Caelius.

19 Corellia, an old family friend of Pliny's, bought some estates from him at a favourable rate in a friendly business deal between co-heirs (Plin. *Ep.* 7.11). In *Ep.* 5.1 he discusses the social consequences of Pomponia Galla's will, in which she had passed over her son in favour or Pliny and other heirs. On the estates of the wealthy Pompeia Celerina, see Duncan-Jones (1974: 324), Pliny (*Ep.* 1.4).

20 On the amphitheatre and temple she built for Casinum, see *CIL* 10.5813 (*ILS* 5628). *AE* (1946, 174) seems to indicate that she restored a theatre which her father had built, but see now Fora (1992).

21 See Tac. *Ann.* 13.12; 13.46 and 14.2 (with qualifications) for her role in palace factions. Inscriptions and papyri which throw light on other aspects of her life include *CIL* 10.7489, 7980, *CIL* 6.15027, *ILS* 1742; *P. Berl. Inv.* 7440 (recto). The presumption is that Acte benefited more substantially from Nero than Pliny's old nurse did for her services to her master. The moral is one that would be drawn by a Roman satirist rather than an orator, perhaps.

22 See Cicero (*Off.* II.87), Cato (*Ag. Pref.* i–ii) on the respectability of land. See also Hopkins (1978: 49–51) and cf. Rawson's examples (1976: 93–5) of humbler landowners, including the retired gladiator of Horace (*Epist.* 1.1.5).

23 On the *Lex Claudia* (or *Flaminia*; or possibly *plebiscitum Claudianum*) see Livy (21.63). On the view of maritime investment, see Cicero (*Off.* 1.150–1), Plutarch (*Cat. min.* 21) and cf. Petronius (*Sat.* 76).

24 See esp. d'Arms (1980, 1981); Finley (1973); also Hopkins (1978: 52); Paterson (1982). Jongman (1988) has a good summary of the more general issue of senatorial investment in commerce.

25 Calvia Crispinilla appears in *ILS* 8574a and b; *CIL* 3.12020, 7; 14371, 7. Her husband was implicated in Messalina's downfall (Tac. *Ann.* 11.36). The Caedicia Victrix who appears in the amphora stamp *ILS* 8573 may be the woman exiled from Italy 65 AD (Tac. *Ann.* 15.71). Cf. *CIL* xi.6695, 23; *CIL* 10.6252.

26 On the profitability, see Cato (*de Ag.* 1.7) (who includes qualifications); on the expense, Duncan-Jones (1974: 34–35). On wine as a respectable source of income, Purcell (1985).

27 Cf. Cicero's catalogue of despicable livelihoods and sources of profit (*Par. St.* 43; *Off.* 1.150–151).

28 And sometimes of the manager (*officinator/officinatrix*). The owner was termed *dominus* or *domina*, apparently owners of the estates on which the factories (*figlinae*) were sited. See Helen (1975: 22–3; 45–6).

29 See esp. Setälä (1977: 107–9, 250–7). For the Domitiae Lucillae, see *ILS* 86 52–5.

30 Since Cicero is our source, we hear most of the services he performed for Cicero himself, before he fell out with his wife (*Att.* 11.24.4 (Ephesus) and 10.5.3). Philotimus ceased to act for Cicero after the breach. See also Fabré (1981: 343–4) and Haury (1956: 189–90).

31 See further below. See also Mohler (1940); Skydsgaard (1976: esp. 46); Forbes (1955).

32 On women's stereotypic acquisitiveness (Tac. *Ann.* 3.33; 13.19; Aul. Gell. *NA* 17.6.2–3; Juv. 8.128–30). Cf. the characterization of Sulla's daughter Cornelia Fausta by Valerius Maximus (4.2.7).

33 See Suetonius (*Claud.* 18–19) on *libertinae* (women freed from slavery) shipowners, Ulpian (*Tit.* 3, 6) on privileges accorded other grain traders. See also Sirks (1980).

34 Kampen (1981a: 114) makes the point that while petty traders had a poor reputation, *negotiatrices* were respectable. The quote above from Cicero suggests that a similar standard applied to men, at least as viewed from higher up the social ladder.

35 The difference was possibly not only one of scale (as elucidated in the *de Officiis* passage quoted above) but of distance from the everyday operations of trading (Wiseman 1971: 79). Cf. Tacitus' scornful reference to the activities of Gaius Gracchus, descendant of a noble line now reduced to trade (*Ann.* 4.13). On the later use of *negotiator*, see the examples in Greene (1986: 166–7).

36 Compare similar rulings *Dig.* 50.16 (e.g. 152, 153.1, 195 *pr.*) confirming the general principle that masculine words, even in the singular, cover female equivalents. Cf. Gardner (1995).

37 See Paul (*Sent.* 2.26.11; *CJ* 9.29) on the legislation imposing penalties for fornication or adultery with free women; Kampen (1981a: 110–11) on the status issues.

38 The usual examples are taken from Plutarch's moralizing description of the 2nd century BC financial practices and *dicta* of Cato the censor (e.g. *Cat. mai.* 21), but it is interesting that Petronius also has Trimalchio speak of giving up his direct involvement with maritime commerce and investing in freedmen (*Sat.* 76.9). See Fabré (1981: esp. 337–9) for a detailed discussion. He considers the eternal question of whether such freed slaves were businessmen in their own right or agents for their patron-investors. Jongman (1988: 172–9) contests the notion of direct upper-class involvement in trade. The main role of the free poor in Roman literary sources is as an undifferentiated mass, a moral or political category (urban mob, disappointed clients, noble peasantry).

39 In addition to other types of patronage, such as inclusion of freed slaves in a tomb monument or will. Consider the example of Iunia Libertas of Ostia, cited below (Calza 1939).

40 See Cicero (*Clu.* 178) on the premises, equipped at Sassia's expense. See also Skydsgaard (1976: esp. 46) on the social and economic meanings of such arrangements. Cf. Kirshenbaum (1987). On the language of patronage, see Hellegouarc'h (1972) and the first chapter of Saller (1982).

41 Interpretations of this skewing have varied. See Garnsey (1980: 44) and the references in n. 42 below. Jongman (1988: 177) believes that it reveals the unrepresentative character of the records and suggests that many artisans were actually slaves.

42 Classic studies include Frank (1916); Loane (1938); Taylor (1961). They have considered the over-representation of servile and foreign workers, *inter alia*. LeGall (1969); Treggiari (e.g. 1975, 1976, 1979) and Kampen (1981a: 107–29) have looked specifically at the distribution of women in such inscriptions. Joshel (1992) has analysed the identification of workers within the workplace.

43 See esp. Treggiari (1979: 76–79), where she also discusses small business structure and Kampen (1982), who contrasts the low incidence of women artisans in iconography with representations of other female occupations in Roman media.

44 Use of the expression *sua pecunia* (e.g. by Veturia Fedra, *CIL* 6.37820), emphasizes that many female dedicators funded the monument independently of any inheritance from the deceased dedicatee.

45 Possibly a loan (*CIL* XIV supp. 4698). Kampen (1981a: fig. 47) shows the reconstructed monument.

46 Jean Andreau's growing body of publications on the financial aspects of Puteoli (e.g. 1983, 1995) have extended our knowledge of this area. See also Camodeca (1999); Gardner (1999).

47 Cf. Ulpian *Dig.* 14.3.7 on the liability of female slave managers (*institores*).

48 See Kampen (1981a, 1982) on representations. Waltzing (1895: vol. I. 348–9) on the probable exclusion of women from trade *collegia*. But see Treggiari (1979: 86).

49 The last line includes the statements 'She kept the house, she made wool' – *domum servavit, lanam fecit*. Cf. *CE* 1988, 14 (Rome, 1st century AD), and the examples of Lattimore (1942: 297). The formula was clearly seen as apt across a great time frame.

50 Not, however, in Roman iconography. The detailed depictions of stages of cloth production in the House of the Vettii murals (Pompeii) and the frieze of the Temple of Minerva in the Forum Transitorium (Rome) are embedded in allegorical or mythological treatments. Realistic depictions are few, e.g. the painting of a woman spinning on the garden wall of the house of Venus Marina (Pompeii) (Jashemski 1979: vol. I, 101, fig. 159), and the painting of a vertical two-beam loom on the Hypogeum of the Aurelii at Rome (Wild 1976: 166).

51 Williams (1958: 21 n. 20). The 'Turia' he cites is the unknown subject of the long inscription, *CIL* 6.1527a = 37053, the so-called *Laudatio Turiae*.

52 Cf. the comments attributed to Cato the elder by Polybius (31.25.5 = 31.24.4), or Juvenal (xi.95–109). Columella's comment in the preface to book 12 (quoted in part above), that women *these days* leave it all to the *vilica* (bailiff's wife) on the rural estate is embedded in the usual general *laudatio temporis acti*. Since women of his own social group and their husbands owned a number of such estates, it would obviously have been impossible to carry out the job personally on each one, any more than a CEO of a multinational can operate without managers of national branches. Juvenal's claim (6.287–291) that the ancestresses were too exhausted from wool-work to commit adultery and the implication that his contemporaries were freed from such constraints should not need any comment from me.

53 The extent to which cloth production was 'industrialized' continues to be debated, (e.g. Jones 1960, 1974). See esp. Moeller (1976) and Jongman's response (1988). On the issue of 'industrialization' in the Roman economy generally, see Duncan-Jones (1974: 19–20, 48–9); Hopkins (1978: 53); Harris (1993: 11–29).

54 Pompeian residential houses apparently accommodating (or converted to) spinning, weaving and fulling include VI.viii. 20–1 (Jashemski 1993: 134) and VI.xiv.22 (fullery of M. Vesonius Primus – Jashemski 1993: 50). And see Brion (1960: 132–133), Moeller (1976: 40, 56); Jongman (1988: 163, 178–9). Jongman (1988) and Laurence (1994) are sceptical about some workshop identifications.

55 Cf. Garnsey (1976: 129) on oil production in commercial quantities in elite residences at Volubilis, and see MacKendrick (1983: 268–9). A review of these differing perspectives on the Roman economy is provided by Harris (1993).

56 The stress on work rather than patronal relations, a theme explored by Joshel (1992), is evident in the commemoration of spinners (*quasillariae*) without the name of their owner(s).

57 Loane (1938: 76–7) and Treggiari (1979: 71–2) interpret the commercial relations in slightly differing ways. See now Dixon (2001c) for a more detailed discussion of these inscriptions.

58 *SIBI ET SVEIS* (l.7), a common formula.

59 Neatly expressed in Kampen's summary of the sources she cites (1981a: 123):

> Fabric work, then, was a low-paying occupation for free women, a duty and attribute of the virtuous matron, and, in the majority of cases, a job for domestic and industrial slaves. It was, at certain times and places, a quintessentially female occupation – born of necessity and fraught with the contradictions endemic in women's situation in Rome – alternately honored and oppressed.

60 MacMullen (1974: 98) describes weaving as 'the most widespread and economically the most important industry of the ancient world'. Cf. Jongman (1988: 155–7) on the significance of the cloth trade.

61 Guilds: according to Waltzing (1895: 348–9). We know very little about apprenticeships in Roman Italy.

62 For more detailed discussion of the representation of such activities by the Roman elite as patronal or as dutiful maintenance of the family estate, see Dixon (2001a: ch. 7).

63 Cf. Cornelius Nepos' observations on the differences between the social roles of the Greek and Roman matron (*Praef. Vit. Ill., On the Lives of Illustrious Men*).

5

MATRONLY PATRONS IN THE EARLY ROMAN EMPIRE

The case of Salvia Postuma

Margaret L. Woodhull

In Book One of Virgil's *Aeneid* the hero Aeneas and his comrade Achates set out to survey their surroundings after landing in northern Africa. In due time they reach a cliff from which they spy the bustling city of Carthage and marvel at the grand new gates, temples, and paved streets that were replaced by the city's monarch the Phoenician queen, Dido. Her fame as a civic founder and patron extended into history as witnessed by her appearance as the quintessential patron in a seventeenth-century tapestry cartoon by Giovanni Francesco Romanelli showing the queen holding plans for her city (cf. Valone 2001: fig. 1, p. 319) (Figure 5.1).[1] In its day it might have provoked viewers to recall great patrons of the ancient world, perhaps even Suetonius' frequently cited observation of Augustus: he found the city built of mud brick when he came to power, but left it encased in marble upon his death (Suet. *Aug.* 28). In both early modern and ancient Italy, a leader's erection of urban structures was symbolic of the civic and sacred authority he held, a measure of his greatness. Yet, for Romans, the similarities between Dido and Augustus extend no further, for the queen of Carthage, unlike Augustus, was fated for ruin – largely because she was a woman. Dido's queenly ambitions matched by uncontrolled desire were not simply unacceptable to the Romans, but ultimately yielded her downfall to Rome's moral *virtus* embodied in Aeneas (and by analogy, Augustus). For epic readers, the moral was that female-led Carthage was no match for Rome's masculine *virtus*. Scholars often compare Dido in Carthage to Cleopatra in Egypt. Her political and personal relationship to another of Rome's powerful men, Antony, brought her demise (Galinsky 1996: 230; Wyke 1992). The analogy perhaps reminded readers that, to the Roman mind, a world ruled by a woman is one turned upside down, and thus doomed, just as Cleopatra's world had fallen to Rome's might.

Figure 5.1 Giovanni Francesco Romanelli: Dido Showing Aeneas her Plans for Carthage, *c.*1630–1635. Gouache and black chalk on paper, laid down on linen (276.9 × 487.7 cm) (The Norton Simon Foundation).

The effectiveness of Virgil's literary trope of a woman empowered threatening civic stability is heavily indebted to a patriarchy that informed it and
all facets of life in Rome. Taken alone, such evidence might suggest that
Romans saw women as aliens to civic politics, with no place in forming civic
culture. Instead, they were more properly anchors of domestic culture, overseeing the household economy, bearing and rearing children, and tending to
familial concerns. Yet, despite such noble ideals of womanhood, in practice
elite Roman women in the last decades of the republic did regularly gain
access to political life particularly through family ties, though not, as Suzanne
Dixon (1983: 91) notes, in the sense of voting and pursuing magistracies or
senatorial authority, but 'in the sense of the pursuit and exercise of real
power.' Women like Clodia, Servilia or Fulvia interceded on behalf of certain
men as behind the scenes patrons. In this way, some elite women wielded
exceptional power via familial relationships within Rome's social network of
powerful families (Carp 1981; Dixon 1983; Skinner 1983). By appropriating
the terms of the family, women could participate in patronal activities and
extend their sphere of influence beyond their traditional domestic roles.

The actions of these late republican figures represent one example that
challenged traditional ideals of feminine behaviour. Others tapped into civic
life overtly by physically fashioning ancient cityscapes using architectural
benefaction (see, for example, Boatwright 1991; Flory 1984; Kleiner 1996;
Van Bremen 1996; Woodhull 1999). Though meagre, the epigraphic
evidence from the western Mediterranean indicates that women of the republican era embellished or refurbished religious precincts, town walls, and gates,
though the physical structures rarely survive.[2] For the imperial period,
however, archaeological evidence is more abundant yet poorly studied. This
reality led to the observation that, '[t]he scholarship on the early empire has
largely ignored the power of women and the impact of their monuments
. . . The evidence exists, but it has not been sufficiently explored' (Kleiner
1996: 40, n.7). In cities and towns across the Roman world, women built
in increasing numbers from early in the imperial period. Their motivation,
as Carolyn Valone writing about women patrons in sixteenth-century Rome
recently observed (2001: 317), was to use architecture to gain a public voice
that allowed them to construct a public persona.

Why is it, then, that women's contributions to the urban landscape have
failed to gain attention until recent years? The answer is multifaceted. For
the most part, architectural scholarship has highlighted the, admittedly more
abundant, corpus of monuments built by men, grand structures that glorify
military accomplishments or demonstrate the inventiveness of Roman engi-
neering, buildings like Pompey's extravagant stone theatre or Nero's Domus
Aurea.[3] Typically women's monuments do not fall into these categories,
though they are often extraordinary, as in the case of the building erected
by Eumachia in Pompeii – the largest structure in the forum (Dobbins
1994). Generally, then, women's monuments are relegated to the margins

of scholarship if they receive attention at all. This essay responds to that lacuna in scholarship on women and architectural patronage in the early decades of the empire. It considers the phenomenon of women's civic bene-faction as a mode of expressing publicly a patron's identity through that most permanent and visible form of civic euergetism, buildings. By erecting large-scale structures, women effectively inserted a feminine voice, an alien presence, into a predominantly masculine culture. In doing so, they influ-enced traditionally militaristic and political overtones that blanketed a city's plan through the symbolisms embodied by its monuments. I assert that women introduced into the public theatre concerns specific to their experi-ences with family and motherhood (see Hallett in this volume). Seen as primary texts, buildings, like literary counterparts, can reveal a patron's self-conception in the broader community. This essay deliberately focuses on a little-known arch, the Arch of the Sergii (c.20–10 BC), built by Salvia Postuma (Figure 5.2), a member of an elite *gens* in the Roman colony of Pola (set at the margins of central Italy in what is now modern Croatia), in order to draw attention specifically to those buildings commissioned by women that stand at the edges of traditional architectural inquiries, so that we may understand a distinctly early imperial phenomenon taking root across the Roman world and not just in the city of Rome. I begin by exploring the rise of women's euergetism in the late republic and early empire as modeled by Rome's imperial women and conclude by suggesting that, through her building, Salvia, like her imperial counterparts, was central to defin-ing womanhood in early Augustan Italy. By appropriating the terms of architectural patronage already practised by men, women gain sanctioned access for the first time in Roman history to an openly public and political voice.

Architectural benefaction in late republican Rome

The last two centuries of the Republic saw an explosion of architectural patronage by prominent men within Rome. Victorious generals returning from the Greek east brought with them the spoils of war and a desire to display these trophies in buildings that demonstrated political hegemony and a newly cultivated taste for the architectural jewels of the Hellenistic world. In time, Rome, particularly the Campus Martius, developed into a monumentalized war trophy, littered with grand colonnades and marble temples offered in thanks for military successes. Few of these projects, however, addressed the essential demands of a rapidly growing city in need of basic urban amenities, like a sound infrastructure or easy access to water (Favro 1996: 55ff.). With Augustus' victory at Actium (31 BC), however, the city, for the first time in centuries, began to experience physical and architectural changes that set her on a par with the Mediterranean's finest capitals, like Pergamon, Alexandria or Athens. To effect these changes, the

Figure 5.2 Arch of the Sergii, *c.* 25–20 BC, Pula, Croatia
(photo: Margaret L. Woodhull).

emperor created civic posts through which private citizens who controlled much of Rome's wealth might attend to urban needs and embellish civic spaces. In his *Res Gestae*, Augustus enumerated his contributions to this effort, indicating that, by the end of his forty-five year reign, his benefactions included the erection or repair of hundreds of temples, roads, theatres, aqueducts, basilicas and other public edifices (Aug. *Res Gestae*, esp. 19–21). Soon civic leaders in colonies and the provinces across the empire (supported in part by money from Rome) followed suit. Building programmes engendered a Romanization of the empire's cities and towns and slowly these dependants began to emulate their mother city (MacMullen 1959: 207).

It is in this context that names and faces of women start to join civic donor lists as benefactors alongside their male counterparts. In Rome, Augustus' own building program engaged the participation of women of the city's first family, specifically the emperor's sister, Octavia, and wife, Livia, whose architectural benefaction is well attested by ancient literature and archaeology. Counted among the earliest benefactions was Octavia's portico (called *porticus Octaviae*) at the southern end of the Campus Martius.[4] Here, the emperor's sister renovated the republican colonnade of Metellus, a monument originally designed to accommodate war trophies. Under Octavia's patronage, the portico received a thorough face lift and two libraries dedicated to her late son, Augustus' intended successor, Marcellus. Soon after, Livia took the stage and commissioned numerous temples, shrines, a portico, and perhaps even a food market (the so-called *macellum Liviae* near the Porta Esquilina), including the Temple of Fortuna Muliebris on the via Latina; the Villa *ad albinas* at Prima Porta now famed for its 'Garden Room' frescoes; and the *Porticus Liviae* and its associated *aedes Concordiae* known from Ovid's *Fasti* (6.637–48).[5]

Although under Augustus architectural patronage and urban renewal followed a systematic plan designed to facilitate life in the city, in many ways, his patronage was a continuation of that same urge to monumentalize that grasped his republican predecessors in Rome. Thus, we might expect to find in architectural patronage by imperial women the continuation of similar efforts on the part of their republican predecessors. Yet this is not the case; instead, it is surprising to find that very little benefaction in the form of buildings was practised by elite women of the late republic, despite their documented political patronage. Even accounting for accidents of preservation, one finds distinctly fewer benefactions by women during the pre-imperial period relative to the output of imperial and non-imperial elite women of the Augustan era. This observation suggests some shift in women's conditions, a change that invited women to more readily practise civic euergetism than had previously compelled them to do so. What was this shift? For the answer we must consider Augustan ideological programmes across Italy that moved emphasis away from a primarily military culture to one dominated by the concerns of a nascent dynasty.

Cautiously, Augustus introduced to Rome a dynastic governance that had not existed since the city's regnal era (753–509 BC). Under such a system, power is transferred not through election of officials but, instead, through inheritance. In this system, women gain central importance in the family structure as producers of heirs (Corbier 1995). Thus, women of the Julian family took on new-found public prominence rarely seen in the days before the beginning of the imperial period. Their place in a broader public discourse on dynasty is attested by the fact that, for the first time, imperial women began appearing in monumental state reliefs, such as the Ara Pacis Augustae. Indeed, Natalie Kampen (1991) argues that imperial women were intentionally publicized in art for political gain. Their expanded representation in state art reveals their legitimizing role in the political and ideological goals of a given dynasty.

Seen through the lens of dynasty with its emphasis on family, the monuments of Augustan Rome take on a new meaning. Though many remained documents of Augustus' victory and his military valour at Actium, many others were named for family members or erected by them as members of the imperial entourage. Thus, formerly militaristic symbolism was suppressed in favour of a new unifying theme: family beneficence. Across Rome, what was once a collection of monuments by diverse patrons, scattered throughout the city and united, for the most part, by having been inspired by war, was now a collection which, when mapped across the civic space, linked like branches forming a genealogical tree of the Julian patrons who had commissioned them, each uniting through and in a central source, Augustus. The *locus classicus* for beginning to understand this transition is the Roman Forum, which, under Augustus, became a virtual museum of monuments glorifying the Julian family (Favro 1996: 195–200). But the Campus Martius is perhaps a better example, for it was here that the staging ground for military display during the republic had found its greatest concentration and it was here that, one by one, new monuments were built and pre-existing ones appropriated, restored, and refurbished in the names of members of the imperial house: the Theatre of Marcellus, the Porticus Octaviae, the Pantheon and Baths of Agrippa, the Mausoleum of Augustus, the Ara Pacis Augustae, a second Octavian portico to name but a few.[6] Elsewhere in the city other monuments erected by the emperor and his wife Livia linked into this web of family patronage, extending its range across the whole of the urban plan.

Each monument bore decoration that, as numerous scholars have demonstrated, addressed an Augustan discourse on the pax Romana, beneficence, virtue, and divine heritage – and therefore justified authority – of the emperor, and the centrality of his family in the smooth workings of the empire. In the case of monuments built by Livia and Octavia, features like decoration and location attest to their intrinsic place in this discourse with their special emphasis on women's roles in the burgeoning empire. For instance, in Octavia's portico, painted and sculptural artworks focused on family themes and idealized matrons, like Cornelia, mother of the Gracchi brothers, who had outlived both her sons and was represented in the portico by a seated bronze portrait (see Hallett in this volume). Octavia's addition to the complex of two libraries commemorating her own late son linked her through a similar loss with Cornelia and indicated that she, too, was an ideal Roman matron, fulfilling social duties of motherhood that included com- memoration in death (Mustakallio 1990). Likewise, Livia's portico and its associated shrine to the goddess Concordia link topographically, symbolically and temporally (through dedication dates) to other shrines and women's cults across the city. In Livia's hands, Concordia shifted from a late republican concept heavily weighted towards accord between distinct political factions to one that privileged family concord and marital harmony – such as that modelled by the empress and emperor.[7] By interweaving familial and femi- nine concerns in their new buildings, imperial women responded to those created by men in the family that emphasized masculinity, such as Augustus' new forum, his civic centrepiece.[8] Together they created a web of family patronage and symbolism criss-crossing the city, such that the absence of any one monument would create a palpable rift in the dynastic agenda.

Honoured as *pater patriae*, Augustus had, indeed, tended to the city welfare as a *paterfamilias* would his family (cf. Favro 1992). If Augustus was cast 'father' of Rome, then Livia was its civic 'mother'; Rome's citizens, their charge and care.[9] Together they were the *parentes urbis*. If we read the changes in Augustan Rome using this domestic metaphor, we may see more clearly, then, how a once alien presence (women in civic life) became mainstream culture in Augustan discourse, integral to conception of Rome in the empire. No longer alien, the feminine was thoroughly entrenched in the urban land- scape; indeed, it was institutionalized and, thus, made more rigid, more mainstream. Instead of subverting traditional gender norms with large-scale architecture, imperial women and their benefactions became models of femininity.

Salvia Postuma's Arch of the Sergii: a case study

Inspired by women of the Julian house, wealthy women beyond Rome turned to architecture as an outlet for the display of civic authority, modeling their own families and casting themselves as mothers of their cities in ways similar to their Roman counterparts.[10] One particularly striking example is the monumentalized city gate/arch erected by Salvia Postuma. Having alluded to the ways in which family is implicated in women's architectural bene- faction at Rome, I shall devote the remainder of this chapter to considering specific ways in which Salvia's arch addressed similar concerns of a woman living far from the centre of power, but close to its ideological project. Through analyses of its design, sculptural decoration and its topographical location, we may see that Salvia's arch addressed a general discourse on ideal womanhood in the project of empire, while also attempting to draw attention to her unique role as a leading lady of Pola.

Commissioned by Salvia Postuma of the *gens Sergia*, the Arch of the Sergii has received little attention in the scholarly record, though, set in the heart of modern Pula, it remains one of the best-preserved ancient examples of a Roman arch.[11] In antiquity, Pola was one of the more prosperous and important colonial ports under Augustus.[12] The monument commemorated three men of Salvia's family and Salvia herself, as is indicated by inscriptions across its attic (Figure 5.3). These identified from left to right: Lucius Sergius, Salvia's husband, an *aedile* and *duumvir* of the town (*L Sergius C F/aed{ilis} II vir*); Salvia Postuma next to him (*Salvia Postuma Sergi*); their son at the centre of the arch Lucius Sergius Lepidus, also an *aedile* and a military tribune of the 29th legion (*L Sergius L F/Lepidus aed{lis}/tri{bunus} mil{itum} leg{ionis} XXIX*); and finally, Lucius' brother, Cornelius Sergius, an *aedile*, *duumvir*, and *censor quinquennalis* (*Cn Sergius C F/aed{ilis} II vir quinq{uennalis}*) (*CIL* 5.50; DeGrassi 1962: 39–44; Forlati Tamaro 1947: 40–1, n. 72).[13] Each inscription accompanied a portrait statue of the family member crowning the arch. None survives, though carved footholds for the statues on the top of the arch indicate where each stood.[14] Where the inscriptions across the attic emphasize civic and military offices of the Sergi men, a fifth, centred in the architrave, declared the patron: Salvia Postuma of the Sergi, from her own money (*Salvia Postuma Sergi de sua pecunia*; *CIL* 5.50).

Figure 5.3 Detail of inscriptions: Arch of the Sergii
(photo: Margaret L. Woodhull).

A single-bay arch, the monument stood immediately inside a prominent and heavily trafficked town gate, framing the portal as visitors exited. In antiquity, its front faced west towards town, while the reverse joined with a pre-existing town gate via two short spur walls that ran from engaged columns on the back of the arch to the city portal thereby uniting them as one. Sculpted reliefs decorated the interior of the piers with scrolling grape vines and acanthus tendrils inhabited by birds and small creatures, a pattern reminiscent of the Ara Pacis Augustae (Figure 5.4). Winged victories floating in the spandrels and figures of Helios and Selene manning chariots frame the dedicatory inscription. A frieze of erotes and bucrania-supported garlands

Figure 5.4 Detail of vine scrolls on arch piers: Arch of the Sergii (photo: Margaret L. Woodhull).

runs from the ends of the dedicatory inscription to its corner where friezes of armour pick up and continue around the sides of the arch. A host of marine creatures and sphinxes embellish the coffers of the arch's soffit. At the centre, a lozenge-shaped panel presents an eagle, wings spread, grasping a serpent in its talons (Figure 5.5).

Stylistically, both the arch and its sculpted embellishments tie the monument to the Augustan era. Comparison of the ornament with similar workmanship on the local Temple of Roma and Augustus in Pola's forum, completed between AD 2–14 and analysis of the epigraphic evidence for Salvia's son Lepidus, a soldier at Actium, locate the monument in the last decades of the first century BC (Traversari 1971: 39–44; Woodhull 1999: 38–9). The high-quality workmanship on the sculpted details suggests that Salvia's expenditures were costly, an observation that raises the question: how exactly might Salvia have paid for her monument?

During the Augustan principate, opportunities for women to represent their public personas became particularly pronounced with the new emphasis on women's role in society as mothers and bearers of new citizen Romans. Ideologically, they were central to propaganda and social legislation that sought to increase the citizen body of the Roman empire. To aid this effort, Augustus enacted legislation, the *lex Iulia de maritandis ordinibus*, which liberated elite women from tutelage when they had produced three or more children and allowed them to inherit great sums of money.

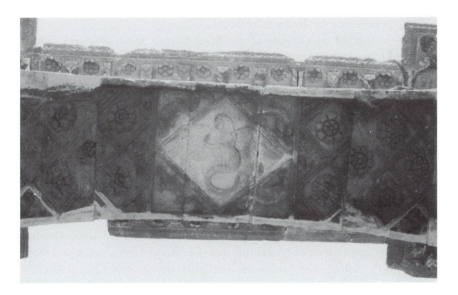

Figure 5.5 Detail of soffit with apotheotic image: Arch of the Sergii
(photo: Margaret L. Woodhull).

With new-found freedoms, women had access to financial capital that they could turn into social capital if they so desired.[15] Not a few chose civic enrichment.

Location, location, location: topography and the Arch of the Sergii

As in modern times, patrons of antiquity observed the dictum that a building's location is its greatest asset. Recent works by Diane Favro and Penelope Davies demonstrate the importance that Roman patrons placed on location. Favro's study of Augustan Rome (1996) applies theories of both narrative and urban planning to analyse how ancient Romans created meaning for city spaces through the relationships between buildings. In Favro's view, Augustus' building patronage and his choices of siting inter-twined to create narratives with historic or symbolic value further shaped by a viewer's response to, and perception of, the new emperor. A patron would consider the kinetic and haptic experience a viewer had of her monument and exploit these features to evoke meaning. By siting monuments near extant structures, a patron's new building could gain and share special asso-ciations with the site (Favro 1996: 10). In a similar vein, Davies (2000) concludes that emperors exploited topography and design in their funerary monuments in order to solidify dynastic claims as heirs to imperial power. The collective memories of a site could also influence a new building's signifi-cance for the viewing public. Thus, a well-chosen location could enhance a patron's beneficence by its mere association.[16]

By situating her monument at the town portal, Salvia Postuma clearly capitalized on its placement. City portals saw some of a community's heaviest traffic and thus guaranteed high visibility. But beyond visibility, the city gate carried other rich symbolism of which Salvia's arch partook. The portal, a symbolic rift in the protective enclosure of a town wall, demanded ritual protection which traditionally took the form of a god's tutelage.[17] This ritualized protection acknowledged the threshold of the town as a place of danger, a liminal zone. By dedicating a portal to a god, the deity's protective watch transformed the structure into a sacred fixture. At Pola, the gate where Salvia's arch rose honoured and was held sacred to the goddess Minerva. Salvia's embellishment of the structure associated her and her family name with the area the goddess protected.

Anthropological theories of liminality provide a model for understanding the significance of Salvia's topographical choice. Rooted in the work of Arnold Van Gennep (1960), the notion of liminality derives from his studies of rituals concerned with a human being's transition from one status to another, for example from being single to married (see also Turner 1969: 94–130). Van Gennep theorizes that these life transitions share a common tripartite scheme. In this scheme, an individual first separates from a particular status, then passes through a liminal period – that is she crosses a symbolic threshold that marks her transition and, finally, re-emerges from the transition into a new status in society. In the liminal phase, a person's status is uncertain, and she is, therefore, considered vulnerable. The rituals surrounding the liminal experience function apotropaically, to protect the individual until she passes through the liminal state into her new identity.

For Van Gennep, an architectural threshold, like a portal or an arch, metaphorically embodied liminality.[18] It marked a transition in space, from indoor to outdoor, or as in the case of a city gate, from an urban environment to a rural one. That space between the two poles was vulnerable in the same way that the person in transition between two life phases is and, therefore, needed ritual protection. In the Roman world, a tutelary deity provided a town's portal sacred protection that extended to all who passed through it from city and country.[19] Indeed, for the ancient citizen of Pola, the countryside beyond the city walls was a dangerous place, and departure from the civilized world of the city for the unruly, often lawless, world of the country, demanded care. For not only might one be subjected to barbarian aggression, but even in times of peace one would have feared wide-spread brigandage (MacMullen 1974: 2–10; Shaw 1984).[20] By erecting her arch here, Salvia not only took responsibility for providing her fellow citizens with an elegant facelift to the gate but boldly she insinuated her family's place as co-guardians with Minerva as she claimed tutelage for them eternally. By casting them as civic caretakers, Salvia, a woman, adopted a paternal role as crafted by the imperial family at Rome and substituted her own family members in their stead as *parentes coloniae*.

Iconography and the Arch of the Sergii

In choosing the arch form specifically, Salvia further alluded to imperial practice. Indeed, Augustus had erected arches for similar purposes in towns outside Rome on the Italian peninsula. In Rimini, the emperor built an arch (*c*.27 BC) at a principal town gate and dedicated it to divinities sacred to his regime, Jupiter, Apollo, Neptune and Roma, adding tondi with busts of the gods to the faces of the arch. The top he crowned with his portrait, indicating his unity with the Olympians depicted below. Together, all protected the colonial precinct and its threshold (Cassius Dio 53.22.2). While it is one thing for an emperor to lay claims to divine congress with the gods, it is quite another for a private citizen, moreover a woman, to do so. The implication that her family were worthy to share in the duties and honours of a divinity, such as Minerva, might have been viewed as rather bold. How Salvia might have affected such claims can be understood by examining the typology and function of a Roman arch.

This particular use of the arch as a sacred portal originated as a typolog-ically distinct monument during the Republic when, according to Livy, it was used in the context of a sanctuary (Livy 33.27 as in Kleiner 1991). Described as votive, these arches generally supported statues of tutelary deities and marked thresholds of sacred precincts. The earliest known votive arch dates to 196 BC, when Lucius Stertinius erected three in Rome. Two of these stood in the Forum Boarium, where they marked the entrances to the sanctuaries (*templa*) of Fortuna and Mater Matuta. They indicated a trans-ition from the space of the city into the realm of the goddesses. Livy notes that Stertinius embellished these with golden statues of the deities connected with the respective cults (Kleiner 1991: 205). Because ancients understood their city to be endowed with a sacred character (through distinct founding rituals, the city was literally constituted as a *templum*, the same term used to describe a sanctuary), the portal evolved to look like the Republican forms that preceded them. Like Stertinius' arches, these would adopt the image of a god and would, as in Van Gennep's theory, mark passage into the sacred precinct of the town. The arch, then, was understood by a viewer as sacred and associated with thresholds. By the early empire, it became a quin-tessentially Roman design and had spread to towns across the empire as a marker of a city's Romanization. To build one was to make claims about a city's or patron's *romanitas*. Perhaps, far from the centre of power, strictures of propriety and hierarchy observed in Rome were less closely regulated beyond the city, thereby enabling a woman like Salvia to boldly proclaim a place for her family with the goddess. Perhaps, too, the Sergii and Salvia merited these claims for other reasons. The iconography of the arch's sculp-ture may provide further answers to this conundrum.

Scholars typically describe the Sergii arch as commemorative, for its deco-rative motifs indicated a funerary character. For example, manned chariots representing personifications of Helios and Selene may allude to life's begin-ning and ending, its dawn and its dusk (see Cumont 1942: 206). The garlanded frieze is commonly found on funerary altars and tombs. Reliefs of armour no doubt commemorating Lepidus' military achievements foreshadow mounded trophies and armour on the later base of Trajan's funerary column that marked the emperor's martial accomplishments (Kleiner 1992: 112). Moreover, inscriptions cement the lifetime accomplishments of the men of the *gens Sergia*, in essence a biographical *res gestae*, a common feature of Roman funerary monuments.[21] Yet, it is the lozenge-shaped panel that secures the funerary character with its classic image of apotheosis. From an early era, apotheosis was expressed visually with an eagle, sometimes bearing a serpent or, as in later imperial imagery, bearing an image of the deceased himself (Cumont 1917; Geyer 1967; Roes 1949).[22] Ancient practice seems to have held that apotheosis was the means by which a deceased's spirit could ascend to the heavens and join the stars in the realm of the divine. In particular, deeds of military or civic valour were often associated with apotheosis (Cic. *de Rep.* 6.4.4–26.29). Apotheotic scenes become common in the imperial period after entering aristocratic funerary practice and imagery in the late Republic (Price 1987).

By its inclusion on the Arch of the Sergii, the panel implied for its viewer that the Sergii deserved to be honoured with apotheosis for lifetime accomplishments marked by their civic and military deeds noted in the inscriptions. They were, in effect, heroes of the town. Moreover, the apotheotic iconography functioned kinetically within the monument's design to activate a theatrical dramatization of this event: approaching the arch, the viewer would first see the portraits; then, moving in closer, she would read the inscriptions accrediting civic and military valour; finally, passing under the arch, she would look up and note the eagle in the soffit, wings spread, 'bearing' the figures just seen on the arch's attic heavenwards. The arch's continual use recreated the moment of apotheosis each time a person passed through the arch. Much as Augustus had joined the tutelary gods at Rimini, here Salvia made her family, now members of a heavenly realm, perpetual guardians of her fellow citizens.

The public face of Salvia

Epigraphic evidence tells us how the men of the *gens Sergia* had served the state well and why they deserved apotheosis, yet by what means might Salvia, a woman with no public office nor military accomplishments to her name, earn the honour of apotheosis? I suggest that Salvia merited this glory by the very benefaction itself, for it embodies her accomplishments in the civic sphere and simultaneously highlights those in the domestic, too. The monument is, in its own right, a permanent marker of her beneficence. A notable act of public piety and generosity, it left a plastic and epigraphic record of this extraordinary measure, in effect a prominent feature of her personal *res gestae.*[23] Indeed, the monument's high quality recorded a generous expenditure to commemorate her family. The full-length portrait and dedicatory inscription further elaborated her biography. Equally significant, the protection the arch offered spotlighted Salvia's motherhood as a caretaker of family. Such references bring to mind similar characteristics adopted by Livia in Rome. As a commemorative monument, the arch reminded viewers that Salvia had fulfilled uxorial and maternal duties.

Finally, the formal composition of the statuary group on the arch's attic seems to address this very facet of her persona, for a reconstruction of the monument reveals that Salvia's portrait and its inscription stand between husband and son, forming a visual genealogy of the primary family structure (Figure 5.6). For the proper aristocratic matron, like Salvia, one's civic duty included familial responsibilities of extending the line of a husband's

Figure 5.6 Reconstruction drawing: Arch of the Sergii (adapted by the author from
G. Traversari, *L'arco dei Sergi*, Padua, 1971, plate 1).

gens. Thus, without Salvia, neither family nor benefaction would exist, and she demonstrates as much by placing herself as the visual link between father and heir. Her place in her family's generation, then, was central. In her visual genealogy, Salvia informed her viewer that she had borne an accomplished son and had been a dutiful wife and citizen. Indeed, the message is all the more emphatic as we note that her off-set portrait disturbs an expected symmetry. Thus, in the end, the design creates an arresting composition that directs viewer attention to Salvia first.

Notes

1 My thanks to Professor Valone for sharing her manuscript.
2 Republican evidence includes the following: *CIL* 1².981 = 6.3089 = *ILLRP* 126 = *ILS* 3423; *CIL* 1². 1688 = 10.292 = *ILLRP* 574 = ILS 5430. I am grateful to Professor Celia Schultz for sharing her thesis research with me.
3 On Pompey's Theatre, see Steinby (1993–2002: s.v. Campus Martius); on the Sanctuary of Fortuna Primigenia, see Boethius and Ward-Perkins (1970: 140–3).
4 On the Porticus Octaviae, see, most recently, Steinby (1993–2002: s.v. *porticus Octaviae* with bibliography). See also Woodhull (1999: ch. 3) where I consider Octavia and Livia's monuments, and Woodhull (2003).
5 On the Temple of Fortuna Muliebris, see Quilici (1981); on the villa at Prima Porta, see Gabriel (1955) and Calci (1984); on the aedes Concordia and the porticus Liviae, see Flory (1984) and Kellum (1990).
6 The Campus Martius housed two porticoes that bore the Octavian name. One was located at the southern end of the field; the other is believed to have been located to the northwest of this one.
7 On the historic meaning and significance of Concordia, see Levick (1978). Cf. Flory (1984).
8 On masculine gendering of the forum, see Kellum (1996).
9 J. Rykwert's *The Idea of the City* (1988) addresses the Roman city as a macrocosm of the home.
10 Cf. similar observations by Nichols (1989) who suggests that a rise in civic patronage by non-imperial women during the late third century AD is inspired by increasingly prominent imperial women.
11 See Kähler (1939: s.v. Pola), Traversari (1971), DeMaria (1988: 251–2 with bibliography) and Kleiner (1992: 111–12) for sculptural decoration. Measurements for the arch are: base, length 8.91 m; depth 2.65 m; height 11 m; front of the pylons 2.20 m; arch width 4.23 m; height 7.27 m.
12 Colonization of Pola, see Fraschetti (1983) and DeGrassi (1962: esp. 914–15).
13 A *duovir quinquennalis* was a censor.
14 Kähler (1939) suggests that Salvia's portrait statue was added posthumously. There is no hard evidence for this assertion. The addition of her portrait statue in this image is my own reconstruction.
15 On Augustus' reproductive and marriage laws, see Galinsky (1981). On women in law generally, see Gardner (1986).
16 Catharine Edwards develops this thesis in *Writing Rome: Textual Approaches to the City* (1996).
17 Rykwert (1988: 97–161, esp. 139–44) explores the ritual importance of guarding the threshold gate of a town's walls. As a vulnerable point in a town's fortification walls, the opening demanded ritual and divine protection.
18 Van Gennep (1960: 20–5) discusses Roman monumental arches as important markers of transitional spaces, like thresholds.
19 Plutarch (*Rom.* 10.2–3) recounts stories of Romulus' ritual laying out of Rome by plowing a sacred circle around the town and lifting the plough at the threshold, thereby leaving it unconsecrated.
20 My thanks to Professor Andrew Riggsby for the latter reference.
21 Augustus' Mausoleum in Rome displayed bronze tablets inscribed with his *res gestae*.
22 The arch of Titus, the Sabina relief, and the column base of Antoninus Pius and Faustina are classic examples of apotheosis of the imperial family.
23 The last two decades have seen important work on biography in funerary art. For example, see Whitehead (1984), Kampen (1981b) and Davies (2000).

6

WOMEN'S INFLUENCE ON REVENGE IN ANCIENT GREECE[1]

Fiona McHardy

In this chapter, I discuss how women influenced revenge culture in antiquity.[2] My thoughts on this subject were initially stimulated by Edith Durham's comments (1928: 164) on how Albanian village women could be more conservative than men in maintaining traditions and less likely to break with traditional ways of doing things. I wanted to examine this theory with reference to the evidence for revenge culture. Here I argue that the association of women with persistent calls for vengeance and the constant memory of past events and traditions is part of the reason why women have been so closely associated with revenge plots in literature. In the first part of this chapter, I discuss the representation of women and revenge in some modern novels based in vendetta societies. In the second part, I compare these to some literary representations of women and revenge from ancient Greece, especially in democratic Athens. It is not my aim to suggest precise equivalence or continuity in these forms of literature, (although Greek tragedy has clearly been influential in some respects on later revenge plots), but rather, I put forward a way of reading tragedy that is suggested by these modern novels.

Women's influence on revenge culture in vendetta societies

The evidence for my study of revenge culture in vendetta societies is derived principally from accounts of Mediterranean feuding societies in the nineteenth and twentieth centuries.[3] Anthropologists have shown that there are several characteristics of the feud which can be observed across different vendetta societies.[4] First, feuding occurs in places with a lack of central authority. So, there is no alternative legal system and participants resort to self-help. Second, feuding is conceived of as equal and is usually characterized by the taking of a life for a life. Third, the feud is related to the quest for honour. Men from these societies are very sensitive to alleged insults to their honour which they prize above life itself. The only way to regain honour is by swift retaliatory action, usually the taking of a life. Fourth, where brothers remain in the same community bringing wives from the outside, there is higher incidence of feuding. Where brothers are scattered feuding is scarce. This is because agnatic kin support one another in the feud. Close agnatic male kin are the most likely avengers. Finally, women are said not to fight in the feud.[5]

There are several possible reasons for this. Women are thought to be weak and they do not carry weapons. Therefore, the killing of a woman in retaliation for the death of a man is not regarded as an honourable or worthwhile action. Even if a woman is shot, this is not an insult which requires washing away.[6] In addition, women are known as 'moving sticks' or 'strongholds' during a feud, because they are not targets and so can continue with agricultural work and other tasks necessary for the survival of the family, while their menfolk fight or stay under protective cover to avoid attack. Further, women are 'sacks for carrying things', in that they may bear a number of male offspring in the future.[7] Finally, if a woman is married, an enemy would be threatened with retaliation by two clans, her natal clan and the one into which she is married. This makes killing a woman a needlessly dangerous act. Nevertheless, women are still just as keenly interested in disputes over family honour as men. Moreover, it is often maintained that women are more blood-thirsty, or more eager for revenge than men (Durham 1928: 164). Indeed, in some instances, men tactically prefer to accept a truce or to receive blood money, while the women of the family are still keen to take blood. Women bring influence to bear on reluctant men in three key ways.

First, they have a significant role in raising children, and if their husbands are killed, they often encourage their sons to take revenge for their father, even if other male relatives might prefer a truce. Durham says of Albania that settled feuds are often reopened by a boy of 15 who has been brought up by his mother to take revenge (Durham 1928: 164; cf. Deliyanni 1985: *Mani* 36; Herzfeld 1985: 89–90; Holst-Warhaft 1992: 87). In this scenario, women raise small children with the idea that when they are grown they must take revenge for their dead father. Where possible, a man might leave instructions with his wife to raise her child to avenge his father. In the following lament, a widow describes how her husband instructed her to raise her son to take revenge for his father. The dead man also identified his killers, who are named at the end of this extract:

Sourdi [murdered husband] who died a bad death,
left me this order
to raise the child,
to reach eighteen,
to give him the gun,

hanging in the gun rack,
to hunt the killers,
Mourmouras and Karkis,
and the child of the whore.
                    (Seremetakis 1991: 127–8;
            see further below, pp. 104–5).

Alternatively, a woman with grown sons might incite them to take revenge for their father (Holst-Warhaft 1992: 87). In both cases, the woman uses her influence over her sons to achieve her aim of revenge for her dead husband.

Second, women influence male relatives into taking revenge by preserving mementoes of the dead man. These are produced constantly in order to remind the avenger of his responsibility towards his dead kinsman. Typically, the memento is an item which is covered in the man's blood, such as his shirt or a piece of cloth (Durham 1928: 164; cf. Glotz 1904: 83). This blood-stained cloth functions as an embodiment of the 'stain that can only be washed out with vendetta' (Deliyanni 1985: *Corsica* 97–9; cf. above, p. 93). If the blood on the cloth turns brown, the hour of vengeance has arrived (Hasluck 1954: 131).[8] Blood is an especially significant symbol in vendetta societies where a great deal of emphasis is placed on the importance of blood kinship through the patrilineal line.

Third, women can publicly shame men by taunts about their honour and by calling for revenge through the medium of lamentation.[9] Men could be goaded into taking revenge, even against their own wishes, by the pressure exerted on them by women's sarcasm and challenges to their honour (Deliyanni 1985: *Mani* 64–5; Holst-Warhaft 1992: 88; Knudson 1988). In Corsica, this challenge to a man's honour is known as the *rimbecco* (see Deliyanni 1985: *Corsica* 96). The seriousness of this insult is revealed in Mérimée's novel *Colomba* (1992: 33): '*Le rimbecco! dit Orso; mais c'est faire la plus mortelle injure à un Corse: c'est lui reprocher de ne pas s'être vengé*'.[10]

Although lamentation is a feature in many preindustrial societies, women's association with the lament is always strongest in vendetta societies. Common features of the lament are: they are composed orally and sung by women, usually in a group expressing shared suffering (Caraveli-Chaves 1980: 146; Holst-Warhaft 1992: 1, 20ff., 97; 2000: 30), they constitute a form of lasting memorial to the dead, assisting the bereaved to remember the person they have lost (Holst-Warhaft 1992: 35ff., 97), they focus on the pain of the bereaved rather than being an encomium of the dead (Holst-Warhaft 1992: 97),[11] and there is a shifting of pain outward by the blaming of an agent of death (Holst-Warhaft 1992: 97). In the absence of a human enemy, God or Charon take this role.[12] Otherwise, vengeance is instigated by the women singing the lament. Constant lamentation at the tomb can also be seen as responsible for stirring up feelings of revenge (cf. Alexiou 1974: 22; see further below, p. 106).

Moreover, laments were perceived as possible fora for political comment by women. For example, in Mani, women found an effective forum for airing their concerns at the *klama*, where women sing laments for the deceased in the presence of the whole community. A focal point in the *klama* is the grave of the dead man around which the women cluster and sing (Seremetakis 1991: 174). Women's participation in the *klama* allows them to enter a public space in which they have an ability to influence social and political matters (cf. Caraveli-Chaves 1980: 129). According to Seremetakis, the female *klama* complements and opposes the male *gerontiki*, although its power is only indirect, as opposed to the formality of the male institution.[13] In this way, Maniat women could influence the decisions of their menfolk concerning revenge by appealing to common moral sensibilities, even though the women's desire for revenge did not always coincide with the political interests of the male council. In the lament cited above, a wife publicly states her opposition to a truce and, instead, favours revenge for her murdered husband. By uttering public slurs against the mother of the killer, she ensures that the enemy group do not want to pursue the truce and therefore that vengeance will not be dropped (Seremetakis 1991: 127–8). So, through the medium of public lamentation, women could influence policy substantially.

Women could also influence individual men into taking revenge by publicly shaming them and suggesting that they had no honour if they did not avenge their kinsmen. In the following example from Mani, men are individually named and called to action:

> Eh, Lazaros and Panayis,
> and you, Fokas and Thodoris,
> what are you waiting for?
> The killer of Panagos is staying in Yerakia.
> Tie up your belts,
> pick up your guns,
> and hunt the killer,
> sunwards, in Yerakia.
> (Seremetakis 1991: 129)

Women might also threaten that they themselves would go and take revenge by arming themselves and dressing in men's clothing (Deliyanni 1985: *Corsica* 94–5).[14] This idea is made clear in a Maniat lament which dates to the early nineteenth century:

> And Ligorou let out a shrill cry
> that made the place shudder all around
> – Did Vetoulas have no brother,
> did he have no first cousin?
> If only I'd been a male
> and could wear pants myself!

To have shouldered the gun myself
and chased the murderer!
(Kassis 1979: vol. 1, 187–8;
trans. Holst-Warhaft 1992: 58)[15]

This lament represents the importance of strong male kin to a murdered man. In it, the female singer drives male relatives to seek revenge by suggesting that they are not truly manly. However, Knudson (1988: 88) maintains that a Corsican girl without male kin does not call for vengeance. She suggests that although women may sing about how they themselves will go and exact vengeance, they say this not because they actually intend to arm themselves, but rather as a jibe to prompt male relatives into taking revenge. By threatening to take revenge themselves, the women are challenging the men to show that they are honourable (Knudson 1988: 91–2).

Deliyanni and Holst-Warhaft, on the other hand, maintain that women did take revenge into their own hands in the absence of male relatives. They find evidence for this view in several laments from the Mani in which a sister or daughter sings that she took vengeance into her own hands.[16] In vendetta societies, ties to natal kin are often felt particularly keenly, so much so that a woman is likely to preference her father and brothers over her husband and even over her own children.[17] The Maniat lament of Kalopothos Sakkakos from the mid-nineteenth century is a good example of this preferencing (Kassis 1979: 274–8). The lament is sung by the sister of the dead man, Paraski. In it she expresses her grief and explains how she plotted vengeance for the death of her brother. She says that she discovered that his murderers were none other than her own husband, her father-in-law and brother-in-law. So, she calmly put poison in the omelette that she cooked for them and watched them die, before returning to her parental home, where she received the congratulations of her parents.[18]

Another lament tells how a different Paraski takes the place of her brother after he is attacked and taken to hospital in Kalamata. Her husband suggests that they go to Kalamata to visit the sick brother, but Paraski insists upon arming herself and going to defend her natal family's tower by firing down upon her brother's enemies (Holst-Warhaft (1992: 84). In a third lament, the mother of Vyeniki urges her daughter to dress as a man and arm herself to kill the enemies of her murdered brother (Holst-Warhaft 1992: 86).

These laments have been used by Deliyanni (1985: *Mani* 62) and Holst-Warhaft (1992: 86) to suggest that women did, indeed, participate in the blood-feud. However, these narratives are in no way straightforward, partly through problems of transmission[19] and partly through the tendency to exaggerate or embellish stories. The laments have come to function more as folk-tales than as laments (cf. Holst-Warhaft 1992: 59). Just as the stories of female warriors, which occur in Greek folk-songs, should be treated with care and cannot be viewed as historical proof of the existence of female warriors in reality,[20] just so, these laments must be treated with care. Moreover, the tendency of participants in vendetta societies to exaggerate events or suppress information in order to offer a more 'pure' account matching social ideals can cause problems with accepting the validity of their claims. For example, during the recent campaign in Kosovo, Ramonda claimed to have joined the KLA to avenge the murder of her young sister. However, after the end of the fighting the reporter discovered the girl alive and well at home (Channel 4 News, 15.9.99). This case reveals the import-ance which local people attach to the ideals of revenge, but discredits oral accounts of their motivations.

It is striking that while the evidence of those who have lived in vendetta societies researching the blood-feud suggests that female revenge was a possi-bility in certain cases, none have actual proof of its existence. For example, Boehm, researching in Montenegro, heard anecdotal tales of women who took revenge in far off towns, but never encountered anyone who had actually taken revenge themselves. Nevertheless, one woman he interviewed claimed that she would do so, if her brother was killed (Boehm 1984: 55). Even in Albania, where tradition dictated that a woman who swore perpetual chastity could take arms and take vengeance herself, providing that she never married, the evidence suggests that women chose this option in order to avoid unde-sirable marriages rather than to pursue revenge.[21] Herzfeld, too, found no evidence of acceptable female participation in his research on 'Glendi' in Crete. He cites an example of a woman who steps out of her expected role by defending her son's name in a coffee house (a bastion of masculinity). For this offence she is described by local men as *athelekarsenikia* (female–male woman)[22] due to her invasion of male space and adoption of the male stance (Herzfeld 1985: 71). Such a woman is making a mockery not only of herself, but also of her husband and his family. Even Holst-Warhaft (1992: 202 n.13) is forced to concede that this example is at conflict with her idea of women taking revenge into their own hands. Herzfeld (1985: 71) notes that women can get the better of men, particularly in singing bouts, but he adds that these are exceptional cases and that they involve the use of mental ingenuity rather than physical violence. Likewise, Seremetakis (1991: 118) attests to the fact that men manage their violence through physical force whereas women manage theirs through verbal power in the lament.

Whether the stories are factually accurate or not, tales of female revenge (or indeed exceptional female behaviour, such as becoming a warrior) are clearly exceptionally popular in folk-songs, laments and anecdotes. It seems to me that the fascination with female revenge is representative of cultural ideals held by the community in question. In vendetta societies, the women of the laments and folk-songs are esteemed because of their loyalty to their blood kin. So, I believe that the stories are offering a kind of paradigm to the community at large. Here, the choice of brother over husband, for example, is an expression of social norms in this kind of society but, nevertheless, it is a difficult choice, and therefore one worthy of discussion and comment in folk-songs and laments. In societies which place such emphasis on the importance of blood (and, indeed, duty to blood-line and its honour), it is inevitable that the stories which hold most interest are those which raise the subject of how individuals were dutiful to the blood-line and how they preserved its honour. The fact that women were placed in a position where this loyalty was more likely to be tested makes them an extremely popular topic for oral poetry, andecdotes and, indeed, novels and myth as I discuss below.

In the laments we have an example of female composition (cf. Alexiou 1974; Holst-Warhaft 1992: 71–2). Not only are certain women able creators of oral poetry, but they are also revered as the composers of sentiments which are imbued with traditional ideas and the values of the community at large.[23] I shall now turn to how their creations inspired male writers when formulating revenge plots in novels based on vendetta societies.

Representation of women in male literature based on vendetta societies

Modern novels about feuding and revenge are of great interest as they place the drama of revenge in its social context. However, the novels should not be viewed as an accurate source for revenge ethics in vendetta societies. Problems with using the novels as a source include: the tendency to select unlikely storylines for dramatic purposes, the tendency to villify feuding participants and the tendency of the authors to make moral and ethical judgements about participants in feuding based on external concepts of justice (in particular the Christian rejection of revenge). However, the novels constitute a useful testing point for me when it comes to discussing how ancient literary texts represent revenge. Here, I shall concentrate on how women are represented in the plots of novels and compare this to the evidence for their roles in revenge in vendetta societies. It will become clear that while certain elements of the novels' representation of women are realistic enough, the tendency to emphasize the participation of women and to associate them most closely with the desire for revenge exaggerates their roles. Nevertheless, it seems that this tendency is inspired by those laments which are most popular among the people of vendetta societies. Moreover, this means that popular revenge plots can be seen as created and inspired by women, the original composers of the popular laments. However, it will be seen that this is not always a positive thing for the women.

Here, I shall focus on two novels: Pandelis Prevelakis' *The Sun of Death* and Prosper Mérimée's *Colomba*. In both of these novels women feature as the embodiment of traditional (primitive) revenge ethics, while the heroes are represented as intellectual outsiders who embody the values of (progressive) education and civilization.

This is very clearly the case in Mérimée's novel *Colomba* which is set in Corsica in 1817. The author was born in France in 1803 and was sent to Corsica in August 1839 to make an inspection of the French *Comité des Arts et Monuments*. Mérimée is clearly an outsider whose rather biased views of the depravity of the Corsican vendetta strongly influence his writing. Throughout the novel, which was first published in 1840, events are seen through the eyes of an English colonel and his daughter who perceive the Corsicans as 'savages' and their customs as barbaric. The hero himself (Orso della Rebbia) is also characterized as sophisticated due to his training in the French army and he is distanced from the beliefs of his fellow islanders (cf. Cogman 1992: 34–9). After the murder of his father, he has no idea of taking revenge, but when his sister Colomba persists in believing that their old enemies the Barricini were involved in her father's death against all apparent evidence, Orso determines upon bringing about a peaceful resolution of the conflict – a policy which is applauded by the young English heroine, Miss Lydia. However, Colomba, who is portrayed as thoroughly Corsican and deeply devoted to the cause of her father to the extent that she rejects marriage, is determined to persuade her brother to take revenge. First Colomba publicly accuses the Barricini of killing her father in her lament for the dead man and she threatens them with vengeance by her brother (Mérimée 1992: 67). This lament becomes so popular that it is sung by other characters in the book. Next she writes to her brother to tell him of these accusations (1992: 67). Then, on the return of her brother to Corsica, she incites him to vengeance by showing him the place where their father died and producing a shirt covered in his blood and the two bullets which hit him. After producing these, she appeals to him saying: '*Orso, mon frère! . . . Orso! tu le vengeras!*' (1992: 103). Colomba is determined not to cease mourning nor to marry until revenge is taken (1992: 100). However, Orso is now 'civilized' by his time in the French army and cannot easily reconcile these two influences (1992: 104). Colomba refuses to accept the prospect of settlement with her enemies (1992: 127), but instead she goes a step further to provoke her brother into taking revenge. She finally manages to put him in the right frame of mind by cutting the ears of his horse and throwing the blame on his enemies. Then she explains to Orso that this is a mortal insult (1992: 155). However, the author clearly exonerates Orso from all blame in the revenge act by making his opponents shoot first and the tale concludes with his pardon and marriage to Miss Lydia. The fact that Mérimée was writing for an external audience who strongly disapproved of revenge (due to the strength of Christian teachings) means that his portrayal of Corsican customs is tainted.

Of greatest significance here is Mérimée's decision to base his plot around the theme of female loyalty and unswerving determination to take revenge. Here, it is clear that Mérimée was inspired by laments and stories which he learnt while living in Corsica.[24] Indeed, it can be seen from the summary of the novel given above that Colomba indulges in nearly all the methods of inciting revenge described in the previous section. However, Mérimée's novel places its heroine in a more controversial position than the folk-tales and laments created and perpetuated by women in vendetta societies. Whereas the women who compose laments are viewed by those in their communities both as great artists and as upholders of social norms and traditions, Mérimée, here, makes his heroine an uneducated savage and a dangerous force through her close association with the instigation of revenge.

Prevelakis' novel *The Sun of Death*, which was first published in 1959 (the first part of a trilogy), also introduces the traditions of Crete through the medium of an outsider. The novel's young hero, Yiorgakis, is represented as an 'intellectual' from the city who desires to become a writer. Nevertheless, Prevelakis emphasizes that he must learn to accept his cultural roots in order to succeed in this ambition.[25] This allows the author to explain traditions through the dialogue to the innocent character of the child who has not grown up with the traditions of the blood-feud. The novel focuses on events in a Cretan village during the First World War. At the beginning of the novel, the central character, Yiorgakis, goes to live there with his father's sister after being orphaned. When his cousin Lefteris kills Ilias, the son of another village woman on the front near Thessaloniki, the dead man's mother calls on her younger son Michalis to avenge his brother. However, when Lefteris is killed in the war, Yiorgakis as closest male blood relative becomes the new target for revenge. The novel culminates dramatically with Michalis' attempt to shoot Yiorgakis who is saved when his aunt steps into the path of the bullet and dies declaring that the blood that was owed has now been paid back.

The central role of women in this novel matches that found in *Colomba*, although Prevelakis is not dogmatic about the depravity of revenge, but expresses a belief that it is part of traditional Crete which a young Cretan writer needs to understand. Nevertheless, his portrayal of women's close association with revenge presents women in a somewhat problematic way.[26]

Throughout the novel, the village women are closely associated with mourning for the dead and, to some extent, with bitterness towards the distant powers who condemn their sons to die in a far off land for an unknown cause. The wives, sisters and mothers, who are left to mourn their kin without a body, place the clothes of the dead man on the bier and gather round to lament (Prevelakis 1989: 118). The bitterness which this can generate is shown especially clearly when the usually moderate character, Aunt Rousaki, is so distraught by the news of how her son perished that she cries out that she will go and set herself alight in front of those who are in power along with all the other mothers who have lost sons (1989: 305). She speaks of forming a chain of burning mothers around the world leaders. She adds that if the mothers had known what would be awaiting their sons, they would not have given birth (1989: 305). Here, the women, through their association with mourning and lamentation, are represented as potential threats to the war effort and to male authority as a whole, as well as to the normal way of life.[27]

Spithouraina, the mother of Ilias, is also represented as a potential cause of trouble to the village community. She is depicted consistently as implacable and insistent on revenge. Although Aunt Rousaki, the mother of the killer, Lefteris, would like to avert revenge by mourning for the dead man herself, going on bended knee to the mother of the dead man to kiss her feet, cutting her hair in mourning and tearing her cheeks alongside the bereaved mother, she recognizes that Spithouraina will not accept this, but will demand blood (1989: 81, cf. 84). She is unforgiving despite the earlier friendship of the two women and their initial sympathy for one another because both their sons are fighting at the front (1989: 50).

Spithouraina is not placated even by Lefteris' death. Instead, she beats the ground with her fist and says 'May my curse bring him out of his tomb' (1989: 138). The village folk, on the other hand, believe that Lefteris' death leaves the matter settled (1989: 139). So, Spithouraina is represented as unreasonable, unable to accept abject apologies or public opinion. Instead, she longs only for blood revenge and it is said that she hates the fact that Yiorgakis is still alive and longs to see him lying in a pool of his own blood (1989: 316). In order to achieve her goal of revenge, she constantly reminds her son Michalis of the necessity of taking revenge for his brother. She says to him: 'The time has come for us to take back what is owed to us. There is no sweeter honey than revenge!' (1989: 308). The strength of her desire to achieve revenge for her beloved son is so strong that she urges on her second boy, although she risks losing him too when he is sent to jail for murder (1989: 84).

The excessive desire for revenge attributed here to Spithouraina, who goes against public opinion, and the potentially violent acts of insubordination suggested by the grieving Aunt Rousaki, show mourning women as threats to male authority (represented by the world leaders) and social order in the village itself.

In both novels, women's association with instigating revenge closely matches that found in vendetta societies. Women are represented as being keen to urge on male kin to take revenge through the use of mementoes, jibes and laments. However, in their literary incarnations, the women come to be seen as hostile forces, a threat to the male order of society. Through their own compositions and actions in vendetta societies, women come to be represented in an excessive and disproportionate manner in literary plots.

Women's influence on revenge culture in ancient Athens

A comparable study of women's influence on revenge ethics in ancient Greece is very much hampered by the lack of suitable evidence. Those discussing this subject in the past have relied much on the use of tragedy to draw inferences about women's behaviour in reality. Although I do not want to dismiss the use of tragedy as a source, I propose here to try the evidence of tragedy against evidence for women's actual behaviour in Athens. This is no easy task for several reasons. Primarily, women have not left any evidence themselves and it is necessary to rely on texts which frequently prefer to dismiss women altogether. Moreover, these texts do not have as their aim a discussion of the behaviour of women in revenge culture in Athens. In particular, the lack of ancient fieldworkers recording women's laments is a great loss to this study. Finally, Plutarch, whose work is much used in the discussion of women's involvement in revenge ethics, is a much later source. However, from both historical and oratorical texts of the fourth and fifth centuries BC, it is possible to derive some idea of the ideals and values of the Athenian people. Forensic oratory, in particular, provides a rich source of such values, as it was intended to appeal to members of the Athenian public who made up the members of the jury.

Athenian society differs from vendetta society in particular in its social structure, but I believe that Athenians shared many ideals and cultural emotions regarding the ethics of honour and revenge (see McHardy 1999; cf. Cohen 1995). These are manifested clearly in forensic oratory, although the importance of revenge ethics is usually expressed differently – it is expected that revenge be taken through the laws rather than violently (cf. esp. Dem. 23.39; A. *Eum.*). One of the key aspects of the move towards radical democracy seems to have been the suppression of women in public life. This is particularly reflected in the funerary legislation I will discuss below. Women in classical Athens had no political rights. So they could not be directly involved in Athenian legal or political activity as orators or jurors. Neither is there any evidence of women resisting these conditions other than in drama – e.g. Aristophanes' *Lysistrata* (cf. Loraux 1998: 26–7; Walters 1993: 194). However, there is some evidence that women could influence men and achieve their aims in the male public world. In this respect, women's ability to persuade and influence family members is of significance (Foxhall 1996; Walters 1993: 195; cf. also Hallett, Harlow and Marshall in this volume).

Although women could not speak in court at Athens, they were still able to bring their influence to bear in the private sphere, usually on cases of importance to male family members. One such example is of Diogeiton's daughter (Lysias 32).[28] When her sons are robbed of their inheritance by Diogeiton, they turn to their mother for help. With the aid of the boys' brother-in-law (sister's husband), a family council is called. At this family meeting, the mother is a prime mover, apparently delivering a speech in which she exposes the dealings of her father in front of the rest of the family (32.12–17). This speech is later related in court in the speech of her son-in-law. In this way, although women could not speak in court themselves, the mother's words are heard by the jury.[29] The speaker relates that the speech of the mother so moved the relatives gathered at the council that they were reduced to tears (32.18). So we can assume that the effect of her words was meant to stimulate a similar response from the jurors.

Other examples provide evidence of the ability of Athenian women to influence men into introducing their children as Athenian citizens. One such is Alce, a former prostitute, who is said to have induced Euctemon to introduce her eldest son to his phratry against the wishes of other male relatives (Is. 6.18–26). She is characterized as manipulative and it is implied that she manages to control the old man through the use of drugs (6.21). Similarly, Neaera and her daughter Phano seek to have Phano's son introduced to the phratry by his father Phrastor, although Phano is not an Athenian citizen. They persuade Phrastor, according to the speaker, by nursing him when he had fallen into ill health. Again, the introduction of the child is said to be against the will of his male relatives ([Dem.] 59.55–7). Plangon also uses her resourcefulness to induce her ex-husband to introduce her son to the phratry. She first tells him that she will swear publicly that the sons are not his if she is paid, but when asked to swear, she publicly declares that the boys *are* Mantias' children (Dem. 39.3–4, 40.11). In so doing, she uses deception to achieve her goal of citizenship for her sons (cf. Walters 1993: 203–8). Elsewhere, women are portrayed as liable to attempt to persuade their husbands not to give evidence for strangers in kinship disputes (Is. 12.5) and as showing male kin their displeasure at an unjust verdict concerning a woman ([Dem.] 59.110–11). Although these arguments are surely rhetorical, and we cannot conclude that Athenian men always paid close attention to their womenfolk on such matters, they nevertheless indicate that women were thought to show their pleasure or displeasure concerning trials to their male relatives, and perhaps to persuade them of their views.

In addition, women are said to help their brothers in their desire to gain estates. Oneter's sister is said to collude with him to defraud Demosthenes of his estate (Dem. 31.11–12) and Diocles' sister constantly pretends to her husband that she is pregnant to help her brother's designs on her husband's estate (Is. 8.36). In these examples, it is recognized that Athenian women did have some ability to influence events, in particular in cases of inheritance. This ability was so feared by the Athenians that they established a law in which questions of inheritance could be challenged if women had improperly influenced a man's will. According to the law, a man without sons could not bequeath property if he was deemed to be mad, senile, drugged or under the influence of a woman (*gynaiki peithomenos* – [Dem.] 46.14; Is. 2.19).

The suggestion of this law and of the examples above is that women were thought to get involved in public disputes involving their close male kin, although this tends to be viewed as problematic. By using their influence in the private sphere, Athenian women could act using persuasion or deception to promote the causes of their children or to help their brothers increase their wealth. There is also a tiny amount of evidence that women could influence political decisions relating to their kin. In some writers' versions of the history of Cimon, Plutarch tells us, Elpinice, sister of Cimon, is said to have been active in persuading Pericles to drop bribery charges against her brother (Plut. *Per.* 10.4–5). She is also credited with brokering a deal between the two men to allow Cimon to return to Athens (cf. Fantham *et al.* 1994: 78). Although it is clear that we cannot put too much credence on this account of events, it is interesting that some ancient writers allowed a woman to have such a significant role in influencing the behaviour of important Athenian political figures.

Moreover, descriptions of foreign women suggest that they were thought able to use their abilities to deceive and persuade in order to incite others to take revenge for them. Women who incite revenge through persuasion include Gobryas' daughter, who asks Cyrus to avenge her brother, murdered by the King of the Assyrians (Xen. *Cyr.* 5.2.7), and Pheretime, who persuades the Persian army to help her get revenge for her son (Hdt. 4.200). Women who use deception include Nitocris, who avenges her brother's death by ordering the construction of a death chamber and inviting a host of Egyptian nobles whom she blames for his death to a dinner in it (Hdt. 2.100), and Candaules' wife, who uses a combination of persuasion and treachery to induce Gyges to murder her husband in revenge (Hdt. 1.10). Although these stories tell us little or nothing about Athenian women's involvement in inciting revenge, they do suggest that women were associated with this ability in antiquity and that the Greeks believed powerful, foreign women were not only liable to desire revenge, but were also capable of achieving it by using these methods.[30]

Athenian women are not shown inciting revenge as directly as foreign queens, but some examples suggest that women were felt to have a significant influence over their children which could lead, as in the modern evidence, to a woman raising a child to take revenge for his dead father. Imprisoned and put to death for being a democrat, Dionysodorus instructs his kin to avenge his death. He achieves this by telling his wife, who visits him while he is in jail, that Agoratus is responsible and through her he charges his male relatives to avenge him. Significantly, he also instructs his wife to tell her as yet unborn child (if male) to avenge his father on his coming of age (Lys. 13.39–42). His cousin (who also happens to be his wife's brother) brings the case to court and asks the jury for revenge (13.1). However, Dionysodorus' instruction to his wife is telling. This is a clear ancient example of the modern parallel where women raise male children to avenge their murdered fathers. The difference here is that the Athenians expected revenge to be taken through the law courts rather than violently.

Other evidence suggests that women were believed to exercise considerable influence over the raising of their children. Because of this, the habit of marrying a woman to a hostile family or in a hostile land could be seen as potentially dangerous (see McHardy 1999: ch. 2). Alcibiades is explicitly criticized for having a child with a Melian woman whose male kin he had killed. This is said to be a particularly risky idea because a child raised by such a woman would be the bitterest enemy both of his own father and of the city (Andoc. 4.22–3; cf. Plut. *Alc.* 16.5). The author exclaims that this is exactly the sort of plot which occurs in tragedy and which the Athenian people deem so terrible.[31] A group of Athenian women is shown as possessing similar strong influence over their children in an anecdotal tale told by Herodotus. He says that when the women were captured by the Pelasgians, they raised their children as Athenians, making them hostile to their Pelasgian fathers (6.138; cf. Philochorus *FGH* 100–1).

While these examples show that there was a fear of the excessive influence which women might bring to bear on their children, influencing them to be hostile towards their fathers, the example from Lysias indicates that women in Athens still had sufficient influence over the raising of their children that they could be expected to raise them to achieve revenge for their father. This example compares directly to the lament cited above in which the dying man is said to have instructed his wife to raise her son to take revenge for him on his coming of age (above pp. 93–4). In both examples, the man identifies his killers to his wife, who thereby becomes a vital instrument in achieving the dying man's desired revenge. This demonstrates that men trusted that their womenfolk would pay attention to their wishes in calling for vengeance and also that women were capable of and perhaps expected to procure revenge through whatever means were open to them. In the Lysias case, the wife who is informed of her husband's desire to be avenged, tells her brother (the murdered man's cousin) of what has happened and it is he who pursues revenge through the law court. However, her brother makes it clear in his prosecution speech that had he been unable to pursue vengeance himself, this task would have fallen to the dead man's son, raised by his widow and informed of the need for revenge for his father. We must infer from the inclusion of this tale in the narrative of the prosecution speech that the jury would have taken seriously the information that the dead man called on his wife to ensure that he was avenged. In addition, it seems that the naming of the accused by the condemned man would have carried weight for the prosecution.

The raising of children in revenge requires an enduring memory of the wrong which has been perpetrated. In the Lysias case it would have taken many years for the child of Dionysodorus to grow to adulthood. The inability to forget wrongs, but instead to focus on future revenge, is a characteristic of vendetta societies. In an intelligent essay on the subject of memory, Nicole Loraux (1998: 98) associates the concepts of mourning and memory with wrath and the desire for revenge, and suggests that this tends to be seen as a womanly characteristic throughout Greek myth and literature. She discusses the Athenians' ban on recalling past wrongs[32] after the reign of the Thirty in 403 BC and states that the desire to forget was related to the desire to preserve the unity of the city (Loraux 1998: 10). Here, the recollection of evils is not so much remembering, as recalling against someone. So the memory is brandished in an offensive manner which can lead to desire for revenge (Loraux 1998: 86–7). In this case, the Athenians are keen to eliminate the possibility of revenge attacks, because of the threat to civic order caused by civil war (cf. Andoc. 1.81; Lys. 18.18). However, it is also possible to speculate that women were similarly viewed as potential threats to the civic order, because they publicly remembered past evils and called for revenge in their laments.

Although no ancient laments composed by women survive, modern scholars have suggested that they were viewed as threatening to the order of male society and have concluded that lamentation of the dead in ancient Greece was often closely associated with blood revenge (Alexiou 1974: 21–2; Holst-Warhaft 1992: 118; Seaford 1994: 84). Evidence for this is most frequently drawn from the texts which refer to the funeral legislation ascribed to Solon and from tragedy, as well as from comparison to modern ritual laments. Our sources suggest that Athenian funerary legislation aimed to curb excessive behaviour in mourning the dead. To this end, many of the restrictions laid down applied directly to women. Demosthenes tells us that the laying out of the body was to take place inside and that the funeral procession had to occur before sunrise on the day after the laying out. In the procession men were to walk in front and no women under the age of 60 except close relatives were to join the procession to the tomb (Dem. 43.62). Here, it appears that the legislator is attempting to diminish the large groups of women who could gather at the grave side. This is probably because the tomb of the dead man, as a visual symbol of his demise, could become a potent focal point of grief as in the evidence seen above (p. 94). Moreover, it can be speculated that the decision to disinter the bones of the Alcmaeonids (Thuc. 1.126.12; *Ath. Pol.* 1; Plut. *Sol.* 12.3) could have been intended to prevent the tombs becoming a focal point where lamenting women could incite revenge (Seaford 1994: 92–4). To the particulars supplied by Demosthenes, Plutarch supplies some additional details about the restriction on excessive behaviour at funerals such as self-laceration, reciting dirges and lamentation by professional mourners (Plut. *Sol.* 21).[33] Again, the focus here is largely on the behaviour of women.

Much has been made of these descriptions of Athenian funerary legislation by Alexiou and Holst-Warhaft in their discussion of lamentation in antiquity. In part, the measures apparently aim to curtail the power of the aristocratic families, whose loyalty would have been focused in large gatherings at funerals (Alexiou 1974: 21; Holst-Warhaft 1992: 116; Loraux 1986: 45; Seaford 1994: 83). As such, the sweep of the legislation is essentially democratic. Also, the legislator seems to have been keen to restrict women's power over the rites of death, so that the state funeral and the male funeral oration are of greater significance (Holst-Warhaft 1992: 3–6; Loraux 1986: 42ff; Seaford 1994: 84–5). Again, the suppression of women and the promotion of state cult is seen as a significant move towards democracy (Alexiou 1974: 21; Holst-Warhaft 1992: 117; Nagy in Loraux 1998: x; Seaford 1994: 82). Here, there is an added implication that women's mourning could be detrimental to the state war effort.[34] However, the law also removes from women the opportunity to voice their concerns in a public forum. The legislation implies that there was a concern about the numbers of women who attended funerals and also about their lamentation. This has suggested to modern commentators that women's laments in antiquity were viewed as dangerous. Through use of cross-cultural comparison with modern laments, the commentators have suggested that the legislator wished to remove women's power to discuss issues in public. So, women could no longer influence decisions about inheritance through public appeals in their laments (Alexiou 1974: 21; Holst-Warhaft 1992: 117; Seaford 1994: 84–5). Women's active role in influencing matters connected with the distribution of estates in classical Athens has been noted above (pp. 102–3). Moreover, the commentators suggest that laments could no longer be used as a forum for inciting revenge.

Here, practices which are acceptable in a pre-state society without legal institutions come into question. The establishment of the Athenian state and its progression towards radical democracy clearly affects the status of women in society. In addition, the desire to quell blood-feuds and, instead, to bring enemies to law brings about a necessity to curb all means of inciting violence (Dem. 23.39; cf. A. *Eum.*). Nevertheless, it is not clear how successful these measures actually were, and it is possible to speculate that lamentation and violent revenge still occurred at Athens, especially in more rural areas. This appears to be an area in which the theory about women's conservatism in preserving ancient traditions holds true (cf. Alexiou 1974: 22–3).

However, much of this discussion is speculative and there is little evidence from classical Athens that women were actually responsible for inciting violent feuds. Nonetheless, the stories about foreign women suggest that inciting revenge was viewed as a female trait in antiquity. Moreover, a small amount of evidence shows that it was acceptable for women to encourage the pursuit of revenge through the laws in Athens. In the absence of the women's laments, it is difficult to draw firm conclusions about the threat which these presented to the orderliness of society, but the evidence does suggest that women did not easily forget misdemeanours against their family, and the concern of ancient legislators also allows us to conclude that women's behaviour at funerals was, in some way, deemed threatening to the order of male society.

Representation of women in male literature of ancient Athens

Here, I want to focus on the character of Electra who is well represented in extant plays by the three great tragedians. The ongoing nature of the feud in the house of Atreus also makes this particular plot of interest. Electra's devotion to the cause of her father is represented in all three plays by her failure to achieve marriage and by her excessive mourning. Electra is also shown as most desirous of revenge in all three playwrights and takes a key role in urging on her brother to revenge.

In Aeschylus and Sophocles, Electra is not married, an unnatural state of being for a grown woman which is characteristic of Electra's strong allegiance to her father's house.[35] However, in Euripides' play Aegisthus marries her to a peasant so that her children will not be strong enough to take revenge (E. *El.* 25–39, 267). He does this because he is afraid that if he does not marry her off, she will have a noble son in secret (22–42). The significance of this decision is that Aegisthus' choice of her partner is not a relative, and so his children would not feel so strongly obliged to avenge a man who was not related through the paternal blood-line. Electra would have expected to marry a relation under normal circumstances; a usual occurrence in the royal house of Argos. She was betrothed to her mother's brother, Castor (312–13), but then marries her father's sister's son, Pylades (E. *Or.* 1658–9; *El.* 1284–5, 1340–1; cf. Hyg. *Fab.* 122). It is perhaps a secret son by Pylades that Aegisthus fears. Here, as in the evidence from Athens and from modern Greece, the possibility of a woman raising children to seek revenge is seen as a threat.

In all three playwrights, Electra is characterized by her excessive mourning. In Aeschylus' play Orestes can identify his sister because her great grief makes her conspicuous (*Cho.* 16–18). In Sophocles' play, Electra says that only a fool would forget. Instead she will grieve unceasingly like Procne and Niobe, both renowned for their unending mourning for their lost children (S. *El.* 145–52). In Euripides' play, Electra makes her entrance with a great song of grief for her own fate, for her father and for her brother. She claims that she constantly tears her cheeks and beats her head as well as wearing her hair shorn in mourning. She refuses to go to the festival with the other women and cannot go on with normal life (E. *El.* 112ff., esp. 146–9). Here, Electra's unwillingness to stop mourning is not only viewed as excessive, but also as threatening to the normal pattern of life. Instead of marrying and raising children of her own, Electra revels in mourning. Even where she is married, she refuses to fulfil the proper roles of a wife, but prefers to focus on lamentation.

The laments of Electra as they are represented in the plays bear close resemblance to modern ritual laments in several of their features, although the structure of the laments differs. Moreover, the fact that the staged laments would have been performed by male actors reciting precomposed lines, rather than being extemporized by female composers would have affected them in ways that it is now difficult for us to perceive (cf. Foley 1993: 102 n.4). Nevertheless, it seems that the audience would have been able to recognize these as literary examples of real laments. First, the tendency to address the dead man directly is evidenced in all three writers (e.g. A. *Cho.* 332–5; S. *El.* 808; E. *El.* 122–4, 157–66). Second, the lamenter often expresses wishes, usually for things which cannot now be fulfilled (Alexiou 1974: 178ff.). For example, in the *Choephori*, while Orestes expresses the wish that Agamemnon had died honourably at Troy (345–53), Electra wishes that his slayers had died instead of him (363–71). The lamenter also tends to focus on her own grief and suffering (e.g. A. *Cho.* 444–50; S. *El.* 807–22; E. *El.* 114–21, 132–4). Further, the tendency to call for revenge during the lament makes the laments of tragedy directly comparable to the modern laments cited above. In Aeschylus' play, Electra calls on her dead father together with her brother. They ask for his help in achieving revenge by appealing to his sense of honour asking him to remember how he died (*Cho.* 491–2). In similar fashion in Euripides' play, Electra reminds Agamemnon of the ignominy of his death (157–66) and appeals to Zeus to bring her brother back to achieve revenge (135–9). In Sophocles' play, Electra refers to how hopeless revenge now seems in her lament for the supposedly dead Orestes (811–12), before working herself up to a decision to attempt revenge herself. Although it is impossible to judge to what extent these laments are true to life, it seems from a comparison to modern laments that they were at least inspired by real laments.

Both through her laments, and through general persuasion, Electra is portrayed in the plays as a key force in promoting Orestes' revenge. Her role is most muted in Aeschylus' play but, nevertheless, Electra prays for the return of her brother (*Cho.* 138–9) and her lamentation aids Orestes' resolve to take revenge (cf. Foley 1993: 113). Further, it is presumably Electra who keeps the robe covered with Agamemnon's blood which Orestes displays at the end of the *Choephori* (985–9). She also refers to this in the lament appealing to her father not to forget his shameful death (492). This appeal intends to provoke the ghost of Agamemnon to support his children, but it also serves as a reminder to Orestes, intended to stimulate his wrath ready for revenge. This is a suggestion in the ancient evidence that, like women in vendetta societies, ancient women preserved mementoes of the dead man covered in his blood to help incite relatives to revenge.

Electra also longs for the return of Orestes in Sophocles' and Euripides' plays (S. *El.* 113, 209–12, 453–8; E. *El.* 137–9, 269) and plays a major part in urging him on to take revenge (S. *El.* 1487; E. *El.* 967–78, cf. 269). In Sophocles' play, Electra is accused of rescuing Orestes to ensure revenge (S. *El.* 601–4, 1133; cf. 12–14, 777–87). In Euripides' play, she also acts as a helper to Orestes (E. *El.* 98–101) by luring Clytemnestra into a trap

(647ff.; cf. E. *Or.* 32) and by holding onto the sword as Orestes kills his mother (1224–6). Significantly, in Euripides' *Orestes*, Tyndareus claims that Electra is more guilty than Orestes for egging him on (*Or.* 615–21). This crime means that she must share equally in the punishment for the murder voted on by the Argives. Tyndareus' comment gives an indication that inciting revenge was not only seen as a threat in the ancient *polis*, but it was also condemned most strongly as antisocial behaviour.

Electra goes one step further than this in Sophocles' play, when she threatens to take revenge herself after she believes that her brother is dead. For help in this plan, she turns to her sister Chrysothemis (954–7). The first dialogue between the girls emphasizes that females are thought to be too afraid to act. Chrysothemis agrees with her sister on the injustice of her father's murder and looks forward to the return of Orestes, but she will not show her feelings out of fear (333–6). Instead, she refers to the necessity of yielding to those in power (396). Similar worries dominate the girls' second dialogue. She tells Electra that it is not possible to act against enemies because they are women and therefore are too weak (997–8). Electra criticizes her sister's cowardice (1027) and accuses her of not being sufficiently supportive of Agamemnon, and of respecting her mother too much (341–2, 367–8).[36] Electra is aware that the sisters will not be allowed normal lives and marriages because of Aegisthus' fears that their sons will take revenge (S. *El.* 963–6, cf. E. *El.* 267–8). The fear of revenge here is not thought to come from the women themselves, but from their sons, raised with the idea that they must take revenge. This notion, based on women's supposed weakness, is supported by Chrysothemis' reluctance to have any part in taking revenge on her father's killers. Electra's willingness to act takes her out of the sphere of womanly weakness, to a place where she would be worthy of honour for preserving her father's house, usually a manly virtue (S. *El.* 975–83). So, she feels that they have nothing to lose, but that their revenge will gain them a good marriage and praise (970–2). However, as soon as Orestes reveals that he is alive, Electra returns to the role of praying and encouraging, leaving the actual killing to her brother (1487).

In these plays, a female character is placed at the heart of the revenge plot, demonstrating excessive and even dangerous behaviour within her own family group. By focusing on a revenge plot within the family, which involves the matricide of a murderous, adulterous wife, the Athenian playwrights are clearly revelling in excessive plotlines which bear little resemblance to everyday events. However, it is equally clear that some of the elements included in their characterization of Electra are drawn from observations about women's association with revenge ethics, although these are blown out of proportion. It is, further, possible to speculate that if ancient laments were in fact similar to modern laments, as Alexiou and Holst-Warhaft maintain, Electra's laments were inspired by dirges originally composed and performed by Athenian women.[37] Indeed, the threat of female revenge in Sophocles' play closely matches similar threats in the modern laments. As above, I do not see this as evidence that women actually ever took revenge into their own hands in ancient Athens. Instead, I see this as a possible example of the manipulation of female songs by male dramatists.

Electra's case is not isolated in Attic tragedy. In some plays, women are actually represented as taking revenge themselves. They tend to act when in a position of isolation, lacking male relatives, and they always act on behalf of their own relatives, usually fathers, brothers and sons.[38] For example, Althaea is said to have condemned her son to death because he murdered her brothers. She is able to achieve this by the burning of a magical fire-brand which is preserving his life (A. *Cho.* 602–11). One fragment from Phrynichus' *Women of Pleuron* tells us how Althaea, the contriver of evil, threw the magical brand on the fire (fr. 6 Snell = Paus. 10.31.4). Hecuba (E. *Hec.*) is able to achieve her revenge against Polymestor by using deceit and with the help of her faithful servants. Medea (E. *Med.*) and Procne (S. *Tereus*) are able to kill the victims of their revenge, because instead of targeting their husbands, they slay their young children (see further in McHardy 2004).

As argued above, this kind of plotline does not seem to reflect reality. Glotz (1904: 82) believes that this phenomenon is caused by poets' fantasies which make them portray women acting in vengeance. He believes that women would have been incapable of such dynamic action and maintains that all they ever did in reality was curse. He refers to stories showing women reproaching or cursing as 'authentic legends', while stories in which women take violent revenge are poetic fantasies.[39] Here, instead of stressing the idea that poets embellish life merely for aesthetic purposes, I would like to suggest that they are embellishing life in order to reflect Athenian social ideals on stage.[40] I suggest, *contra* Glotz, that the Greek audience did believe in the existence of female revenge, especially in the distant past and in distant places. Indeed, like the modern novels, the tragedies have focused in on female involvement in revenge as a potential area for anxiety. Moreover, whereas the evidence for women's participation in revenge acts in Athens is extremely light, so strong is the association of women with desiring and inciting revenge, that female characters in tragedy are closely involved in revenge plots or represented as actually taking revenge themselves in ten extant plays.[41] Here, I would like to suggest that ancient women's laments and their close connection with the traditions of revenge ethics have inspired the tragedians, just like the modern novelists, to place female characters at the centre of their revenge plots. However, just as in the modern novels, where women conflict with Christian ethics or the institutions and norms of civilized male society, the vengeful women of tragedy become embodiments of uncivilized values which cannot be condoned in civilized democratic Athens. They do not merely incite revenge, they are involved in problem-atic revenge plots within the family or with a guest-friend. Ethics which could be considered honourable are sullied by the tendency to kin-killing, where a son is urged to kill his own mother, and mothers murder their own children in vengeance. Here, I want to argue that the women of Athenian tragedy embody the danger of allowing the vendetta to continue unabated at Athens. The implication of this is that Athenian society rejects bloody feuds in favour of due process and pursuing revenge through the laws (cf. A. *Eum.*).

Women's unwitting influence

Throughout this chapter I have drawn a distinction between the evidence for women's actual influence on revenge culture and how men represent this in literary plots. Real women appear to have made positive artistic contributions through their composition of laments and to have influenced a traditional area of society. Moreover, in both ancient and modern sources there is some evidence of respect for women who ensure that revenge is pursued at the request of a dying man. However, women's possible influences on revenge are construed as dangerous in democratic *polis* society in Athens. This leads to legislation on the behaviour of women and to the re-allocation of lamentation to the male actors and male playwrights who portray women in tragedy. Moreover, the close association of women with encouraging revenge ethics and with the rituals involved in mourning, leads to female characters in tragedy being represented at the heart of nearly every revenge plot. Not only is it possible to speculate that tragic laments are based on the oral creations of women, but also the plots of the plays appear to be inspired by folk beliefs about women's role in revenge ethics. Although the evidence for women's actual influence on male revenge culture in Athens seems scant enough, the threat of this influence is exposed clearly in tragedy with its focus on excessive mourning, antisocial behaviour and, even, women's revenge against their own children. In this way, we can see that women did, indeed, have an (albeit unwitting) effect on one of the greatest aspects of Athenian male culture – tragedy.

Notes

1 I would like to thank Barbara Goff and Richard Seaford for their helpful comments on drafts of this chapter.
2 For the significance of revenge ethics in Greek society, see Dover (1974: 180–4); Mossman (1995: ch. 6); Vlastos (1991: ch. 7); Whitlock-Blundell (1989: esp. ch. 2); McHardy (1999).
3 These include: *Northern Albania*: Durham (1909, 1928), Hasluck (1954); *Bedouin society*: Abu Lughod (1987), Ginat (1987), Peters (1967); *Corsica*: Deliyanni (1985), Knudson (1988), Wilson (1988); *Crete*: Herzfeld (1985); *Mani*: Deliyanni (1985), Holst-Warhaft (1992), Seremetakis (1991); *Montenegro*: Boehm (1984). Black-Michaud (1975) writes about feuding in Mediterranean societies in general. See McHardy (1999) for a detailed discussion of the scholarship on revenge in these societies.

4 However, while anthropologists have pointed out these so-called 'rules', most frequently it is not possible to retrieve how individuals actually lived or acted. Rather, the evidence is strongly coloured with cultural ideals and values.

5 See further below (pp. 96–8) on arguments for women having an active role in the fighting.

6 For the metaphor of washing see Pitt-Rivers (1965: 25) who quotes the saying '*La lessive de l'honneur ne se coule qu'au sang*'.

7 This may seem a reason for killing a woman in preference to a man, but the equality of the code of blood revenge allows only one death in return for another.

8 Alternatively, the man's blood is stored in a bottle to remind the men to take revenge when the blood has fermented (Hasluck 1954: 231).

9 These laments are also significant in their own right as uniquely female compositions.

10 See further below on this novel.

11 In this respect they are the opposite of the male funeral encomium which makes a virtue of death in the service of the state (Foley 1993: 105; Holst-Warhaft 1992: 5).

12 See, for example, Alexiou (1974: 124): 'Cruel Charos, most cruelly have you taken my child, who was my pride, who was my life'.

13 For further description of this male council which deliberated on matters of importance to villagers in Mani see Seremetakis (1991: ch. 7).

14 The adoption of male clothing by ancient Greek women participating in 'male' spheres such as philosophy and medicine is discussed by Hawley (1994: 73); Finnegan (1995).

15 This is one of several versions of this lament. See Holst-Warhaft (1992: 56–9) for discussion of the lament.

16 Sisters and daughters might be associated with such revenge as blood kin, but wives do not sing of avenging their husbands. As noted above, wives with young sons could raise them to take revenge for their fathers. Women without children could return to their father's home and remarry.

17 For more on this see McHardy (1999 and 2004). Seremetakis (1991: 31) notes that a married Maniat woman retains the surname of her natal family. If she is addressed by her husband's name the suffix *nyphe* (bride) is added.

18 Cf. Holst-Warhaft (1992: 77ff.) for discussion of this lament. She notes the use of poison is a woman's method.

19 The oral nature of the laments means that when they are recalled or reused on other occasions, details change. There is no definitive version of these compositions (although some collectors have been keen to try to establish the 'original' version). Cf. Janko (1998: 2–3) on the flexibility of wording even in short oral poems.

20 See Constantinides (1983) on the occurrence of warrior maidens in Greek folk-songs. Cf. also Boehm (1984: 47) on esteem for female warriors in Montenegrin folk-poetry, and Durham (1928: 75–6, 149, 171) on women and vengeance in folk-poetry.

21 Durham (1928: 194) met four such virgins on her travels in Albania, but they did not dress as men or carry arms.

22 See Aeschylus (*Ag.* 11) for a comparable reference to Clytemnestra.

23 Seremetakis (1991) discovers many men in the Mani who recall great *moirologistrias* (lament singers) and can recite parts of their verses. Cf. also Caraveli-Chaves (1980: 129–57; 1986: 170–94) on men's differing reactions to laments. Many express admiration. The popularity of some composers is also attested by the many different versions of some laments which are current.

24 See Pierre Salmon's preface to Mérimée's novel (1992: 7–12) which describes the historical feuds on which Mérimée based his novel. However, it will be noted that the story differs in important details, specifically, that the real Colomba was married

with children. In this it seems that Mérimée could have been influenced by the myth of Electra (further below, pp. 108–10).

25 This aspect of the novel is partly autobiographical. Prevelakis, although born in Crete in 1909, was educated in Paris. He found his western education an impediment in getting back to his Cretan roots. Cf. Mackridge (1986: 146).

26 There is also a tendency to embellish the role of women. The key role played by Yiorgakis' aunt, Rousaki, in dying to preserve the life of her brother's son, is a moving and effective way of closing the novel, but it is not representative of reality.

27 Cf. Holst-Warhaft (1992: 89ff.) on laments which place women at conflict with the authorities, especially over foreign wars and (2000: 18) on the Serbian 'Women in Black' who were arrested for their protests against the war in which they had lost menfolk. See further below (pp. 106–7) on this problem in ancient Greece.

28 See Walters (1993: 195–200); Gagarin (2001) for discussion of this speech. Cf. also Blundell (1998: 63).

29 Although Gagarin (2001: 167) emphasizes that these are not the woman's actual words, he believes that she did originally make a speech in her own 'feminine' style on which Lysias based this 'masculine' version. Cf. also Foxhall (1996: 149).

30 Cf. also Schaps (1982: 198) on literary representations of women urging their men to make war.

31 On the disputed authenticity of this oration see Edwards (1995: 131–6).

32 Jury men took an oath not to recall grievances, but to vote according to the laws (Andoc. 1.90–1).

33 See Alexiou (1974: 14ff.); Holst-Warhaft (1992: 114ff.); Loraux (1998: 19ff.); Seaford (1994:74ff.) for descriptions of similar funerary legislation from other Greek cities.

34 See Fantham et al. (1994: 78) for discussion of Plutarch (Nic. 13) where women's lamentation at the Adonia is said to challenge the war effort because it stresses the consequences of death for the survivors. Cf. also Holst-Warhaft (1992: 119ff.); Loraux (1998: 11). See above, pp. 100 n.27.

35 Even in Euripides' version where she is married to a peasant the marriage is not consummated (E. El. 43–4, 255, 311). Cf. also Antigone (S. Ant. 905–12; E. Pho. 1683–4), Macaria (E. Hkld. 531–2). See Foley (1981: 152); Seaford (1987).

36 Cf. Ismene in Sophocles' Antigone (61–4) who is afraid to act, but agrees with her sister and even attempts to share the blame later (536–7).

37 Cf. Murnaghan (1999: 203–4) for a similar view of laments in epic.

38 Except Medea, who acts for herself.

39 I do not accept his division into 'authentic' and 'inauthentic' legends.

40 Contra Burnett (1998: xiii–xviii) who believes that revenge in tragedy is for entertainment's sake alone. Cf. Gilbert (1999) for a perceptive review of her book.

41 A. Ag., Cho.; S. El.; E. Med., Hec., El., Or., Hlkd., Andr., and Hipp. Fragmentary plays such as Sophocles' Tereus also seem to have featured central female revenge plots.

7

A WOMAN'S INFLUENCE
ON A ROMAN TEXT

Marcia and Seneca

Rebecca Langlands

In the introduction to her ground-breaking work on women in the ancient world, *Goddesses, Whores, Wives and Slaves*, Sarah Pomeroy comments on ancient Greek and Roman civilization, 'rarely has there been a wider discrepancy between the cultural rewards a society had to offer and women's participation in that culture' (1975: 9). As illustration of her terms 'cultural rewards' and 'culture' she offers the examples of the philosophy of Socrates and the histories of Herodotus and Thucydides, the linguistic products of elite society. The textual traces of these kinds of products are precisely the sources which classicists today scrutinize in our search to understand ancient cultures. Yet almost all the texts written in ancient Greece and Rome which survive today were written by men, and the implications of this have long been appreciated; the texts offer male perspectives on their cultures; they do not allow the reader direct access to women's voices; they contain no expression of women's ideas.

However, in this chapter I shall argue that Roman women did exert influence over male-authored texts. Even when a text was written by a man, women could participate in the production of his text and influence what he wrote and how he wrote it, both as individuals and, more generally, as members of his society whom the writer could not ignore. Even when women were not writing themselves, they were affecting the literature of the culture in which they lived. The influence is felt particularly keenly in a situation where the author anticipates that women will read a text (for example as patrons or addressees). I shall suggest that the effects of this influence are visible in my sample text (Seneca's *Ad Marciam*) and that they may be recovered by the modern reader.

I shall illustrate this thesis by discussing one particular ancient male-authored text which explicitly anticipates a female reader: the philosophical treatise of consolation (*consolatio*) written by the Stoic philosopher and statesman Seneca the Younger some time in the late 30s or early 40s CE,[1] and addressed to Marcia, daughter of the historian Cremutius Cordus.[2] Marcia's young adult son Metilius has died and three years have passed in which her grief has apparently persisted (1.7). Such a *consolatio* presents itself as aiming to educate the addressee, to strengthen their moral fibre so that they may best cope with their bereavement (Wilson 1997: 48–9; cf. also Braund 1997: 70). Seneca describes his treatise at 1.8 with the anatomical analogy of a medical remedy which must be applied to the hardened and festering wound of her mature grief; he cannot treat her as gently as he might if the bereavement were fresh, but must fight more violently against it and shatter her sorrow. Philosophy works not on the body, but on the mind, and Seneca's tools are those of the philosopher: persuasion, language, ideas. Following the conventions of this genre, Seneca addresses to Marcia a combination of stock philosophical precepts – we are all mortal, the dead cannot suffer, she must look to her remaining children and grandchildren for comfort – and apposite *exempla* which she must follow: examples of illustrious figures who have suffered a similar blow and borne it well. In sections 12.6 to 15.4 he offers Marcia the figures of Lucius Sulla, Horatius Pulvillus, Paulus, Lucius Bibulus, Gaius Caesar and the emperors Augustus and Tiberius.

In this chapter I will show how the fact that the named addressee of this particular piece, Marcia, is a woman, has an effect on what Seneca writes and on how he writes, and thus on his expression of Stoic thinking. I shall focus upon two key passages which illustrate two aspects of the impact of a female reader. The first is the opening passage (1.1–2.2, and especially 1.1), where Seneca shows himself grappling with the application of conventional Stoic language and ideas to a situation which threatens to expose their inadequacy. The second passage (16.1) is Seneca's reflection upon his own use of *exempla*, which ends by suggesting that male and female readers may interpret *exempla* in radically different ways. Here, Seneca raises the worrying question of how much control an author has over the interpretation of his own work and thus acknowledges the power of a female reader to contribute alternative or subversive meanings to male-authored texts.

The lack of control that a thinker has over the reception and interpretation of his or her own ideas by other people once they have been disseminated in textual form was clearly a source of anxiety for ancient authors; a classic discussion is that in Plato's *Phaedrus* (275Dff). Seneca raises the spectres of such anxieties early on in this consolation, during his sketch of Marcia's reaction to her father's death and her current situation (1.2–6). In this passage he describes Marcia as having made an immense contribution to Roman scholarship and to posterity (1.3). In itself this is an interesting characterization of a Roman woman, worth bearing in mind in the context of my argument. The contribution Seneca refers to here is in the secondary role of preserving and publishing the ideas of another. Her father, Aulus Cremutius Cordus, was the historian who was convicted of treason during the reign of the emperor Tiberius, according to Tacitus because in his history of Rome he praised Brutus and Cassius, the men who killed Julius Caesar. He was ordered to kill himself and his works were ordered to be burned, but, Seneca tells us, Marcia managed to hide some of his writings until a change in regime meant that they could safely be made public once more. Now 'he is read, he flourishes, taken up once again in people's hands and hearts' (1.4).

Cremutius Cordus' story is one of a man whose text is fatally (mis)interpreted as a political attack upon the imperial family. The story closely associates the author with his works, as the above citation shows; the two are condemned as one to destruction, and the life of the work which Marcia's action guarantees means that the author himself will, after all, never grow old. It is a tale which vividly demonstrates the possibility that a text might be received in a way which the author had not intended or anticipated, and which might have dire consequences for author and text.

Shortly after this, Seneca introduces the figure of Marcia herself as someone whom grief has rendered an uncooperative reader. During the past three years, he tells us, her friends and relatives have tried all means of persuasion to console her, but all in vain (1.6). The scholarly pursuits which she used to love, following in her father's footsteps, now fail to evoke the required response from her – they fall on deaf ears. This opening characterization of Marcia, outlining her past and present relationships with literature, also introduces two different aspects of authorial anxiety about readers; Cremutius Cordus' fate highlights the possibility of dangerous readings which have repercussions for the author, while Marcia represents a reader who may resist the right sort of engagement with the text, thus rendering the words and philosophical ideas impotent.[3]

In general terms it is important to emphasize here that I do not wish to suggest that there are essential differences between men and women which cause them to interpret texts differently. The possibility of Roman women reading differently from Roman men arises because Roman structures of gender ideology place men and women in different subject positions and different circumstances which may affect their relationship to the text. For example, when Seneca praises the benefits of Cremutius Cordus' history to Marcia, he claims that its memory will not fade as long as there are those who wish to learn moral and political lessons from the past. Yet, Seneca's formulation of the key lesson that may be learnt from Cremutius Cordus' work might cause Marcia to wonder about her own role in Roman history: memory will not fade as long as there is anyone who wants to know 'what it is to be a Roman man'.[4]

The language of philosophy

In the Latin language (at least in the register of language that we are able to access in the written texts produced by educated men), the vocabulary that describes moral qualities often overlaps with vocabulary which denotes difference and opposition between male and female. Thus, for example, the term *muliebris* is the adjective describing the word for woman (*mulier*), and so means 'womanly', 'like a woman', but it also means 'cowardly' or 'morally weak'. *Virtus*, from which our own word 'virtue' derives, can mean virtue in our broad sense of moral strength, or more specifically 'courage', or it can mean, 'manhood' – the state of being an adult male, or *vir*. The core terms of ethical philosophy are thus strikingly gendered. The Latin we find in extant sources is, in Dale Spender's phrase 'man-made language', which privileges men and male experience, and makes masculinity synonymous with all that is good, while the female is the weaker sex. Spender (1990: x) writes of the English language 'men controlled the language and . . . it worked in their favour', and this assertion holds true for Latin as well. This linguistic polarization is, of course, no accident; it reflects ideas about the differences between male and female, excluding and denigrating women, which ran deep through Roman society, and affected and reaffirmed political, legal and social structures.

These linguistic structures cause problems for a man who wishes to talk philosophy with a woman. When Seneca addresses a woman in a philosophical treatise, the language he has at his disposal makes less immediate sense than it does when he is writing to another man. This becomes clear when we compare his consolation to Marcia with another treatise in the same genre whose addressee, Polybius, is male. When he is urging Polybius to respond to Stoic teaching, to control his grief at his brother's death, and not to fall prey to weakness and self-indulgence, Seneca writes: 'Nothing lowly, nothing base is appropriate for you; yet what is there so base and cowardly/woman-like (*muliebre*) as to allow oneself to be consumed by grief?' (*Consolatio ad Polybium* 6.2). He tells Polybius that he is surrounded by people watching whether he will be able to bear adversity like a man/courageously (*viriliter*), that grief must not be borne *molliter et effeminate* (both adverbs associated with Latin terminology for women and denoting moral weakness) for though it is inhuman not to feel grief at all, to be unable to bear it is 'not appropriate for a man': *non est viri* (17.2). The gendered terminology can be used unproblematically. Indeed, it lends persuasive impact, for to grieve is not only morally reprehensible in itself, but would be, for Polybius, inappropriate behaviour for his sex.

Addressed to Marcia, of course, these same words would have an altered significance, and her status as a woman would complicate matters. Urged not to behave like a woman but to 'be a man', Marcia might well ask: 'why shouldn't I continue to grieve and be like a woman? It is appropriate, since

I am a woman'. Or she might ask: 'how can I hope to achieve a virtuous state, since it seems it would be in conflict with my womanhood?' If Seneca takes Marcia seriously as a philosophical pupil – as he seems to – then modifications are required to his persuasive techniques. In order to use effectively the conventional language of his Stoicism, Seneca is compelled to set up a new interpretative framework, to gloss terms, to argue in new ways, and, as we shall see in the second part of my chapter, to alter and to explain the way he employs traditional *exempla*.

So, in his very first sentence, Seneca acknowledges that his reader's sex changes the situation. Marcia's sex presents a challenge which he must at once address. I give the passage first in Latin, with the gendered terminology highlighted in bold, and then in two alternative translations which tease apart the different nuances of these phrases; the first translation brings out the moral significance of the vocabulary used, the second its reference to sexual difference:

> *Nisi te, Marcia, scirem tam longe ab infirmitate **muliebris animi** quam a ceteris vitiis recessisse et mores tuos velut aliquod antiquum exemplar aspici, non auderem obviam ire dolori tuo – cui **viri** quoque libenter haerent et incubant . . . Fiduciam mihi dedit exploratum iam robur animi et magno experimento approbata **virtus tua**.*
>
> (Seneca Ad Marciam 1.1)

> If I did not know, Marcia, that you have withdrawn as far from the weakness of **a cowardly mind** as from the other moral failings, and that your behaviour is looked to as if it were some ancient exemplar, I should not dare to meet your grief (which even **heroic figures** happily fixate and brood upon) head-on . . . The strength of your mind, which has already been put to the test, gives me confidence, as does **your moral excellence**, established through extensive trials.

As the first translation makes clear, Seneca begins his treatise by stating that he is confident about taking the step of addressing to Marcia the consolations of Stoicism because he knows that she possesses the moral qualities necessary to benefit from philosophy, and that his admonitions will take root. This sort of preamble, asserting the intellectual and moral qualifications of the reader, is common in didactic philosophy (cf. Lucretius to Memmius, *DRN*1). We will discover in the following pages that it is the force of Marcia's grief for her son's death, which has already lasted three years and shows no signs of abating, before which Seneca quails. The second translation shows, however, that the Latin language renders the association of moral weakness with being a woman inescapable. In a passage which praises Marcia's moral standing, therefore, Seneca is also endeavouring to explain how this moral standing is possible in a woman, and how Marcia may be disassociated from the apparently inevitable moral weakness of the female:

> If I did not know, Marcia, that you have withdrawn as far from the weakness of **a woman's mind** as from the other moral failings, and that your behaviour is looked to as if it were some ancient exemplar, I should not dare to meet your grief (and **men** happily fixate and brood on grief too) head-on . . . The strength of your mind, which has already been put to the test, gives me confidence, and **your manliness**, established through extensive trials.

Trying to describe a woman as morally excellent exposes the limitations of the Latin language, and, like many Latin authors,[5] Seneca takes a certain delight in foregrounding the ensuing paradox: to describe Marcia as good is to describe her as a man. This situation is familiar to anyone who has studied the ways that women are written about in patriarchal cultures. Within a general framework of opposition between the sexes, some individual women may have qualities not usually associated with their sex, because in some respects they are not like other women. A detailed discussion by Judith Hallett (1989) of this phenomenon in ancient Rome argues convincingly that praise of women is enabled by their kinship with men. Her bipartite model is very useful for making sense of the paradoxes inherent in the Romans' attitudes towards the praise of women; my chapter aims to show, however, that the paradoxes are ultimately irresolvable, based as they are on categories of differentiation between the sexes which are difficult to maintain under pressure.

Seneca's opening formulation, then, is not a solution, but a fudge or compromise which brings with it its own contradictions, and in this passage Seneca's attempt to resolve these leads to further problems. Since Marcia is to be his reader, he is obliged to clear conceptual space in which a female reader may stand and to explain how his addressee is capable of engagement with the work he is writing for her.

There are at least three separate strategies at work here (and the very multiplicity of techniques may be suggestive of a cornered man firing on all cylinders). First, Seneca uses the metaphor of physical removal to describe Marcia's distance from the mental infirmity associated with women. This evokes the idea that Marcia has set herself apart from other women, she is not part of the common herd. The comparison of her with an ancient exemplar strengthens this explanation: like the heroes of old she stands apart from ordinary people, and this alone might explain why she is not like the rest of womankind. Second, Seneca uses a phrase which describes humanity inclusively and partially breaks down the opposition between the sexes (while at the same time drawing attention to it): *viri* (men, or on another reading *great* men), too, may suffer excessively from grief. Third, Seneca endows Marcia with manhood as far as her mind or *animus* goes.

Shortly afterwards Seneca claims that the quality of her mind means that he is compelled not to take her femaleness into account or to allow it to deter him from his project: 'This greatness of your mind forbade me to take any notice of your sex, or of your facial expression, which is occupied with the continuous sadness of so many years . . .' (Seneca *Ad Marciam* 1.5). Implicit in this is, of course, the notion that writing to a woman consumed with grief is an unusual thing to do – and a difficult one. Her femaleness and her grief are highly visible – her body, the expression on her face – and the strength of the verb 'forbid' (*vetuit*, twice repeated in the Latin) does suggest that to ignore her sex requires some effort on Seneca's part. Seneca represents Marcia as a paradox, and the situation as unusual and as a dilemma, in which he has to force himself to turn away deliberately from some facts which confront him.

Seneca also announces at the beginning of Section 2 that because Marcia is his addressee he must introduce a radical change to the conventional structure of a *consolatio*. Usually an author would begin a treatise with the rational arguments against grief (precepts), and then go on to offer illustrations of famous historical deeds (*exempla*) which inspire the reader to follow these precepts. However, while some people, he tells us, respond to reasoning (*ratio*), others must be impressed and held in thrall by famous names, and he swiftly follows with the introduction of two exemplary figures which will guide Marcia's behaviour: Octavia and Livia.

Now, not to be amenable to reason, the key attribute which marks out human beings from animals, is clearly a sign of inferior intellect. The nature of the group to which Marcia implicitly belongs is conveyed in a phrase which heightens this idea: the kind of person who is more impressed by illustrious examples is *ad speciosa stupenti* – 'awed by splendid things', or, gaping at/stupefied by things which are in fact specious. Seneca does not claim that her inferiority is due to her femaleness; in the context it is clearly a reference to the earlier passage in which he has described how tenacious and far advanced is her grief. Yet, in associating her with excessive grief, with lack of reason and with a tendency to be won over by show and superficies, Seneca is, despite his opening protestations, ascribing to Marcia stereotypical attributes of women, echoing language he uses elsewhere in his writings about women (see Vidèn 1993).

It may be argued that the passages discussed so far do not move beyond traditional sexist formulations, and that while attempting to acknowledge Marcia's intellect and moral strength, Seneca also undermines this very acknowledgement. Yet the fact that the picture is confusing and contradictory and that the arguments are unconvincing is, in itself, telling. His treatment of the issues may be read as ultimately serving to confirm Marcia's exclusion from the male world of philosophy, but along the way the inadequacies of the Latin language in the face of a woman reading philosophy have been exposed. Marcia's status as a woman has affected the structure and the content of the work, and the meaning of the language used in it. It has compelled Seneca to raise issues and to explore ideas as he would not have done had he been writing with a male reader in mind. When he writes to Polybius the polarized structure of gender and morals can comfortably be left in place. Here, however, Seneca must offer from the start convoluted explanations about how it is possible that he write to Marcia at all, given conventional attitudes towards the moral incapacity of women. When a woman is posited as the reader, key terms such as *virtus* show up in a different light, and assumptions in the language which ordinarily might be taken for granted become visible.

Exempla

Inspiring exemplary stories (*exempla*) play a crucial role in a Roman *consolatio*; they provide illustrations of virtue in the shape of great figures who have, for instance, overcome their grief in the past, and models of the behaviour to which the addressee should aspire.[6] The first examples that Seneca places before Marcia's eyes as illustrations of different ways of coping with their grief at the death of their sons are those of Livia and Octavia. As he points out, these are the greatest examples both of her own sex and her own era. With this comment, Seneca underlines the fact that these exemplary figures are like her because they are contemporaries and because they are women, drawing attention to the notion that will become important later in the text, that certain kinds of *exempla* work best when the reader identifies very closely with the protagonist.[7] Livia and Octavia, however, are by no means the conventional examples which we would expect to find in a consolation, and this again underlines the unusual nature of this situation. Seneca presents them in conventional terms: in the phrase which introduces his account of the two women's grief (2.2) he calls them '*exempla*', and he ends this section of the piece by using this term again: *elige itaque utrum exemplum putes probabilius*: 'choose, therefore, which *exemplum* you think more commendable' (3.3; see also 3.4). His descriptions of the two women's responses to bereavement, presented to Marcia as alternatives between which she must choose, are framed as traditional examples. Yet these narratives of recent events are, in fact, not part of the wider Roman exemplary tradition, and the very length of the accounts and the detail included in them are an indication of this.

A list of traditional examples does follow, however, from section 12.6; these conform to the conventions of *exempla* both in their concise and pointed presentation and in their familiar content.[8] 'I shall set before you', Seneca tells Marcia, 'certain examples . . . so that you may know that there have been many who have assuaged painful experiences by bearing them with equanimity' (12.5). He tells of L. Sulla, Pulvillus, Paulus, L. Bibulus and Gaius Caesar, all of whom lost sons but were not deflected by their loss from service to their state (12.4–15.4). Inevitably, all these precedents for dealing with bereavement are the deeds of men: the majority of Roman *exempla* are (cf. Litchfield 1914).

Eventually, Seneca imagines Marcia interjecting to complain that these *exempla* are unsuitable for her since she is a woman: 'You have forgotten that it is a woman whom you are consoling, you are relating examples of men' (16.1). His response has often been pored over by those asking whether Stoicism could be thought of as 'feminist' or as believing in the equality of the sexes (see e.g. Loretto 1977; Manning 1973; Ward 1996). It is to tell her that women have the same capacity for virtue as men, and to cite as evidence for this the exemplary tales of Lucretia and Cloelia, which function as historical illustrations of female moral strength in Rome.

> Yet who has said that nature has dealt grudgingly with the dis-
> positions of women, and severely reduced their virtues? Believe me,
> they have equal force and equal ability, if they like, to perform noble
> deeds; they can suffer pain and labour just the same if they are accus-
> tomed to them. In which city, for heaven's sake, are we having this
> discussion? In the city in which Lucretia and Brutus drove out the
> king who was oppressing the Romans: we owe our freedom to
> Brutus, but Brutus' deed to Lucretia; in which we have almost
> written Cloelia into the lists of heroes because of her astonishing
> bravery – fearing neither the enemy nor the river. Sitting on her
> equestrian statue on the Sacred Way, the busiest part of the city,
> Cloelia taunts our youths as they go up to take their seats for
> proceeding in such a way in a city in which we have granted
> equestrian statues even to women.
>
> (Seneca *Ad Marciam* 16.1–2)

In this passage, Seneca attempts to reassure Marcia that she should not be discouraged that all the exemplary figures that he has offered so far are men, and that she should not necessarily assume that, as a woman, she is ill-equipped to emulate their fortitude. He suggests, with his initial rhetorical question, that women are not necessarily naturally disadvantaged, and goes on to talk in terms of their equal potential. There is no reason why a woman such as Marcia should not strive to imitate the virtues displayed by great men; the figures of Lucretia and Cloelia, famous women from Roman history, are presented as evidence that women in that past have indeed achieved greatness, and as models for Marcia herself to follow. References to the tales of Lucretia and Cloelia, the familiar Roman heroines, illustrate Seneca's claim that Rome, the very city in which he and Marcia live, is one which particularly nurtures and acknowledges women's valour. The passage is designed to encourage Marcia to feel confident in her own potential as a woman, and to aspire to imitate the virtues of men.

Yet, if we turn to look more closely at the description of Cloelia's statue with which the passage leaves us, we find a very different message – a message which, in fact, undermines the very principle which the passage earlier claims to be affirming. Cloelia's equestrian statue, standing in the centre of Rome on a busy urban street, is not pictured merely as an inspiring and uplifting image of Roman heroism. Rather, it draws on another tradition of thinking about *exempla* and about women; that which sees a woman's heroism necessarily as a denigration of men.[9] Seneca uses the term *exprobat* (taunt) to describe the effect that Cloelia's statue has upon the slack young men of Rome who pass by her daily: the statue and the story that belongs to it stand as a criticism of them, an accusation of their inadequacy. 'Even women' have been honoured in this city, and this reflects badly upon those men who have not achieved greatness. This taunt rests on the underlying assumption that for a woman to outperform a man is a shameful thing, and this in turn makes sense only if we assume that men are naturally more capable and virtuous than women. The *exemplum* which started out as reassurance to Marcia that women are not inferior to men, can end by functioning as a challenge to Roman youths by drawing on assumptions which seem to run directly counter to this – women *are* naturally inferior – all in the space of eight and a half lines.

How does such as brief passage convey two such conflicting messages at once? It works by setting up (within the text) two different kinds of readers who read from different perspectives and respond differently to the material. The meaning of the exemplary story of Cloelia's escapade is shown to be affected by who the audience or reader of the story is. On the one hand we have Seneca's characterization of Marcia – an anxious woman who has queried her ability to live up to the standards set by male examples, and who should be reassured by the passage of her own potential and inspired to virtue by the figures of famous women. On the other hand, we have the degenerate Roman youth who should (if they bother to take notice of it) be stung by the disapproval which it expresses of their lifestyle, and embarrassed into reforming their own lives. The two posited readerships relate in different ways to the exemplary figures and draw different conclusions about the way that the message they convey can be applied to themselves; Marcia is invited to identify with and emulate Lucretia and Cloelia, the young men to see themselves as fundamentally different from and to aspire to outdo them.

Seneca's passage neatly illustrates how an *exemplum* is open to different readings and how, in this case, the gender of the reader is an important factor in the definition of its message. It also demonstrates his awareness of the above: in order to write the passage Seneca has had to imagine reading as a woman and as a young man, and to acknowledge diverse perspectives and identities, and alternative possibilities in interpretation based on these. In this passage we see once again the tentative development of ideas which would not have seen the light of day had Seneca not been required to bear in mind the perspective of a female reader. The awareness of Marcia as a potential reader has sent Seneca's thoughts in new directions. In addition, this notion delineated here by Seneca, that a female reader may read from a different perspective, and that this may affect her interpretation of a text, has broader implications: all male-authored texts may be at risk from the off-beat interpretation of potential female (-identified) readers. We have already seen that ancient authors expressed anxiety about the lack of control that they had over the interpretation of their ideas once they had become reified in text; the possibility of female readers, with their alternative concerns, identifications and interpretations, posed an invisible threat to men's ideas.

Conclusion

Seneca's struggles with the structures of Roman thought and language and his reflection upon them will not necessarily have had a lasting effect upon Roman culture, but they do, themselves, reflect a woman's influence. The text I have examined cannot show us (alas) what Marcia would have made of it; however, her real presence in Seneca's life enables us to see a male writer beginning to think about what it might be like to 'read as a woman', and the implications of this. In this *consolatio*, we see Seneca attempting to deal with the problem that traditional ways of thinking about women as different from and inferior to men do not work well when they are confronted with the prospect of a real and intelligent female reader. We also see him manifesting awareness of the fact that women may read from a different point of view from men and that this may affect their interpretation of a text. In conclusion, women, as hypothetical thinkers, moral agents and readers cannot help but influence the ideological products of their own culture, even when the media are directly controlled by men.

Notes

1 Dating by Waltz (1955). Unless otherwise specified all following references are to this text, *Consolatio ad Marciam* (OCT edition), and all translations are my own.
2 Seneca discusses her relationship with her father 1.2–4, but see also Tacitus' account of his writings and his death under the emperor Tiberius, *Annals* 4.34.
3 For an outline of Stoic thought about the author's inability to control the interpretation of his text see Schiesaro (1997: esp. 107).
4 '*quid sit vir Romanus.*' *Vir* is the Latin term which is used to mean 'man' in opposition to 'woman', but it also has an emphatic sense of 'great man' or 'hero' – it is translated as 'hero' in this passage in the Loeb edition (1932: 5). I shall use both translations in what follows. For more on the nuances of this term see Santoro L'Hoir (1992).
5 See, for example, Livy 2.13.11 on Cloelia or Valerius Maximus 6.1.1 on Lucretia.
6 For general introductions to *exempla* in Roman society and literature see Chaplin (2000: 5–31) and Skidmore (1996: 13–22).

7   See Quintilian *IR* 5.11 on different kinds of *exempla*.

8   For the conventional form of an *exemplum* (exordium, brief narrative and concluding reflection on the tale) see Guerrini (1981: esp. 13–16). To see how conventional is this list of men who have combatted their grief at the death of sons, compare with Valerius Maximus 5.10 and see the catalogue of examples in Litchfield (1914).

9   For female examples used to inspire men see Quintilian *IR* 5.11.10. Cf. e.g. Cicero's citation of a taunt probably also referring to Cloelia at *de Officiis* 1.18.61 'you young men are acting like women, that maiden like a hero', and Pliny the Elder's indignation about her statue at *NH* 34.28.

8

WOMEN AND THE TRANSMISSION OF LIBYAN CULTURE

Eireann Marshall

In this contribution, I would like to explore the role played by Libyan women in the transmission of Libyan culture in Cyrene. I believe that this north African city offers a good case study of the way in which women can act as transmitters of culture for two reasons. First, there is strong evidence to suggest that Libyan women intermarried with Cyrenaeans throughout much of the city's history and, second, we can, to a degree, distinguish between Libyan and Cyrenaean culture. This means that the influence Libyan women exerted in Cyrene can, to an extent, be detected. This having been said, we are, as usual, at the mercy of sources which are mostly silent about the transmission of Libyan customs and, in particular, about the role which Libyan women played in this transmission. I have divided this chapter into two sections: the first will examine the evidence for intermarriage between Libyans and Cyrenaeans while the second will review the evidence for the role Libyan women played in the transmission of Libyan customs.

Intermarriage between Cyrenaeans and Libyans

Libyan women intermarried with Cyrenaean men certainly by the late fourth century when Ptolemy Soter passed his *Diagramma* which granted citizenship to the offspring of Cyrenaean fathers and Libyan mothers (*SEG* 9.1.2–3).[1] It seems likely that Ptolemy Soter passed this edict in order to appease the Libyan population that provided him with mercenaries. As such, it appears as though Ptolemy Soter was appealing to a group in Cyrene who had Libyan mothers. Therefore, while the *Diagramma* indicates that Cyrenaeans had previously restricted their citizenship, it also suggests that marriages between Cyrenaean men and Libyan women occurred despite these restrictions.

Other evidence suggests that Cyrenaean men and Libyan women intermarried throughout the city's history. Onomastic studies of Cyrene carried out by a number of scholars indicate that there are a considerable number of Libyan names in the city's epigraphy (Masson 1976: 377–87).[2] Carrhotus, the brother-in-law of Arcesilas IV and a charioteer at the Delphic games, is an example of a Cyrenaean who bore a Libyan name.[3] The proliferation of Libyan names in Cyrene suggests that Cyrenaeans and Libyans forged close relations with one another, including marriage alliances and guest friendships.

Fifth and fourth century BC sources also relate that Cyrenaean colonists intermarried with Libyan women. Herodotus clearly says that the colonists who founded Cyrene were male. He relates (4.153) that Thera decided to send men from the seven regions which made up the island; the quota of colonists was obtained by selecting by lot one brother of every household which had at least two brothers (Graham 1964: 98–9; Jeffrey 1961: 139–40; Osborne 1996: 1–13). The *Stele of the Founders* (*SEG* 9.3) also states that the Theran colonists were male. This is a decree from the early fourth century BC that confirmed the citizenship rights of Therans who settled in Libya; these rights are said to have been granted to Therans upon the foundation of Cyrene (Applebaum 1979: 35; Chamoux 1953: 108; Graham 1964: 104; Jeffrey 1961: 139). The decree is supported by a text entitled *horkion ton oikisteron*, which is represented as the original terms by which the city was set up. It is this *Pact of the Founders* which states that one son from every Theran household was required to take part in the expedition (*SEG* 9.3.28–29). While neither source says that the colonists intermarried with Libyan women, the exclusively masculine nature of the colonization suggests that marriage with native women was an essential element in the foundation of Cyrene (Compernolle 1983: 1041).

It is difficult to use Herodotus and the *Pact of the Founders* as sources of the colonization of Cyrene in the seventh century BC. Herodotus was writing two centuries after the colonization and did not have reliable records on which to base his account. Anachronisms in the *Pact of the Founders*, such as the allusion to an *ecclesia*, demonstrate that it is not a genuine seventh-century document (Chamoux 1953: 110–11; Dusanic 1978: 55–76; Nicolai 1992: 160. See also Jeffrey 1961: 139–47). While it may have been based on an earlier text, it was written some time after the colonization of the city. I would suggest that Herodotus and the *Pact of the Founders* reflect the societies which produced them. Since it is represented as an ancient text and since fourth-century BC Cyrenaeans must have believed it to be genuine, the *Pact of the Founders* is an excellent source for Cyrenaean views of their colonization. Taken together, Herodotus and the *Pact of the Founders* indicate that fifth- and fourth-century BC Cyrenaeans thought that Libyan women had intermarried with Cyrenaean colonists. Since foundation accounts served to explain and order cities' realities, it may be postulated that Cyrenaeans peopled their foundation myths with Libyan women in order to explain the presence of Libyan women in their city.[4]

This hypothesis can help to explain why the marriage of Libyan women and Cyrenaean men plays a central role in the city's foundation narratives (see Marshall 1999). Pindar concludes his ninth *Pythian* with the depiction of the union between the Cyrenaean Alexidamus and the unnamed daughter of the Libyan Antaeus (*Pyth.* 9.105–25).[5] He relates that many Cyrenaeans travelled to Irasa in order to marry her (9.105–6). As a result, Antaeus emulates Danaus and establishes an athletic contest in order to decide who would marry his daughter (9.111–16). He places his daughter on the finishing line and proclaims that the first man to touch her robes will gain her hand (9.118–20). Alexidamus wins the race and takes Antaeus' daughter through a crowd of nomad horsemen who fling leaves and crowns at the new couple (9.122–5).[6]

While Pindar only mentions the union between Alexidamus and Antaeus' daughter, the fact that he describes the wedding in order to glorify the city suggests that this wedding is symbolic of the intermarriage between male Cyrenaeans and female Libyans (*Pyth.* 9.103–105; cf. Calame 1990: 303). He also describes this union as part of Cyrene's heritage when he says that he will recount the tale of Alexidamus' wedding in order to recall Cyrene's ancient glory (9.103–15). By comparing this marriage to that of the Danaids, Pindar emphasizes that the marriage of Alexidamus and Antaeus' daughter is a union of two different peoples (Calame 1990: 306; Dougherty 1993: 152, 156 n.52).[7]

In his *Hymn to Apollo*, Callimachus also associates the marriage of Cyrenaeans and Libyans with the foundation of his city. The poet describes Apollo rejoicing as blonde Libyan women watched the Theran settlers perform the first Carneian festival in Cyrene (*Hymn to Apollo* 85–6). Although he does not explicitly describe Cyrenaeans and Libyans intermarrying, the inclusion of Libyan women in this narrative only makes sense if the two groups are thought to intermarry. Callimachus may also be alluding to the intermarriage between Cyrenaeans and Libyans by describing them as participating in a Carneian festival. As Nicolai has argued, it is likely that wedding rites were normally associated with the Carneia (Nicolai 1992: 168–70; cf. Calame 1990: 306).[8] In this case, the blonde Libyan women described by Callimachus could be seen as brides. Callimachus can be seen as celebrating the union between Cyrenaeans and Libyans and including female Libyans into Cyrene's social order. As the Carneia which he describes is performed at the time of the foundation of the city, Callimachus can be seen to include Libyan women into the original core of people who made up Cyrene (Nicolai 1992: 172).

To a large extent, Pindar and Callimachus reflect Cyrenaean views of the foundation of their city. Since the ninth *Pythian* was performed in Cyrene, it is likely that Pindar followed local traditions.[9] In addition, it is likely that Callimachus remained faithful to the myths of his homeland. It follows that Cyrenaeans believed that Libyan women had intermarried with the Theran colonists. It is hard to explain why they believed this if there were not Libyan women living among them. They would hardly have interwoven the inter-marriage of Libyan women and Cyrenaean men into the fabric of their foundation myths if this concept were alien to them. As such, while found-ation myths may not tell us that Libyan women actually married Theran colonists in the seventh century BC, they do suggest that they married Cyrenaean men by the fifth century BC and that this practice was established enough to have seeped into Cyrenaean folklore.

In sum, sources indicate that Libyan women were integrated into Cyrene by the fourth century BC. The proliferation of Libyan names, as well as the important role played by Libyan women in the city's foundation narratives, suggest that Libyan women had married Cyrenaean men before that time. Since only Libyan women could produce Cyrenaean citizens, it can be deduced that Libyan women could be incorporated in Cyrene in a way that Libyan men could not. One might, therefore, expect much of the Libyan influence found in Cyrene to have derived from Libyan women rather than Libyan men. As such, by examining the Libyan influences in Cyrenaean remains, one can view how Libyan women may have acted as transmitters of their own culture to the Cyrenaeans.

Libyan women as transmitters of Libyan culture

Ancient texts and material culture indicate that Cyrenaeans were influenced by Libyans in a number of ways. As marriage customs dictated that Libyan women were more integrated in Cyrene than men, it seems reasonable to suppose that many of these Libyan practices were transmitted to Cyrene by Libyan women. In order to gauge the role these women played in trans-mitting Libyan customs to Cyrene, I will first examine customs normally associated with women to show how they are Libyanized. While they may have exerted influence in other spheres of Cyrenaean life, it seems most certain that they influenced those areas of civic life associated with women.

In his Libyan *logos*, Herodotus relates that Cyrenaean women refrain from eating beef and that women from the Cyrenaican city of Barca eat neither pork nor beef. He ascribes this practice to Libyans and the Egyptian vener-ation of Isis:

> The coast of Libya, then, between Egypt and Lake Tritonis is occu-pied by nomads living on meat and milk – though they do not breed pigs, and abstain from cows' meat for the same reason as the Egyptians. Even at Cyrene women think it is wrong to eat cows' meat, out of respect for the Egyptian Isis, in whose honour they cele-brate both fasts and festivals. At Barca the women avoid eating pigs' flesh, as well as cows'.
>
> (Hdt. 4.186; trans. de Sélincourt 1954)[10]

130

This passage indicates not only that Cyrenaeans followed Libyan customs but also that Cyrenaean women, in particular, did so. The simplest explanation why women alone practised these dietary restrictions is that there was a sizeable portion of Libyan women who influenced Cyrenaean religious customs. There was nothing in the Egypto-Libyan cult of Isis which dictated that women alone should fast. Indeed, Herodotus says that Egyptian men as well as women do not sacrifice cows; as such, it was not due to cultic practices that the prohibition of beef in Cyrene and Barca was limited to women (2.40). The fact that Herodotus refers to them as Cyrenaean women suggests that Libyan women were fully integrated within the city and that they had spread their customs to non-Libyan women. After all, Herodotus does not say that some Cyrenaean women follow these practices, but says that they all do so.

It is interesting to note that Herodotus says Barcaean women follow Egypto-Libyan practices more closely than their Cyrenaean counterparts, in that they refrain from eating both beef and pork. Literary and epigraphical evidence suggests that Barca had a sizeable group of Libyans. After all, the city was founded by the brothers of the Cyrenaean King Arcesilas II in alliance with Libyans who rose up against the king (Hdt. 4.159). The scale of the Libyan presence in the city can be gauged by the fact that the Barcaean king who reigned during the time of Arcesilas III had a Libyan name, namely Alazeir (Hdt. 4.164). Since he was a descendant of one of Arcesilas II's brothers, I would argue that Alazeir was a Cyrenaican who received his name either through guest friendship or through a Libyan mother.[11] The fact that Barca both followed these religious practices more fully than Cyrene and may have had a greater Libyan presence, suggests that the transmission of Libyan dietary practices was linked to the presence of Libyan people. In other words, Barca, like Cyrene, received Libyan customs through Libyans and, in particular, Libyan women.

Libyan women may also have influenced the cult of Demeter and Kore in Cyrene (cf. Fabbricotti 1987: 233–37; White 1987: 79–84). These goddesses are represented in a series of Hellenistic reliefs found right outside Cyrene. These reliefs appear to represent cave sanctuaries, along with the gods worshipped there and their worshippers.[12] The reliefs depict Demeter and Kore either sitting or standing next to one another; Kore often has her hands on Demeter's shoulders. What is particularly interesting is that they are represented in a way which is idiosyncratic to the region: they are depicted with the same corkscrew curls worn by the goddess Libya and wearing leather mantles usually associated with Libyans (for the curls and mantles see below). In other words, these goddesses appear to be represented in a Libyan guise. Just how Libyans influenced the cult of Demeter and Kore beyond the appearance of the goddesses is impossible to gauge. It is possible that Libyans influenced the rituals associated with the cult; however, this kind of information is impossible to glean from material evidence alone and the literary sources are scarce. In any case, Libyan influence was strong enough to alter the way in which Demeter and Kore were represented.

It seems likely that the Libyan influence in the cult of Demeter and Kore was transmitted by Libyan women. After all, cults of Demeter, such as the Thesmophoria, were often associated with women who were guardians of the city's fertility in both the agricultural and the biological sense. As such, it seems that Libyan women influenced a religious cult which was central to a city famed for its agriculture. The importance of the cult of Demeter and Kore to Cyrene can be gauged by the fact that the city had both an intramural and an extramural sanctuary dedicated to them (Goodchild 1971; Stucchi 1967; White 1976). Therefore, the apparent influence exerted by Libyan women was felt at the very heart of the city.

Libyan women may have influenced other fertility cults practised in the city. One such cult seems to have focused around peculiarly Libyan deities. A number of terracotta figurines representing these female divinities have been found in different parts of Cyrenaica, including a sanctuary on the slopes of Cyrene's Acropolis. These goddesses wear leather mantles which are short in the front and long in the back as well as *poloi*; they also frequently hold silphium, while a gazelle is sometimes shown at their sides (Bacchielli 1994: 45; Davesne 1986: 195–204; Davesne and Garlan 1987: 199–226; Parisi Presicce 1994: 88; Pensabene 1987: 193). Some goddesses are shown holding crowns (Bacchielli 1994: 49, 54; Davesne and Garlan 1987: 199–226; Parisi Presicce 1994: 88). Very similar goddesses are depicted on the Hellenistic reliefs mentioned above. They are represented sitting next to one another, wearing leather mantles and holding offerings or gazelles (Fabricotti 1987: 236). In addition, the deities have the same characteristic corkscrew curls as the above figurines. These deities represented on the reliefs and figurines resemble the goddess Libya in that they are represented with the same curls, are shown wearing leather mantles and are holding crowns.[13] Because of the similarities between them and Libya,[14] I would argue that these are the Libyan nymphs whom Apollonius and Callimachus describe attending to Libya. Apollonius says that they wear goatskin mantles which are short in the front and long in the back (4.1309, 1323, 1358; Callimachus fr. 602 Pfeiffer).

The prevalence of Libyan nymphs in Cyrene's material culture and in literary sources suggests that they were important to the city. However, how these nymphs were venerated or the type of cult they were given is unknown. On the basis of their iconography, I would suggest that the nymphs must have been the focus of a fertility cult.[15] Material and literary sources represent Libya and Libyan nymphs as embodiments of Libyan land. Authors, such as Pindar, refer to Libya as fertile or fruitful (*Pyth.* 9.55, *Pyth.* 4.6). In turn, Callimachus refers to Libya as flourishing (fr. 602 Pfeiffer). Ancient sources also describe Libya as overseeing the land and guaranteeing the fertility of the region. Apollonius describes Libyan nymphs looking after Libyan land (4.1209, 4.1323, 4.1358). The fact that these nymphs are associated with the region's most characteristic flora and fauna, namely silphium and gazelles, also suggests that they were linked to Libyan land, either as personifications or as protectors.[16] These Libyan nymphs may be linked to human as well as agricultural fertility: one figurine represents a Libyan nymph as a *kourotrophos* (Pensabene 1987: 105).

The way in which these nymphs are represented suggests that they were originally Libyan. Libya and Libyan nymphs are depicted as Libyan women in both literary and material sources. Herodotus relates that most Greeks believed that the Libyan continent was named after a native woman (4.45). In doing so, he implies that Libya was envisaged in terms of a Libyan woman. Libya is also characterized as a Libyan woman in artistic representations. The heavy mantle worn by Libya is similar to the goatskin mantles that Herodotus describes Libyan women wearing (4.189).[17] It is also possible that the cork-screw curls worn by Libya and Libyan nymphs were reminiscent of Libyan women's hair. The fact that Libya and Libyan nymphs are represented as Libyan women suggests that Libyan women played a role in developing their cults in Cyrene. The importance of Libyan women in the city's regeneration is emphasized by the way in which the city's fertility symbols are based on them. I would argue that the Libyan nymphs either derived from the Libyan pantheon or were created by, or for, Libyan women in order to quantify their roles as reproducers. In any case, since Libyan nymphs appear to have belonged to a fertility cult, it seems likely that they were venerated primarily by women. As such, it is plausible that Libyan women were responsible for introducing the cult of these Libyan nymphs to Cyrene.

I have, so far, only looked at areas in which women were most likely to have influenced Cyrene in order to show that they played an important role in the transmission of culture. However, in implicitly defining spheres as feminine, there is a danger in compartmentalizing values and practices into gender-specific areas and making these areas discrete from one another. This is the implication van Compernolle makes in his discussion of the role women played in the transmission of native culture in colonial situations. In particular, he has suggested that women may have introduced indigenous religious beliefs to colonies, as well as native domestic equipment (1983: 1047–9). Therefore, while Greek males are said to be responsible for the socio-political structure of colonies as well as for the introduction of civic gods, indigenous women are said to influence the domestic sphere.[18] I would argue that this model is simplistic because women's influence is not limited to narrow spheres (see Rowlandson in this volume). While fertility cults may have been organized by women, they were important to the city as a whole. The importance of the cult of Demeter and Kore in a city such as Cyrene which was famed for its production of grain can be gauged by the location and size of its main temples. The sanctuary of Demeter and Kore on the Wadi bel Gadir is the largest of the city's extramural sanctuaries, while the intramural temple of Demeter and Kore is in the *agora*, the heart of the city. Therefore, by influencing the cult of Demeter in Cyrene, Libyan women not only disseminated their religious practices to other Cyrenaean women but to the city as whole.

Furthermore, to limit oneself to looking at women's influence in traditionally feminine spheres of influence is to suggest that they only affected such areas. Libyans influenced Cyrene in ways that cannot immediately be traced to Libyan women. For example, a number of different sources indicate that Ammon was an important deity in the Cyrenaean pantheon.[19] The god is represented on many of the city's coins as well as on the Hellenistic reliefs found in the Cyrenaean *chora* that represent Ammon.[20] While the oracle at Siwa might, at first sight, suggest that Ammon was Egyptian, literary and archaeological evidence suggests that Libyans venerated Ammon from prehistoric times.[21] A cave painting in Wadi Graga of a ram god has provided evidence of the cult of Aries in Libya in the Neolithic period (Paradisi 1966: 95). In addition, several literary sources, which are unfortunately late, indicate that later Libyans venerated Ammon.[22] Macrobius writes that Libyans depict Ammon with rams' horns because they are his chief strength (*Saturnalia* 1.12.18).[23] Likewise, Saint Athanasius says that Libyans venerate Aries whom they call Ammon (*Contra Gentes* 16.6; 46.1).[24] Cyrenaeans appear to have received the cult of Ammon from Libyans living near them rather than from Egyptians. Libyan influence is evidenced from the fact that some representations of Ammon in Cyrene differ from those found in Siwa; in particular, several coins and sculptures from Cyrenaica represent Ammon alongside Aries.[25] In these representations, the ram is not completely syncretized with Ammon. Conversely, in Siwa, Ammon and Aries are entirely syncretized; as a result, the ram is represented as Ammon's head and not as a distinct figure.[26]

While it seems clear that Libyans introduced the cult of Ammon to Cyrene, it is not clear how they did so or which Libyans did so. One might be tempted to postulate that women introduced this cult of Ammon since they were more integrated in Cyrene than Libyan men. However, other Libyans, including non-citizen Libyans, could have influenced Cyrenaeans. While it is not possible to tell whether Ammon was brought to Cyrene by Libyan women, there is no reason to think that Libyan women would only introduce cults normally associated with women. After all, Ammon is venerated in cave sanctuaries outside Cyrene alongside a host of other deities, including Libya, Demeter and Kore. As the gods were sometimes worshipped together, it is difficult to argue that Libyan women influenced the cult of fertility goddesses such as Demeter and Kore or the Libyan nymphs, but did not influence the cult of Ammon. In these circumstances, it cannot be maintained that worship of civic gods was solely the preserve of men, while only fertility goddesses pertained to the feminine sphere.

By intermarriage, then, Libyan women would have had the opportunity to impart Libyan culture directly to their non-Libyan husbands and to their children. Moreover, through the ties of marriage, Libyan men would have been able to develop relationships with their non-Libyan in-laws. In this way, women could have facilitated the transmission of Libyan culture to the Cyrenaeans. One area in which Libyan women could have had this kind of indirect influence is equestrianism, a sport for which the city was famous.[27] Although women could have imparted equestrian skills to Cyrene themselves, it seems more likely that they were imparted by Libyan men, the relatives of those married to Cyrenaeans. A variety of sources indicate that Libyans imparted equestrian skills to Cyrenaeans. Herodotus (4.189) says that Libyans taught Greeks how to use the four-horse chariot (Applebaum 1979: 84; Chamoux 1953: 235; Lazzarini 1987: 172).[28] Cyrenaeans also attributed their skills to Libyans. For example, Pausanias (6.12.7) writes that an Olympic victor from Cyrene, Theochrestus, dedicated a chariot on which an inscription recorded that he bred his horses after the traditional Libyan custom. While women may not have transmitted Libyan customs directly in these circumstances, it is possible that they enabled these practices to become transmitted. Since equestrian sports were normally the preserve of the elite, it is likely that the Libyans who introduced these skills were elite. The Libyan elite with whom Cyrenaeans came into contact forged guest friendships which were frequently sealed through marriage alliances; as such, women were often the means by which Libyan and Cyrenaean men forged relations. Therefore, these equestrian activities in Cyrene may have become Libyanized through a nexus of relations surrounding Libyan women.

Conclusion

I have argued in this chapter that Libyan women were integrated into Cyrene more easily than men. By the fourth century BC at the very latest, they were the mothers and wives of Cyrenaean citizens. Onomastic studies and the foundation narratives suggest that Libyan women intermarried with Cyrenaean men some time before this. Since they were able to become part of Cyrenaean society more easily than their male counterparts, it stands to reason that Libyan women were more responsible for transmitting Libyan culture to Cyrene. The most direct evidence of the influence Libyan women exerted comes from the passage in which Herodotus tells us that Libyan women introduced dietary restrictions associated with the cult of Isis. Other religious customs normally associated with women appear to have been Libyanized. It seems as though Libyan women influenced fertility rites such as the cult of Demeter and Kore as well as the cult of Libyan nymphs. Since Libyan women played an important part in the regeneration of the Cyrenaean population, their role in influencing these fertility cults is to be expected.

One can surmise that these religious cults were Libyanized by Libyan women because these are cults which are normally associated with women. However, I would argue that it is unwise to make a sharp distinction between male and female spheres of influence. When Libyan women influenced traditionally feminine religious cults, such as the worship of Demeter and Kore, they influenced the city as a whole. Furthermore, while it is more difficult to ascertain how Libyan women influenced other aspects of Cyrenaean culture, there is no reason to think that they only influenced cultural areas usually linked with women. Ammon, who was a very important member of the Cyrenaean pantheon, was sometimes venerated alongside Libyan nymphs and Demeter and Kore. It is possible that the Libyan women who introduced the cult of the fertility goddesses could have introduced the cult of Ammon. In any case, Libyan women seem to have been instrumental in the transmission of Libyan culture both by acquainting Cyrene with their customs and by facilitating the transmission of their practices through their male counterparts.

Notes

1 For this edict see Laronde (1990: 178); Applebaum (1979: 52); Bacchielli (1978: 609, 613 n.138, 614); Lazzarini (1987: 173); Parisi Presicce (1994: 86); Moretti (1987–88: 237–41). For a recent discussion of the intermarriage between Cyrenaeans and Libyans see Mitchell (2000: 98–9).

2 For a discussion of Libyan names in Cyrene see Chamoux (1953: 174); Bacchielli (1978: 613, 621n. 87); Bacchielli (1987: 473); Reynolds (1987: 380); Lazzarini (1987: 172); Moretti (1987–88: 341); Camps (1993: 39–73); Zimmermann (1996: 364–6).

3 A scholiast on Pindar (*Pythian* 5.33–4) specifically states that Carrhotus was a Libyan name. The fact that he competed at the Delphic games also demonstrates that he was Greek.

4 For the exegetical nature of foundation myths see Dougherty (1993), (1994).

5 See Chamoux (1953: 129) for this passage.

6 See Dougherty (1993: 139) for the role which the throwing of leaves played in marriage rituals.

7 As Dougherty has emphasized, the marriage of Alexidamus and Antaeus' daughter differs from those of the Danaids in that, while the marriages in Danaus' family are violent, this union is peaceful.

8 Nicolai argues that the Carneian festival was an initiation ceremony. According to him, the protagonists of the feast were young men who had completed their initiation cycle and who were ready to be warriors. In this logic, the Carneia marked their entry into adulthood and into the life of the warrior. He believes that the presence of women suggests that Carneian festivals were also linked to wedding rites. He also argues that a wedding ritual would be appropriate to a festival which celebrates the completion of an initiation cycle.

9 See Calame (1990: 278); Dougherty (1993: 96, 160) for epinicians being performed in the cities which they glorify. For Pindar's account of the foundation of Cyrene, see Osborne (1996: 8–10).

10 For a discussion of this passage see Boardman (1980: 155); Compernolle (1983: 1044); Gallo (1983: 716); White (1987: 80–1, 84); Gasperini (1987: 404–5); Corcella and Medaglia (1993: 376).

11 Masson (1976: 380) suggests that Alazeir was a Cyrenaican who bore a Libyan name. Conversely, Bacchielli (1978: 613, 615) argues that Alazeir could have been either a Cyrenaican or Libyan, while Applebaum (1979: 26 n.114) argues that Alazeir was Libyan.

12 For these reliefs see Fabricotti (1987); Paribeni (1959: no. 238); Pensabene (1987: 107); Giannini (1990: 68 no. 45); Wanis (1992).

13 Pausanias (10.15.6) describes a bronze statue dedicated by Cyrenaeans in Delphi in which Libya holds a crown. See also Pensabene (1987: 105); Bacchielli (1994: 54).

14 The most important representation of Libya is on the Antonine relief in the British Museum (BM Reg. No. 6 1127–30). See Smith and Porcher (1864: 98); Huskinson (1975: 31–2, 25 no. 60).

15 See also Bacchielli (1994: 49); Pensabene (1987: 105–6); Fabbricotti (1987: 236) for these nymphs being linked to fertility.

16 Gazelles and silphium are both frequently represented on coins and become emblematic of the city. For coins representing gazelles and silphium together, see Robinson (1927: xxvi, pl. v, 4; cvii, pl. xxv, 16; xxiv pl. iii, 6; xx pl. i, 8; 59 pl. xxv, 14–18, 4 pl. ii, 7).

17 Diodorus (3.49) and Strabo (17.3.7) also describe Libyans wearing animal skins. For further discussion of these mantles, see Pensabene (1987: 105); Bacchielli (1994: 49–50, 54) and Wanis (1992: 41).

18 So Compernolle attributes the geometric designs of amphorae in Gela to native women.

19 For the cult of Ammon, see Chamoux (1953: 320–41); Bisi (1985: 307–18); Fabbricotti (1987: 231–3).

20 For coins of Ammon see Robinson (1927: ccxxiv–ccxxix); Jenkins (1974: 30–1); Bisi (1985: 309). For statues of Ammon see Paribeni (1959: 78 no. 183 pl. 107; 81 no. 190 pl. 18). For the Hellenistic reliefs, see Fabbricotti (1987: nos. 1, 3, 6, 7, figs 1, 3, 8, 9). Ancient sources also refer to Cyrenaeans making dedications to Ammon. See, for example, Pausanias (10.13.5); Strabo (1.3.4, 1.13.15).

21 For the oasis at Siwa and the cult of Ammon in north Africa see Bates (1914: 189); Chamoux (1953: 333); Stucchi (1975: 565); Bisi (1985: 307); Fabbricotti (1987: 232); Desanges (1981: 431); Mattingly (1994: 38–9).

22 See Fabbricotti (1987: 232) for source problems regarding the early cult of Ammon. The difficulty with the sources is that it is unclear whether the Libyans who are mentioned are indigenous Libyans or Cyrenaeans.

23 He says that Libyans identify him with the setting sun and equates rams' horns with the suns' rays.

24 For this passage see Desanges (1981: 435).

25 These representations of Aries include several double herms of Ammon and Libya or Isis holding up Aries. See Paribeni (1959: 144 no. 144 no. 416 pl. 181); Kraeling (1962: 39, 180, 202 nos. 56–60); Bacchielli (1987: 477); Catani (1987: 391); Fabbricotti (1987: 233). In addition, the Hellenistic reliefs found outside Cyrene depict Ammon with Aries: Fabbricotti (1987: relief nos. 1, 3, 6, 7, figs 1, 3, 8, 9). Last, Ammon is shown with Aries on some coins: Robinson (1927: liv, nos. 25–6, pl. xiii, 3–9).

26 Bisi (1985: 309–10) and Fabbricotti (1987: 232) have argued that the representations of Ammon alongside Aries indicate that Libyans influenced the cult of Ammon in Cyrene. The cult of Aries seems to have preceded the cult of Ammon who was only later conflated with the ram. For the cult of Ammon and the conflation between Aries and Ammon, see Bisi (1985: 307–8). See Herodotus (4.181) for Ammon being represented with a ram's head in Siwa.

27 Cf. Aristophanes (*Clouds* 68–70) in which a son is said to have been influenced by his mother and mother's brother in his love of horse-racing. Cf. also Bremmer (1983) on a man's relationship with his maternal uncles.

28 Exactly what Libyans are meant to have imparted to Cyrenaeans and Greeks in general is unclear since Homer describes chariots. See Mattingly and Hitchner (1995: 174) for chariots in Libyan prehistoric art.

9

GALLA PLACIDIA

Conduit of culture?

Mary Harlow

The western Roman empire was in a period of rapid political and cultural transition in the early fifth century AD and the role of Galla Placidia (388–450) presents a unique view on how these transformations played out. As the daughter, sister, wife and mother of Roman emperors her potential as a player in the groups controlling power in the period was enormous. In the latter part of her life, after her son's accession in 425, she can claim a place in the more traditional role of imperial women in the area of culture as patron of buildings and monuments. The exquisite mosaics of her so-called mausoleum in Ravenna are still frequently used as part of the advertising of the city to encourage tourists and promote Roman mosaic art. While her true association with this building may not be known, other evidence demonstrates her desire to fulfil the role of patron. She commissioned a church to St John the Evangelist, also in Ravenna, in which the mosaic decoration stressed her family lineage back to Constantine and highlighted links across the empire to the Theodosian dynasty in the east. Churches in Rome dedicated by her father Theodosius, and brother, Honorius, were also refurbished by Galla Placidia (Brubaker 1997: 53–5). This interaction of politics and culture embodied in building programmes and their decoration was part and parcel of the role of imperial men and women, in this Galla Placidia is no different from her forebears (see Woodhull in this volume).

This chapter, however, examines a more tangential aspect of 'culture'. It considers the portrayal of Galla Placidia's early life from her late teenage years to the accession of her son, Valentinian III, as emperor of the west in 425 and concentrates on her two marriages: the first to the Gothic king Athaulf (d. 413), the second to the Roman *magister utriusque militiae* and soon-to-be emperor, Constantius (d. 421). The portrayal of Galla Placidia's behaviour in these marriages in the primary sources of the period betrays a series of subtexts on the roles of the various individuals concerned. Not all of these will be explored here; my main interest is in the portrayal of Galla

Placidia as a conduit of Roman culture as embodied in traditional Roman marital virtues. Her first marriage to the non-Roman and periodic enemy of the emperor, Athaulf, is presented in terms of a Roman wedding and a relationship that exemplified *concordia*, the primary virtue of Roman marriage. Conversely, her second marriage, to a man whom Romans accepted as emperor, is presented as a marriage riven with strife in which husband and wife had a deleterious effect on one another.[1] My secondary interest is the implicitly gendered rhetoric of the narrative of these marriages and the overt dominance of a male discourse which uses 'woman' as a narrative tool in the depiction of male actors.[2]

The literary sources for this part of Galla Placidia's life are 'better' in terms of quantity, at least, than those of the subsequent period of her regency for Valentinian III and beyond, but it is difficult, despite Oost's comprehensive biography (1968), to create a plausible and nuanced narrative for most of her life. As a woman, Galla Placidia has very little voice of her own. For her later life we have the evidence of inscriptions, buildings and monuments, while for the early period we have the voices of male historians, some of whom were far more experienced in the ways of the eastern empire than the west. Galla Placidia plays a surprisingly central role in the surviving fragments of Olympiodorus of Thebes (fl. 405–25) who lived through the period he describes and had first-hand experience of some of the different ethnic groups that made up the later Roman empire.[3] While he was not an eyewitness to all the events he recounted, he may have visited Rome for the coronation to Valentinian III in 425 (Matthews 1970: 80; 1975: 383). He certainly travelled widely and served on embassies to the Huns (fr. 19). His work only survives in fragments collected in the work of later historians; but it is known that he wrote a history in twenty-two books, dedicated to the Emperor Theodosius II, covering the years 407–25. Other works that cover the period are Orosius; the fifth-century Gallic chronicles of Hydatius; Prosper and the anonymous chronicler of 452; and Procopius. However, only in the work of Olympiodorus does Galla Placidia play a central role. In the other authors, she merely has a bit-part – a much more usual place for a woman in Roman historical writing.

By accident of birth Placidia was destined to play a part in the politics of the fifth century – she was the daughter of the emperor Theodosius, the half-sister of emperors Arcadius and Honorius; and wife of the emperor Constantius III – she was also mother of an emperor, Valentinian III, and, in addition to this superficially 'Roman' pedigree, the wife of a Gothic king, Athaulf. While the Theodosian dynasty came to rule the Roman empire and thus embody what it meant to be Roman in the later empire, the origins of their dynasty, as with most of the previous dynasties, had long since ceased to be Italian. From its inception, part of the success of the Roman empire had been due to its ability to absorb and assimilate different groups from outside its boundaries. In the late fourth and early fifth centuries Roman identity was, again, in flux. In the west, outsiders were closely identified with people of Gothic or German origin. Despite the accommodations made for them, particularly by Galla Placidia's father, Theodosius, and the fact that the army was manned and commanded by them, Goths and Germans developed as the rhetorical embodiment of the non-Roman.

It is the groups and individuals, with whom she is associated in the histories of the period, that make Galla Placidia different from Roman women who came before her, though in this she set a precedent for those who came after.[4] All textual images of women, particularly imperial women, are stereotyped to a certain extent. In the late antique world positive stereotypes tended to be linked to two images: either the traditional matrona figure of loyal and obedient wife and mother; or the celibate Christian virgin or, if that was not possible, widow (Richlin 1995: 67). For the purposes of studying Placidia, it is the first model that fits the early part of her life, while the second may well have suited her in her old age, in that she remained a widow after the death of Constantius and was increasingly involved with the Church. It is now generally accepted that the way in which women are portrayed in ancient texts, the virtues and vices they present, function as more than just the creation of a female stereotype. They often have a specifically political function and meaning, and are employed to represent something else – usually to stress by opposition or inversion, characteristics or behaviour of the woman's male relations and/or the political situation or social morality. The inherent and implicit discourse of Roman society was that of the male power structure and this view is unquestioned by any ancient writer (Cooper 1992: 151–3). Galla Placidia is not presented as a character in her own right but as a complement to, or antithesis of, her husbands. Her role is to qualify their actions. However, there is no doubt that she was also a player in the politics of the early to mid-fifth century and a product of the social structures that encompass the text. So while Olympiodorus successfully discredits Constantius and praises Athaulf, he is also providing information about later Roman ideas about women. In this case he may be commenting on their ability to rule given that at the time of publication both eastern and western halves of the empire were controlled by women.[5]

As the daughter of Theodosius I, Placidia was always a potential candidate for dynastic machinations. However, since her father died when she was aged six or seven and it is not known where she spent her early years, it is unclear whether there were plans for her at a young age. Oost claims that it is generally accepted that she spent her youth in Rome, in the household of Serena, the niece of Theodosius and the wife of Stilicho, the western *magister militum*. However, the evidence for this is very slim and based on passing comments and dubious identifications in Claudian (*IV Cos Hon.* 204–9; cf. Oost 1968: 63 and notes). Also, according to Claudian, Placidia's earliest proposed husband was Eucherius, son of Stilicho and Serena. Stilicho's dynastic ambitions appear fairly clear in the marriages he arranged for his daughters, both of whom, in turn, married Honorius. Nothing came of the arrangement for Placidia and his son, if it existed. It is only mentioned in the panegyric for Stilicho, in a sort of wish list that also depicts Maria, the daughter of Stilicho and wife of Honorius, as pregnant, another event that never came to pass (Claudian *De Cos. Stil.* ii, 354–9 and 341–9). There is no mention in any of the sources of any other marriage plans for Placidia who was still unmarried at the age of twenty-two when she was taken hostage by Alaric after the sack of Rome in 410. This was quite a late age for a Roman girl to be still unmarried, particularly among the upper classes – time for people to start wondering what was the matter with her, even at a time when choosing to remain celibate was becoming less problematic.[6] It may be, as Oost speculated (1968: 73), that Serena had prevented any other suitors, and thus potential rivals for the throne, from making their play. However, if she could do this, surely she could also have married Placidia off to her son?[7]

Placidia became a bargaining tool for the Goths in the years immediately after the sack of Rome in 410. Alaric had swung to and fro on the pendulum of Gothic–Roman relations, being in turns ally and enemy, and now his successor, Athaulf behaved similarly. The Goths moved from Rome to southern Italy with the intention of crossing into Sicily. However, on the death of Alaric in 411, Athaulf led the group north again, crossing into Gaul. Here, Athaulf sided with the newest western usurper, Jovinus. This alliance was short-lived due to internal Gothic politics and the elevation of Jovinus' brother as co-emperor (Olymp. fr. 20). Athaulf then offered his services to Ravenna and defeated Jovinus in the name of Rome. After this, negotiations were re-opened for the return of Placidia to Ravenna in exchange for land and grain. Olympiodorus says that the return of Placidia was at the urging of Constantius (fr. 22.1). However, Honorius' constant prevarication on keeping his side of the bargain (the provision of land and grain), pushed Athaulf back into an adversarial position. According to Olympiodorus, Athaulf was already planning to marry Placidia and increased his demands so that when they were not met he could seem to be acting reasonably in marrying her (fr. 22.3).[8]

The marriage of Galla Placidia and Athaulf took place in Narbonne in 414. The sources that provide detail about the occasion stress both its *roman-itas* ('Romanness') and the mutual celebration of both Goths and Romans:

> With the advice and encouragement of Candidianus, Athaulf married Placidia at the beginning of the month of January in the city of Narbo at the house of Ingenuus, one of the leading citizens of the place. There, Placidia, dressed in royal raiment, sat in a hall decorated in the Roman manner, and by her side sat Athaulf, wearing a Roman general's cloak and the other Roman clothing. Amidst the celebrations, along with the other wedding gifts, Athaulf gave Placidia fifty handsome young men dressed in silk clothes, each

bearing aloft two very large dishes, one full of gold, the other of precious – or rather, priceless – stones, which had been carried off by the Goths at the sack of Rome. Then nuptial hymns were sung, first by Attalus, then by Rusticus and Phoebadius. Then the ceremonies were celebrated by both the barbarians and the Romans amongst them.

(Olympiodorus fr. 24; trans. Blockley 1983)

Olympiodorus presents the wedding as truly Roman – all the trappings of a Roman imperial ceremony are here, and many of those of a traditional wedding.[9] It takes place in the house of the leading citizen of the city with the encouragement and goodwill of another Roman, Candidianus. This may be the same Candidianus who supported Placidia on her return from the east to put Valentinian on the throne in 425 (Blockley 1981: 34 and *contra* Harries 1994: 62 n.25). Placidia is dressed as a member of the imperial family and, more importantly, Athaulf is shown wearing the *chlamys* of a Roman general/high official and other Roman clothing.[10] He would have had the right to wear this at the time as he had spent his last campaign fighting for Honorius against the usurper Jovinus. All the same, it is significant that the dress stresses his identification with things Roman and associates him with the Gallo-Roman elite among whom he is celebrating his wedding. As at traditional Roman weddings, songs are sung, the first by Priscus Attalus, a man whom Athaulf had intermittently upheld as emperor.[11] The marriage is apparently agreeable to both Goths and Romans (Olymp. fr. 24; Matthews 1975: 316; Oost 1968: 117 ff.). This Olympiodoran image is paralleled later in the century in Spain when Hydatius refers to the occasion as a marriage of the king of the north to a daughter of the king of the south in fulfilment of a prophecy of Daniel (11.6; Olympiad 298.XX, from Burgess 1993: 84).

Obviously we cannot know what the couple themselves thought about this union, although the advantages for Athaulf are fairly clear. In marrying the sister of the emperor, at the very least he could ensure the protection of his people, while at best he could hope to produce an heir who would be next in line to the childless Honorius. This marriage fired the imaginations of both ancient and modern historians – Jordanes (*Geta.* 160) claims that Athaulf was attracted by Placidia's 'nobility, beauty and chaste purity'. He further claims that, when the 'barbarians' learned of this alliance, they were more effectively terrified, since the Empire and the Goths had become one. Rather more recently, Oost gives the impression that there was genuine affection between the two, although his reading of the situation is based on some fairly stereotypical ideas of how 'barbarians' behaved. Of Placidia's abduction, Oost consoles the reader who might be anxious about the well-protected and high-class Roman virgin forced to consort with barbarians that: 'cultures classed as barbarian have many disadvantages from the point of view of civilized persons, one of the advantages however, is frequently a sort of rude chivalry' (Oost 1968: 94). So the reader can rest assured that Placidia was probably well treated, as far as these barbarians were concerned. Not much later in his text, in order to give some explanation as to why Placidia might not have found being a prisoner of the Goths too arduous, Oost describes Athaulf as 'not without masculine charms' (Oost 1968: 104). It may be that Oost saw the Goths as Procopius did, having 'white bodies and fair hair, . . . tall and handsome to look upon' (3.2.4), and Athaulf himself, according to Jordanes (*Get.* 158), was 'a man of imposing beauty and great spirit; for though not tall of stature, he was distinguished for beauty of face and form'. This style of description is one of the great disadvantages of Oost's biography. It is a marker of moves in historiography since the 1960s that this type of characterisation has been seriously revised. However, to give Oost his due, his opinion of Athaulf and Placidia's well-suitedness is based on the evidence of another contemporary, Orosius:

> Placidia . . . [was] . . . taken to wife by Athaulf, a kinsman of Alaric's, as if, by divine decree, Rome had given her as a hostage and special pledge; thus by her marriage with this most powerful barbarian king, she was of great benefit to the state.
>
> (Orosius 7.40.2)

> For I myself heard a man of Narbo, of renowned military service under Theodosius, also religious, prudent and serious, relating at Bethlehem, a town in Palestine, to the most blessed priest Jerome, that he was a very close friend of Athaulf at Narbo, and that he often learned from him under oath what he was accustomed to say when he was in good spirits, health and temper: that he, at first was ardently eager to blot out the Roman name and to make the entire Roman empire that of the Goths alone, and to call it and make it, to use a popular expression, Gothia instead of Romania, and that he Athaulf, become what Caesar Augustus had once been. When however he discovered from long experience that the Goths, by reason of their unbridled barbarism, could not by any means obey laws, nor should the laws of state be abrogated without which the state is not a state, he chose to seek for himself the glory of completely restoring and increasing the Roman name by the forces of the Goths, and to be held by posterity as the author of the restoration of Rome, since he had been unable to be its transformer. For this reason he strove to refrain from war; for this reason to be eager for peace, being influenced in all the works of good government, especially by the persuasion and advice of his wife, Placidia, a woman indeed of a very keen mind and very good religiously.
>
> (Orosius 7.43)

Orosius presents the marriage as made in heaven. In the second extract his informant is set up as highly reliable – he is a good soldier, a holy and serious man, talking in a holy place to another serious and holy man – presumably, therefore, to be believed without question, especially since we are additionally reminded that his words were said under oath. Significantly, here Placidia is presented as a direct conduit of 'Romanisation'. She is influencing her Gothic husband in the proper Roman ways, and these ways are significantly identified as the ways of law. Here, laws and the rule of law are one of the ways of defining Roman from barbarian. Goths are defined as barbarian because they cannot follow the rule of law. Athaulf, through the influence of Galla Placidia, sees himself as the restorer of Rome rather than the destroyer. The barbarian imagines himself the champion of Rome, a figure presumably reminiscent of Stilicho to the listener. Ironically, given the fact that law has been used as a marker of *romanitas*, the 'marriage' of Placidia and Athaulf may have been contrary to Roman law which had not altered the prohibitions on marrying outside of one's rank. A law of the 370s (*CT* 3.14.1) expressly forbade the intermarriage of Romans and barbarians (Sivan 1996: 136–45). It could be argued that all this shows, of course, is that, despite the fact the Romans might imagine that laws defined the state, they were no more likely to obey them than any other group. However, it also suggests that Olympiodorus, Orosius and the chroniclers accepted this as a *bona fide* marriage, thus implying approval for it.

Athaulf and Placidia are again seen working as a partnership in Olympiodorus (fr. 26). When their son was born, he was named Theodosius, expressing both past reminders of Placidia's father, one of the early patrons of the Goths, and imperial ambitions for the future. After his birth, Olympiodorus reports that Athaulf became 'even more friendly towards the Romans. But his and Placidia's desires [presumably for a rapprochement with Honorius] went unfulfilled in the face of the opposition by Constantius and his supporters'. They grieved together at the death of their infant son. The marriage ended with Athaulf's assassination in 416. Athaulf is reported to have told his brother to hand Placidia back to the Romans in order to ensure their friendship (fr. 26).

In this tale Placidia is represented as a marker of Romanness – she is hardly a personality, and we cannot ascribe motivation to her. It was certainly in her interests for the empire to be at peace with the Goths. Indeed, Honorius and his generals had so much to deal with on other fronts, that it is to be imagined that they might welcome an alliance. It appears, however, that Honorius did very little to ensure his sister's return. The impetus for this allegedly came from his general Constantius, who, according to both modern and ancient commentators, wanted to marry Placidia himself. Whether this was the reason or not, Constantius does appear to be implacably opposed to Athaulf gaining any imperial recognition or position. Placidia's thoughts on her capture, marriage and position as the wife of her brother's enemy are not recorded. The only indication of her emotion is recorded in the shared grief for their child. However, in one area she is presented as taking an active role: her Roman identity is stressed in her attempts to instil Roman values into her husband. Indeed, they are presented as the ideal conjugal couple acting in *concordia*. This implicit 'Romanizing' of Athaulf via Placidia suggests that Olympiodorus is sympathetic to his position. Orosius also stressed the fact that by her marriage Galla Placidia was of value to Rome. In these narratives Placidia serves as a foil for the barbarian/Roman dichotomy – the partnership that is implied by the narrative suggests that Romans and Goths could work in partnership against mutual enemies and for the joint glory of Rome.

In the relationship between Placidia and her second husband, her character undergoes subtle changes. She is presented as much more of an actor in events, while Constantius, the Roman, comes off poorly by comparison with the Gothic king. As Blockley notes (1981: 40), the introduction to Constantius, which describes his behaviour in public processions, is in direct contrast to the picture of Athaulf:

> downcast and sullen, a man with bulging eyes, a long neck and a broad head, who always slumped over the neck of the horse he was riding, darting glances here and there out of the corners of his eyes, so that all saw in him 'a mien worthy of a tyrant', as the saying goes.
>
> (Olympiodorus fr. 23)

In the reconstructed version of Olymipodorus' text, this section comes immediately prior to the very Roman celebration of Placidia's marriage to the leader of the 'barbarian' Goths. It is also so reminiscent of the famous passage in Ammianus (16.10) of Constantius II's *adventus* into Rome as to be almost pastiche.[12]

The period of Constantius' rise to high office in the west paralleled the time of Galla Placidia's sojourn with the Goths. Constantius was a Dacian born Roman who had served under Theodosius, Placidia's father (Olymp. fr. 37). By 411 he was *magister utriusque militiae* in the west and successful in strategy and battle against the usurper Constantine in Gaul, and instrumental in the retention of most of Gaul for Roman rule.[13] He is also known for avenging the downfall of Stilicho by approving the killing of Olympius (Olymp. fr. 8). According to Olympiodorus (fr. 22) Constantius was initially in favour of negotiating with Athaulf, as long as the return of Galla Placidia was on the table, as he wanted to marry her himself.[14] When Galla Placidia finally returned to Ravenna and the court of her brother, both she and the eligible marriage partners in both west and east must have recognized her potential in a dynastic marriage, given the fact that it was, by now, apparently unlikely Honorius was going to produce an heir.

The partnership that was presented in the union with Athaulf is patently missing in descriptions of her second marriage. According to Olympiodorus, Placidia initially refused to marry Constantius and was eventually handed over by her brother despite her protests and the marriage celebrated with all due pomp on 1 January 417 on the occasion of Honorius taking up his eleventh consulship and Constantius his second (fr. 33). Oost offers a number of reasons why Placidia might not be in favour of her second marriage: that it was Constantius' influence that had thwarted the ambitions of Athaulf which she herself had encouraged; that Constantius 'was ugly to look at and had unpleasing mannerisms'; that Placidia's Christian beliefs were against a second marriage; that having been married to a King of the Goths and being an imperial princess she thought Constantius beneath her socially (Oost 1968: 142 and see his references). Some or all of these may be valid or even true, but there is no substantive evidence to support them. Imperial women, in fact most Roman women, could expect to spend their fertile years married, to several husbands if necessary, despite admonitions from certain churchmen. Galla Placidia was still only twenty-eight and had proven herself to be fertile, unlike her brother. The imperial ambitions of Constantius must, all the same, have been evident to all parties, Placidia included.

Placidia had two children by Constantius, Justa Grata Honoria, born 419, and Flavius Placidus Valentinian, born 421, their names reminding all of their imperial lineage. On the birth of their son, Constantius was elevated to Augustus by an apparently reluctant Honorius, who appointed him 'unwillingly' (fr. 33) and 'out of respect for his familial relationship' (fr. 33.2). It is improbable, however, that Honorius actually was reluctant as he had pushed for the marriage in the first place and the elevation of Constantius must, in reality, have been planned. It may be that Honorius is as much a cipher in the text as his sister and that Olympiodorus is taking the eastern imperial line here – for Constantius' title was never accepted by Constantinople. At the same occasion, Placidia was made Augusta, and Valentinian was made *noblissimus.* Olympiodorus suggests the recognition of Valentinian was only done under pressure from Placidia, and is evidence of her ambitions for her son (fr. 33). However, these are hardly unreasonable expectations on her part. Valentinian's status was, likewise, unrecognized by Theodosius II at this stage. Constantius was an unhappy emperor by all accounts, regretting the activities he could no longer participate in because of the duties of state and resenting non-recognition by the eastern empire to the extent that he was attempting to raise an army and march east at the time of his death (Olymp. fr. 33; Oost 1968: 164–5).

Olympiodorus recounts the influence that Galla Placidia had over her second husband. Here, her role is represented as controlling and detrimental to both the character of Constantius and the ideal of matrimonial *concordia.* One episode from their marriage is recounted: a certain Libanius, a magician, came to Ravenna offering to get rid of the barbarians without the use of arms. He was given permission to try his hand but when Placidia learnt of this, she is said to have threatened her husband with divorce if he did not have the magician executed (Olymp. fr. 36). While Placidia's attitude is in keeping with the prevailing Christian and Roman mores of the day, the telling of the story highlights a tension in the marriage with Constantius that is absent in the narrative of her time with Athaulf. It also gives the impression of Placidia's power over her husband, a reversal of the accepted and ideal Roman marital relationship that reflects badly on the male. Husbands should be neither controlled nor threatened by their spouses, even if their wife is the conduit to imperial legitimation. This is not the persuasive wife of her first marriage, inculcating Roman ways to her Gothic husband. Constantius is not seen as a husband acting in concord with his wife. Instead, Placidia's ability to control him is a sign of his weakness (cf. Fischler 1994: 127). The ideal conjugal couple was presented in the non-ideal marriage of Goth and Roman.

Olympiodorus also claims that Constantius, 'in addition to his other virtues' was free from greed until he met Placidia. After their marriage he fell into lust with money and, after his death, Ravenna was full of people trying to get recompense for his misappropriation of their property (fr. 37). The text suggests criticism of Placidia and Honorius in their attitude to the petitioners, who were unsuccessful. Oost (1968: 143) again lists a number of reasons as to why Constantius might have become more careful with his money. Olympiodorus recognizes the good qualities of Constantius but remains fundamentally hostile to him, taking the line of Constantinople and this hostility is expressed in his poor marriage. While Placidia is associated with him, she becomes part of the creation of his image as a tyrant – he could not rise to the duties of ruling, he was greedy and avaricious, vices he did not have before his marriage. Placidia is instrumental in this change for the worse in her husband's character. Again, the message is the inherent weakness of the male who is influenced adversely by a woman. Oost (1968: 163) interprets the situation somewhat differently and argues that 'anyone acquainted with the methods of women will have little doubt of the nagging pressure Placidia brought to bear'![15]

To return to my original question – what purpose does Placidia serve in these narratives? I have argued here that Olympiodorus expressed sympathy for Athaulf, and his politics, in the way he has drawn the good relations between husband and wife. Likewise, hostility to Constantius, and his politics, is expressed by the tension in his union. The strengths and weaknesses of both men as individuals are expressed in the nature of their marital relationships. Obviously there is more than that to the question of both the image of Galla Placidia and the politics of the period as expressed in Olympiodorus – Galla Placidia was a real person, and a real actor in the politics of the period, and should not be reduced solely to a narrative tool. It is also worth considering how she benefited from both her marriages in terms of her own political ambitions. Despite a short crisis and exile after the death of Constantius (Olymp. fr. 38, 43), by 425, after she had concluded a peace with the barbarian troops, she was, in effect, regent in the western empire, surrounded by a powerful coterie of loyal generals (fr. 43.2).

It has been suggested by Blockley that one of Olympiodorus' prime sources for the period of Placidia's time with Athaulf was Candidianus. Blockley (1981: 34) identifies the Candidianus who led part of Placidia's army in 425 (and was responsible for raising her spirits when she was sunk in despair and distress, fr. 43.1) with the man who encouraged the marriage of Athaulf and Placidia. This Candidianus certainly gets a good press from Olympiodorus, where other historians ignore him. This may also account for both the favourable treatment that Athaulf receives and the negative evaluation of Constantius. However, rumours that Constantius intended to wage war against the east may have been enough to ensure his bad reputation there (Matthews 1970: 91).

Placidia's centrality in the narrative, and in historical reality, acts as a link between all the male power brokers in the west in this period. More importantly, Olympiodorus is writing about the western empire in Greek for a readership in the east – and at the time of writing Placidia's son Valentinian III was technically ruling in the west. However, it remains that she is presented in a far more sympathetic manner while she is with Athaulf than when married to Valentinian's father. Olympiodorus is surprising for his favourable opinion of Stilicho, whom almost all western sources denounce for his willingness to negotiate and conciliate the Goths, for his alliances and plans for Alaric, and for attempting to put his son on the eastern throne (Matthews 1970: 90 lists Orosius, Jerome and Eunapius). Olympiodorus, however, presents Stilicho as a loyal servant of the western empire, acting in its best interests in trying to annex Illyricum. The suggestion is that the sources for this early part of Olympiodorus' history were not only western, but also supporters of Stilicho. It may be that Olympiodorus has absorbed a similar rhetorical stance in the presentation of the marriage of Placidia and Athaulf. His criticism of Constantius, from his derogatory physical description to his inability to stand up to a wife who did not want to marry him in the first place, may be due to Constantius' hostility to the eastern empire. While Olympiodorus' sympathies appear to lie with Athaulf, Constantius was not opposed to conciliation with the Goths. After the death of Athaulf, Constantius was happy to come to an accommodation with his successors. In 417 he was instrumental in settling the Goths in Aquitania where their kingdom, centred on Toulouse, lasted for nearly a century. It is also true that Constantius' 'Roman' credentials allowed him to achieve where Stilicho had failed – he became emperor and so did his son.

Is the portrayal of Placidia a portrayal of an imperial woman and her actions, or is she a foil for the actions of her male kin, or is she a tool of the subtext of the historian, that Rome should come to an accommodation with the Goths? What is certain is that we can derive no information about Galla

Placidia's own feelings and little about her motivation in the way she is portrayed. We can speculate (but not to the extent of Oost), and we can, with hindsight, see how the dynastic machinations played themselves out. Placidia probably had little choice in whether or not she married either of her husbands. She may have been as unwilling to marry Athaulf as she was alleged to be to marry Constantius. However, it is interesting that even historians of the period had a tendency to romanticize her first marriage – there are certainly echoes of the Hellenistic romance genre in the telling of it.[16] Here, depictions of both Galla Placidia and her two husbands are gender-based. Athaulf and Constantius are subject to similar rhetorical play: the virtues associated with non-Roman and Roman are inverted; traditional masculine virtues of control and reason are lost to Constantius and taken up by his wife. Olympiodorus' text reflects a commentary on the ambiguity of what it meant to be Roman in the fifth century and how *romanitas* should best be defined.

Notes

1 This is an idea first expressed by Blockley (1981: 27–47). He is interested in the political subtext of Olympiodorus' work. My interest in Galla Placidia began with Blockley's interpretation of Olympiodorus and with Oost (1968).

2 There is an extensive and growing body of work that addresses the gendered nature of the text and the reading of women's roles. See, for example, Brubaker (forthcoming, 2004); Clark (1998); Cooper (1992, 1996); Dixon (2001a); Fischler (1994); Richlin (1995).

3 This article is based on the translation and commentary of R.C. Blockley (1981 and 1983). For the most recent summary of Olympiodorus' work, see Rohrbacher (2002: 73–81). See also Baldwin (1975); Gillett (1992); Matthews (1970); Thompson (1944).

4 Galla Placidia's daughter, Justa Grata Honoria, appealled to Attila to avenge the murder of her lover (Priscus, fr.17; Blockley (1983: 301); Holum (1982: 1).

5 For the role of Pulcheria in the reign of Theodosius II, see Holum (1982: 79–111).

6 For discussion of age at marriage, see Shaw (1987). For more general consideration see Evans Grubbs (1995). In the east Pulcheria, the daughter of her half-brother Arcadius, took a vow of virginity at the age of fourteen, a few years after Placidia's abduction in 413. Pulcheria used her virgin state as a power base from which to control those around her younger brother, the Emperor Theodosius II. See Holum (1982: 93 and 79–111).

7 Oost (1968: 73) claims that there was a growing enmity between Galla Placidia and Serena in this period – but this is based on the fact that later Olympiodorus and others claimed that Placidia assented to Serena's death. For debate on Stilicho's plans for his son, see Matthews (1975: ch. 10).

8 For the internal politics of this period, see Matthews (1975: 307–76).

9 For an outline of a traditional Roman wedding, see Treggiari (1991: 163–6).

10 For the use and symbolism of *chlamys* by late Roman generals and officials, see Smith (1999); Harlow (forthcoming, 2004).

11 Priscus Attalus was eventually abandoned by Athaulf and ended up humiliated by Honorius in a triumphal procession, mutilated and banished to an island (Olympiodorus fr. 26.2; Orosius 7.42.9; Oost 1968: 132–3).

12 Ammianus (16.10.10) records Constantius II's visit to Rome in 357 and among other comments describes him as 'gazing straight before him as if his neck were in a vise and turning neither to right nor left (as if he were a statue of a man). When a wheel jolted he did not nod, and at no point was he seen to spit or to wipe or rub his face or nose or to move his hand'. Ammianus continues by saying that this behaviour was a demonstration of Constantius' self-control, also evident in other areas of his life. However, this reading of the text does presuppose that Olympiodorus knew of Ammianus' work, which may not be the case.

13 For Constantius' generalship, see Jordanes (*Get.* 164); Orosius (7.42.15; 43). For his policies see Matthews (1975).

14 See Oost (1968: 113) for an assessment of Constantius' character based on readings of Olympiodorus.

15 The inappropriate assumptions of modern scholars concerning the activities of ancient women are discussed elsewhere in this volume.

16 For Hellenistic romances see Cooper (1996: 20–44); Hägg (1983).

10

GENDER AND CULTURAL IDENTITY IN ROMAN EGYPT

Jane Rowlandson

Roman Egypt was a multi-cultural society. Even before Alexander the Great 'liberated' Egypt from Persian rule (332 BC), there were pockets of Aramaic, Greek and Carian speakers in the Nile valley and Delta, as well as Nubian and other African influences especially in the south. And the military and civilian immigrants welcomed by the early Ptolemaic rulers over the following century included a diverse range of settlers not only from the cities of Old Greece, but also from areas of Ptolemaic overseas power such as Cyrenaica, Thrace and Syria-Phoenicia, including Judaea. The Jewish cultural impact on Alexandria is, of course, well known; but there was also a significant Jewish population in the *chora* (the rest of Egypt) until it was virtually obliterated in the Jewish revolt of AD 115–17. However, although all these settlers left some mark on their adopted country (the Thracian god Heron became an important deity in the Fayum; and the magical spells combine Egyptian, Greek, Semitic and other Near Eastern influences), it was the cultural encounter between the Egyptians and their new Graeco-Macedonian rulers which had the most pervasive impact.[1]

The Ptolemies quickly appreciated that they could never attract enough immigrants to create a Greek bureaucracy; the existing Egyptian scribal class had to be persuaded to retrain in the language of the new rulers. Thus, while 'Hellenes' formed 16 per cent of the civilian population in the Fayum, an area of intensive Greek settlement, this included Egyptians serving in the administration who had received a Greek education as well as ethnic Greeks (Thompson 1994, 1997, 2001). The immigrants themselves were predominantly (though certainly not exclusively) men, and settler families seem to have continued the Greek practice of exposing unwanted daughters, perpetuating the relative shortage of Greek females. So demography added to the social incentives for immigrant men to seek wives among the daughters of prosperous Egyptian families, whose wealth was mostly based on hereditary priesthoods of the local temples. The converse, marriage between Greek women and Egyptian men, is found rarely, if at all (La'da 2002; Thompson 2002: 152–3). By the second century BC, therefore, there were many families in Egypt which were of mixed ancestry, or at least could draw on both Egyptian and Greek cultural traditions. There was surprisingly little obvious 'mixing' of the two traditions, at least until the very late Ptolemaic period, although more subtle forms of mutual interaction are increasingly recognized (Koenen 1993; Selden 1998; Stephens 2003). But many people were 'bi-cultural' as well as bilingual, moving from using a Greek name and identity in a military or administrative context to an Egyptian persona when serving as a priest (Clarysse 1992; Yoyotte 1969).[2]

For the reasons just given, the 'Greek' element in these families normally derived ultimately from the male ancestral line, the 'Egyptian' element from the female. It is also tempting to see this correlation between gender and cultural identity as being reinforced through the generations by the men's participation in military or civilian occupations demanding a Greek education and identity, while the 'private' sphere in which the women operated remained more Egyptian. But matters are a little more complicated than this. In bi-cultural families, women also commonly had double names, Egyptian and Greek, although this is perhaps not quite so prevalent as among the men. And the temptingly neat polarity of Greek/public/male versus Egyptian/private/female soon breaks down in face of the evidence. The Egyptian identities of men were played out in roles no less public than the Greek, especially through priesthoods and agricultural work. While some of the most important Greek cults were headed by priestesses (this included the Alexandrian cults of Ptolemaic queens), women in the Egyptian temples occupied subordinate roles.[3] And, despite the widespread ownership of property by Egyptian women, there is scant evidence that their contribution to work in the fields was more than supplementary or exceptional (Rowlandson 1998: 218–45, esp. 219, 231–2).

Women's position regarding the management of property and conduct of business, implying involvement with legal contracts, complicates the issue further. The law spanned the gap between the private world of the household and the wider public community, and women's ability to own and inherit property, even if it mainly served to articulate their relationships with other family members, could lead to lawsuits and other public situations which actively involved women (with or without male assistance).[4] In addition, the population of Ptolemaic Egypt could also, in effect, choose between the application of Egyptian or Greek law, exploiting the significant differences between the two systems, particularly with respect to the position of women. Thus, a family's papers might include marriage agreements in Egyptian (because Egyptian law offered greater security to the wife), but loans and sales in both languages.[5] And we find examples of Egyptian women acting as parties to Greek contracts without using a guardian as Greek law required, because guardianship of women was not a feature of Egyptian law (Vandorpe 2002: 331).

By the time Egypt was made a Roman province in 30 BC, therefore, the population of the Egyptian *chora* was ethnically and culturally so thoroughly mixed that the Romans simply classed everyone as '*Aegyptioi*' except citizens of Alexandria and the other Greek *poleis* (Naukratis, Ptolemais and, after its foundation in AD 130, Antinoopolis), and Roman citizens. Unlike under the Ptolemies, new immigration into the province was minimal (clearly the result of Augustus' policy of 'setting Egypt apart' from the rest of the empire), but the number of Roman citizens progressively increased through individual grants to prominent families. Although certain distinctively Roman principles and patterns of thought can be seen throughout the administration, the overall impact, as elsewhere in the eastern provinces, consisted primarily of an intensified hellenization and urbanization of the province (Bowman and Rathbone 1992; cf. Woolf 1994).[6] This involved encouraging the development of a hellenized elite among the *Aegyptioi* of the *metropoleis* (the central town of each of forty or so *nomes*, or districts into which Egypt was traditionally divided), who, alone, enjoyed hereditary membership of the gymnasium, the focal point of Greek cultural identity, and who were privileged by paying a reduced rate of poll-tax (from which Romans and Alexandrians were wholly exempt). The basic principles of this system can be traced to the reign of Augustus, but over the next century it was gradually refined, in particular, demanding proof of maternal as well as paternal descent for those claiming metropolite or gymnasial status.

The role of women within the gymnasial order has been the subject of a recent provocative and stimulating paper by Peter van Minnen, to which the present article is essentially a response (van Minnen 2002).[7] His emphasis on the Egyptian antecedents of this apparently most hellenized group reminds us how incomplete and limited the hellenization of the *metropoleis* remained. But his (consciously paradoxical) suggestion that the women of the gymnasial order remained culturally more Egyptian than their brothers and husbands, and were the main vehicle by which Egyptian culture was perpetuated down the generations of this class, is not tenable without qualification. The relationship between gender and cultural identity, both within the gymnasial order and more widely in Egyptian society, deserves further investigation.

Potential evidence is embarrassingly abundant, but not always helpful. For instance, interpreting the significance of the vast numbers of terracottas of Isis, Harpocrates, or Bes is impossible without knowing who owned or dedicated them (see e.g. Dunand 1979). I shall, therefore, focus on three 'case-studies' (nomenclature, literacy and funerary representations) which offer some secure basis for argument while also highlighting the difficulties of interpretation, both empirical and conceptual.

Nomenclature

Names constitute a huge resource as yet only partially exploited by scholars (Fikhman 1996; Hobson 1989; Samuel 1981). Since patterns of naming demonstrably varied from place to place as well as over time, generalization is dangerous unless based on a full and systematic study. No full study exists of the nomenclature of the gymnasial order as a whole, and thus it is diffi- cult to be sure that the examples of gymnasial families in which, over several generations, males have Greek names but those of the women are more Egyptianized, are actually as typical as they appear to be (Bingen 1991; Montevecchi 2000).[8]

There has, however, been a systematic analysis of the nomenclature of the equivalent to the gymnasial class in the Fayum, the graphically named '6475 Greek settlers in the Arsinoite nome'. The reservation of the label 'Hellenes' for the elite only of this nome reflects its distinctive history of intensive development and settlement under the Ptolemies, although even these 'Hellenes' possessed a mixed Greek and Egyptian ancestry through the processes of intermarriage and social mobility described earlier.[9] The '6475' are attested over some two hundred years from AD 55, when Nero confirmed their existing privileges by letter (Montevecchi 1970). Given the explicitly Greek official identity of this group, it is not surprising that the several hundred names of men and women who belonged to it are predominantly Greek in form. But Bagnall (1997, based on the prosopography of Canducci 1991) has shown that this superficial appearance conceals a more compli- cated picture (see Table 10.1).

Names of Egyptian formation are indeed rare, though proportionately less so among the females.[10] But much the commonest type for both sexes are theophoric names which probably or certainly allude to Egyptian deities. This includes not only the understandably popular Apion/Apia, Isidoros/ Isidora, Sarapion/Sarapias/Sarapous, but also less obvious allusions to Egyptian gods

Table 10.1 Nomenclature of 'the 6475 Hellenes in the Arsinoite nome' (derived from Bagnall 1997).

	Male			Female		
	Names	Cases	%	Names	Cases	%
Theophoric (Egyptian)	8	13	2.8	6	14	9.5
Theophoric/calques (Greek)	50	206	44.8	32	90	61.2
Macedonian/dynastic/settler	12	111	24.1	8	11	7.5
Common Greek	44	84	18.3	10	17	11.6
Roman/Latinate	15	23	5.0	4	7	4.8
Other/uncertain	15	23	5.0	8	8	5.4
Total	144	460	100	68	147	100

such as Apollonios/Apollonia (Apollo was the Greek equivalent of Horus), or Kronion and its variants (popular in Tebtunis, whose crocodile god was equated with Kronos).[11] Among men, the next most popular names derived from the period of early Ptolemaic settlement, although the range of these names was quite restricted, for both men and women.[12] Bagnall makes the important point that if we consider this category along with that of the theophoric names, over two-thirds of the men and three-quarters of the women have names which emphasize their specific heritage in the Greek settlement of Egypt in preference to a broader Greek identity.

Within the group of the '6475', therefore, there is perhaps more common ground between men and women in terms of nomenclature than real difference between them, despite the somewhat greater tolerance for overtly Egyptian names among the women than among men of this class. A more marked difference in naming emerges between this elite class as a whole and groups taken from other sections of the population. For comparison with the '6475', Bagnall first analysed the names of around six hundred poll-tax payers at the village of Karanis, where the Egyptian element in nomenclature was much more pronounced, at 40 per cent; Greek theophoric names accounted for a further 26 per cent, and Roman names a similar proportion to those of the '6475'. Karanis was an untypically large village of several thousand inhabitants (better described as a town, though technically a *kome*), popular with army veterans and their families. But as Roman citizens, veterans did not figure in the poll-tax records, along with Alexandrians and all women (no women paid poll-tax). A complete analysis of residents at Karanis would undoubtedly increase the percentage of both Greek and Roman names, although Egyptian names would probably remain the largest single group.[13]

An even higher proportion of Egyptian names is found in the 'archive of Petaus', the papers of a (largely illiterate) village scribe of Ptolemais Hormou in the Fayum in the later second century AD. Bagnall's percentages, based on the name index of the edition, are not differentiated by gender; but the index includes a significant number of female entries, which I have analysed in detail using the same criteria as Bagnall (see Table 10.2).[14]

While most of the women appear in the Petaus documents only as a means of officially individuating their sons (i.e. 'x son of y, whose mother is z'), some women are included in their own right, for instance as landholders.[15] In any case, there is no reason to think they are less representative a sample of overall village nomenclature than the men. The pattern of female names at Ptolemais Hormou essentially seems to combine the features of the other two cases considered so far. It shares with the '6475' an increased preference, compared to the men, for Greek theophoric names at the expense of the various other categories of Greek and Roman names. But, like Karanis, the incidence of Egyptian names is vastly higher than among the '6475', indeed, these form a clear majority of all names, particularly among the women. This

Table 10.2 Female nomenclature in the Petaus archive.

	Women			All names (Bagnall 1997)%
	Names	Cases	%	
Theophoric (Egyptian)	88	184	57.5	53
Theophoric/calques (Greek)	26	101	31.6	26
Macedonian/dynastic/settler	3	3	0.9	5
Common Greek	9	11	3.4	8
Roman	1	1	0.3	3
Other/uncertain	11	20	6.3	5
Total	138	320	100	100

difference in the proportion of Egyptian names between village populations and the elite '6475' is much more striking than the relatively subtle gender differences within each group.

We know little about the considerations which lay behind the choice of names for children in Roman Egypt, except what can be inferred from the names themselves. Names tended to run in families, with children named after grandparents, parents, or other family members. Thus one father wrote (probably to his mother, or his mother-in-law) that had his new-born child been male, he would have been named after his brother, but since 'it was a little girl child, she was called by your name'.[16] Apart from such universal favourites as Isidora, Sarapion, Thaesis (= 'she of Isis') or Petosiris (= 'gift of Osiris'), names tended to be so strongly localized that sometimes the origin of a document can be determined purely from the names occurring in it. Thus, at Soknopaiou Nesos, a remote village on the northern fringe of the Fayum whose economy was almost entirely based on its temple and camel-transport over long distance desert routes, the nomenclature was overwhelmingly Egyptian (Samuel 1981). A census register found at Oxyrhynchus can be confidently attributed to Upper Egypt on the basis of nomenclature, including the characteristic feminine names starting Sen- ('daughter of') (Bagnall 1998; Bagnall *et al.* 1997). While much of this local specificity consists in names derived from local cults, this is not confined to names of Egyptian formation, so that in the census register we find Lykos and Lykophron alongside many Egyptian names referring to Wepwawet, the jackal god worshipped at Lykopolis (cf. the case of Kronion above). Even if we cannot assess how strongly individual choices of such names represent personal attachment to that deity as opposed to simply following local fashion, they suggest that even those families who regarded themselves as sufficiently Greek to adopt a hellenized form of name were content to bear names which clearly associated them with a particular place and its Egyptian zoomorphic cult.[17]

While the precise construction to put on names as indicators of identity may be uncertain, the clear class and geographical differences in nomenclature which we have examined surely point to their having some usefulness in addressing cultural identity. The gender differences are, by contrast, much less extreme. To sum up the argument rather schematically, most men and women's names in Roman Egypt distinguished them either as 'Egyptian Egyptians' (often from a particular place) or as 'Egyptian Greeks'; women were slightly more likely than men to fall into the first category, or into either of these as opposed to the alternatives which offered no particular identification with Egypt. But these are nuances; nomenclature offers only limited support for the idea that cultural identity in Egypt was significantly gendered.

A brief look at slaves' names offers an instructive coda to the discussion of nomenclature. Despite the fact that the vast majority of slaves in Egypt were female domestic servants, their nomenclature is the most strongly Hellenic of any social group. This is no doubt partly because household slavery was basically a Greek import into Egypt, and (for obvious economic as well as cultural reasons) remained more prevalent among the more hell-enized and wealthy families of the *metropoleis* than in the villages.[18] But their nomenclature does not merely reflect that of the families whom they served. Some slaves actually were of foreign origin, like Tyrannis 'of Asian descent' bought by a woman from Oxyrhynchus in AD 215 (*P. Oxy.* XII 1263); but most were home-bred, or rescued from exposure on the dungheap (e.g. Rowlandson 1998: nos. 212, 213). And while some were well-educated, like the girl Peina who was injured on the way to her music lesson, other slaves could barely speak Greek (*P. Oxy.* L 3555; LI 3616, 3617). The choice of common Greek names for slaves had nothing to do with Greek cultural identity, but was a means of emphasizing their deracination, and denying them a share in the local ties enjoyed by the free population.

Literacy

Turning to the question of women's literacy and education more generally, the documentary papyri again provide a large body of data from which to compare the ability to write in terms of both gender and social class. Throughout the Roman period, and particularly after the mid-first century AD, the overwhelming majority of documents are in Greek; it is, therefore, convenient to begin by looking only at Greek writing before considering the relationship between written and spoken Egyptian and Greek. The factual groundwork laid by Herbert Youtie in a series of articles remains valid, despite the publication of many new documents, and the questioning or refinement of some of his interpretations (Youtie 1971a, 1971b, 1975a, 1975b; Hanson 1991; Harris 1989; Hopkins 1991; Thomas 1992). Essentially, the government of Roman Egypt faced the whole adult male popula-tion, to an extent hitherto unprecedented, with the need to use written documents such as receipts for taxes or seed, and various sorts of declaration; with this also went an expansion of the 'elective' use of written private leases, loans, sales, and so on. While the body of these documents would be drawn up by professional scribes who wrote fluently and knew the correct format, for the first time even receipts routinely required the recipient's signature.[19] Since only a small minority of men could even clumsily produce a signature, let alone read the document they were signing, there was widespread resort to 'subscribers' or *hypographeis*, who signed on behalf of those unable to do it for themselves. These men (never women, even if they could write) were often relatives, colleagues, or friends – anyone who could be trusted to undertake a role which potentially offered scope for deception. Among men, there was a strong correlation between the ability to sign for oneself and social status and wealth; while the vast majority of tenants and debtors were '*agrammatoi*' (unable to sign – in Greek; the ability to write Egyptian did not count), most male landowners and creditors could write. But even among gymnasium members, for whom one might expect a Greek education to be de rigueur, there are instances of men who could not comfortably write.[20]

Literacy, even at this most basic level, was very much less common for women of all social classes. Although illiteracy carried no real social stigma even for men, it did put them at a disadvantage in their dealings with the state and private business. Women, even if they were property owners, were not expected to undertake such activities without male assistance, and although some women certainly did take an active and independent role in the management of their property or other business, they did so by choice, and only because they possessed sufficient confidence in their abilities. While literacy was never an official prerequisite for women to undertake business independently, it seems to have been widely perceived as necessary. Most telling are the cases where women invoke their ability to write in connection with their exemption from guardianship by the Roman *ius liberorum*, even though the law itself did not require literacy. For the women of Roman Egypt, literacy in Greek was a relatively rare and greatly prized skill, even when their penmanship was clumsy and much less cursive than that of professional male scribes (although many men shaped no better).[21]

Legal requirements interacted with women's practical achievements and sense of confidence to produce sometimes paradoxical results which can be illustrated by the document already mentioned concerning the sale of a slave (*P. Oxy.* XII 1463). It dates from AD 215, and probably everyone involved in the transaction (except, of course, the slave) had acquired Roman citizenship just three years before, through Caracalla's universal grant (the Constitutio Antoniniana). The surviving document is not the sale itself, but an application for 'examination' of the slave, which both contracting parties needed to sign. Aurelia Claudia, the purchaser, was able to sign for herself, but since she did not possess the *ius liberorum*, the signature of her guardian, who was her husband, was also necessary. Surprisingly, and particularly so since he was a citizen of Alexandria and thus would presumably have gone through the ephebate and entered the gymnasium, he did 'not know letters', and a fellow-Alexandrian had to sign on his behalf. In contrast, the vendor, a villager named Aurelia Artemeis, whose parents' names are clearly Egyptian, was able to dispense with a guardian by the *ius liberorum*; but since she did 'not know letters' she, too, needed male assistance from a *hypographeus*, who was her brother-in-law. The number of women who were both legally and educationally empowered to act without any male assistance was small.

One possible explanation for the very restricted literacy in Greek among women is that substantially fewer women than men could even speak Greek, let alone write it. Is this likely to have been the case? Much is made of a letter which begins: 'By Sarapis! You, the man who reads this letter, whoever you are, expend a little effort and translate for the women the matters written down in this letter and communicate it to them. Ptolemaios to Zosime his mother and Rhodous his sister, greetings' (*SB* XVIII 13867, trans. Rowlandson 1998: no. 246). The letter is unusually long and detailed, but reveals nothing specific about the family's social or cultural background. But if women with such impeccably Hellenic names were ignorant of the Greek language, should we not infer that this was a very common situation, not confined to the lower classes, but extending to the apparently more hellenized levels of society? This text is, however, conspicuously unique. For a society in which Egyptian, Greek and, to an extent, Latin were all in simultaneous use, the papyri provide puzzlingly few references to the need for translation, and hardly any outside the context of legal documentation and law courts, including the well-known legal precedent involving an Egyptian woman being questioned through an interpreter whether she wished to remain living with her husband (*P. Oxy.* II 237 col. vii 37).[22]

The reason for this silence about translation between Greek and Egyptian must be that it was too commonplace to require comment (hence the proportionately more references to the rarer need to translate between Latin and Greek). Generations of use of the two languages side by side meant that most people could shape up adequately in the appropriate language for the circumstances which they were likely to encounter, and there were always people to assist (like the assumed reader of Ptolemaios' letter) if need arose. An increasingly sophisticated understanding of the complex shades of bilingualism in contemporary situations helps us to imagine how the languages co-existed in Roman Egypt, even if the silence of our texts prevents us being sure that we are right (Fewster 2002).

The pervasive impact of Greek on the spoken Egyptian of the Roman period is shown by the fact that Coptic took from Greek not merely most of its alphabet, but also about 20 per cent of its vocabulary. This went far beyond the biblical words to be expected (since Coptic originated as a vehicle for translating the Christian Bible into Egyptian), to include many common conjunctions and prepositions, nouns and verbs (Ray 1994). This seems to imply that even the Egyptian-speaking rural population had become familiar with many everyday Greek words through the need to communicate with officials and landlords. But, just as the need to use Greek documents was greater for men than for women, so one imagines that in the villages, many women may largely have escaped contact with Greek speech, except as loan words adopted into common currency.

The pattern of linguistic usage in the *metropoleis* seems to me much more uncertain. The impression from our documents of the dominance of Greek may fail to reflect what was actually spoken, either in the streets or at home. But there seems no justification in the evidence (apart from Ptolemaios' letter, which may not anyway refer to a metropolitan family) for supposing a significant gender difference here in the use of Greek, particularly among the gymnasial class. Once this class became hereditary in the maternal as well as paternal line, wives basically shared the same cultural background as their husbands – indeed, as is well known, they were sometimes full siblings (e.g. *P. Oxy.* XII 1452).

The shared Greek culture of a wealthy metropolitan family emerges most clearly from the family correspondence of Apollonios, governor of the Apollonopolite Heptakomia at the time of the Jewish Revolt (Cribiore 2001: 94–100; 2002; Rowlandson 1998: nos. 92–9, 236–7). It includes twenty-five letters (some very fragmentary) sent by women, including ones that reveal literary pretensions of script or vocabulary, or sophisticated phraseology. Both Apollonios' mother Eudaimonis and his wife Aline were well-educated in Greek, and the education of his daughter Heraidous is a frequent preoccupation of the letters (one mentions providing her with school materials, including a book to read). Female servants, as well as family friends, also joined in the correspondence, sometimes in their own hands. This archive offers an unusually detailed insight into a family thoroughly familiar with Greek language and culture, but many other women's letters point in a similar direction (Cribiore 2001: 88–94; examples in Rowlandson 1998).[23]

Women were infinitely less likely to be able to write Egyptian than Greek.[24] Written Egyptian, always the preserve of a specialist scribal class, shrank rapidly under Roman rule, although some of the finest literary manuscripts in Demotic script date from this period (Lewis 1993; Zauzich 1983). An oral tradition of story-telling is widely assumed to stand behind the written narratives and prophecies, which prompts speculation how far women may have contributed to their creation and transmission. But unfortunately there is no evidence (the stories themselves abound in magicians and books, but no story-tellers), and it was surely male scribes in the temple scriptoria who wrote the texts down.[25] Any part that women played in Egyptian literary culture was shared with men.

Funerary representations

Burial practices in Roman Egypt have, again, generated a vast amount of evidence, which varies enormously between regions, within localities, and over time. While mummification remained the standard treatment for the dead, including among the hellenized sections of the population (a Greek verse epitaph was an optional extra), the iconography of mummies developed ways of representing the deceased as an individual, rather than in an idealized manner representing assimilation with the god Osiris, and thus the hope of eternal life (Borg 1997). But this individuality could be conveyed in many different ways, such as by a mask or portrait, and including only the head, or extending to the chest or the entire body (Walker and Bierbrier 1997; cf. also Rowlandson 1998: 335–53). For instance, the Graeco-Roman burial site recently discovered near el-Bawiti in the Bahariya Oasis includes four different types of mummy (Hawass 2000: esp. 53). The majority have gilding on the face, and sometimes also gilded and embossed chest-pieces. Others are encased in painted cartonnage (i.e. papier-mâché), with inlaid eyes. The third sort are carefully wrapped in linen, but without painting or gilding, while the poorest category are sketchily and inadequately wrapped. Although apparently none of these mummies includes the strikingly Roman-style portraits found on some Fayum and Nile valley mummies, they, and the tombs where they were found, are no less characteristic of that period.

Funerary evidence is potentially our richest source for investigating issues of gender and cultural identity, since we almost always know the dead person's gender, and often their name and age at death; and much of the iconography seems intended to represent the deceased as a social being (e.g. women are shown with jewellery such as formed part of their dowry; men may appear as soldiers or athletes).[26] But this intricate evidence poses many technical as well as conceptual difficulties of interpretation, and here there is space to focus only on one example to illustrate how a cautious understanding of the context can help to overcome these difficulties.

Some of the earliest portrait mummies come from a burial excavated by von Kaufmann at Hawara in the Fayum in 1892, and now in the Egyptian Museum, Berlin.[27] At the bottom of the grave were three portrait mummies, of a woman and two very young children. The woman's portrait is highly realistic and Romanized, and she wears a white tunic decorated with two vertical purple stripes (*clavi*) (see Figure 10.1). Her hairstyle and jewellery, and the fact that the portraits are painted on linen rather than wood, are evidence for an early date, probably the first half of the first century AD. A small limestone stela lying beside the woman's head was inscribed in Greek: 'Aline alias Tenos, daughter of Herodes, worthy (woman), many salutations. Year 10, 35 years old, Mesore 6th'. If, as seems likely, this refers to the mummified woman, she perhaps died in AD 24 (year 10 of Tiberius).[28] Across these three mummies were placed two more, a bearded man and another girl (aged about nine), each with gilded masks rather than portraits (Figure 10.2). Finally, three undecorated mummies were placed crosswise on top of the rest.

Does this burial represent a family group? Most scholars would accept that 'Aline' was the mother of the two young children with portraits, but

Figure 10.1 Mummy portrait of 'Aline', Hawara, Egypt, mid-first century AD
(Ägyptisches Museum, Berlin, inv. 11411).

opinion is divided over whether the two gilded mummies (let alone the three plain ones) also belong to her family, or are even contemporary (Roberts 1997: esp. 21–2). But, supposing they do belong to a single family, what are we to make of the apparently very different forms of representation? How a deceased person was commemorated may reflect less their own preferences than those of the surviving relatives, although it was possible to include instructions about funerary arrangements in one's will, and some of the mummy portraits may have been painted during life (though this seems unlikely to apply to these early examples on linen, or to any portraits of young children). Certainly, someone needed to make choices: first-century Hawara has produced large numbers of gilded and undecorated mummies in addition to the much smaller number with portraits; and there are also painted plaster masks. This could

Figure 10.2 Gilded mummy mask of an adult male found in the same grave as 'Aline', Hawara, Egypt (Ägyptisches Museum, Berlin, inv. 11414).

have been an area in which women's choices influenced the artistic representations of their family (cf. Woodhull in this volume).

But the choices in this case precisely accord with the contemporary fashion at Hawara, where portraits of women, several with children, begin to appear in the early to mid-first century AD, continuing alongside the more traditional gilded mummies, both male and female. Both formats clearly cater for 'the top end of the market' (these Hawara burials are thought to represent the wealthiest elite of the Fayum), but it is not known how the cost of a portrait compared to that of gilding. However stylized the gilt mummies seem to us, they too exhibit some new and Romanized features; in the men, this is largely confined to the hairstyle, but the females have more individualized facial features, and wear tunics with prominent *clavi*. Only from around the reign of Vespasian do portraits of adult men start to appear, and they remained less common than those of women (Germer *et al.* 1993; Walker and Bierbrier 1997: esp. 37, 77).

It would clearly be absurd to suggest, from the superficial appearance of these decorated mummies, that the elite women of the Fayum were actually *more* Hellenized (or Romanized) than their menfolk. All in their own way reflect an accommodation and identification with the new order. But, for some reason, it was felt appropriate to introduce more radical innovations to the funerary representations of women or young children; for elite men, the iconographic emphasis remained for a while more traditional, perhaps even self-consciously archaizing. As in previous centuries, it was the accompanying inscription (now in Greek rather than Egyptian) that revealed a man's individual identity.[29] After about a generation, male funerary iconography largely caught up with the innovations in female portraiture, and began to depict them as social individuals.

To sum up, as we saw earlier with nomenclature and literacy, the evidence of funerary representations exhibits some undoubted gender differences, but shows that these are much too complex to support any schematic correlation between gender and cultural identity. In the Egyptian temples, women played a role, although their roles were subordinate to those of men. The Ptolemaic legacy of Graeco-Egyptian law allowed women to act as parties to business dealings, but very few felt able to dispense entirely with male assistance, even those entitled to act without a guardian through the Roman *ius liberorum*. It is also difficult to assess how far there is a real contrast between Egypt and other provinces of the Greek East in this respect, and how far the apparently greater independence of women in Egypt is the product of our much more detailed evidence, especially contracts and letters (van Bremen 1996). It does seem though that both men and women contributed to a shared, and immensely varied, culture.

Perhaps paradoxically, a Greek education seems to have been the most potent factor in shaping women's confidence to act independently in what was essentially a male world. The extent to which women had access to the activities of the gymnasium is very uncertain (as, indeed, is the question of whether the gymnasium provided education, even for males), but the requirement for heredity through the maternal as well as paternal line produced a greater emphasis on women's contribution to the identity of the gymnasial class. But for neither women nor men did possession of this elite status involve abandonment of the Egyptian side of their family background. It was possible for both sexes to retain a recognizably Egyptian identity while also assimilating the attitudes and modes of behaviour which qualified them as Greeks within the Roman empire (cf. Woolf 1994).

Notes

1 This essay was written during my tenure of a Major Research Fellowship from the Leverhulme Trust (whom I thank for their support) for work towards a book on *The Culture of Roman Egypt*. I cite Greek papyri by their standard abbreviations, listed in Oates *et al.* (2001).

2 The classic instance is Dionysios son of Kephalas, alias Plenis: see also Lewis (1986: ch. 8).

3 Women gradually ceased to hold priestly titles during the Pharaonic period: Robins (1993: ch. 8); but see Cohen (1996); Rowlandson (1998: 55–62); Colin (2002).

4 See the celebrated case of Chratianch v. her brother-in-law Tefhape: H. Thompson (1934) *P. Tebt.* I 52 records the petition of a woman, Tapentos, complaining of the theft of the contract concerning her house and other business papers by another woman and her son. Note that (in contrast to Classical Athenian law) the Greek law applied in Egypt allowed women to own property in their own right and to enter into legal contracts, so long as a male guardian (*kyrios*) was present; see Rowlandson (1995) and (1998: ch. 4).

5 E.g. *P. Adler*, a family archive from Pathyris probably found intact in its original storage jar.

6 While scholars are now wary of the term 'romanization', for its implication of a deliberate imperialistic project, the hellenization and urbanization of Egypt does seem to have been a conscious policy inaugurated by Augustus, and pursued with varying degrees of interest by his successors.

7 On the other related controversial arguments in his paper, I do not share his reservations about describing the gymnasial order as an 'elite'; but am attracted by his suggestion that the relationship between the gymnasial group and the *metropolitai* paying reduced poll-tax is less that of 'an elite within an elite' (the standard view) than of overlapping definitions of essentially the same class.

8 The names in *P. Oxy.* XII 1452 conform to expectation, but Egyptian male names are common in the series of gymnasial applications *P. Oxy.* XLVI 3276–84.

9 See pp. 151–2. The ethnic mixing gained further momentum in the second and first centuries BC; thus Maron son of Dionysios, Macedonian of the catoicic cavalry, had been known as Maron alias Nektsaphthis son of Petosiris before promotion from the ranks into the elite cavalry (Crawford 1971: 134–5). The Romans were presumably aware that the Greek credentials of the Arsinoite 'Hellenes' were not all they might seem; in legal terms, even this group counted as '*Aegyptioi*'.

10 Even the Egyptian names have Greek endings and declensions, reflecting the long tradition of adapting Egyptian names for writing in Greek (cf. Quaegebeur 1982). Typical examples are: Marsisouchos, Psenkebkis (male), or Tamystha, Tapetsiris (female).

11 Note that the theophoric dominance could easily be made even greater: Bagnall includes as Roman/Latinate names Apollinarios/Apollinaria; and Philantinoos, formed in the same way as Philosarapis, and alluding to the deified Antinoos.

12 Among men, the three names Herakleides, Ptolemaios and Lysimachos account for 90 of the 111 cases. Note that 'Herakleides' could also have an Egyptian reference, to Herishef, the ram-headed god of the neighbouring Herakleopolite nome, although Bagnall considers that in the Arsinoite, this significance would be secondary to the association of Herakles with the gymnasium and with the Macedonian kings; this multivalency must account for the popularity of the name (and of its female equivalent, Herakleia, which Bagnall lists as 'theophoric', presumably because the gymnasial and royal connotations were less appropriate to women). Much of Bagnall's 'Common Greek' category could also be considered 'dynastic' or 'settler', such as 'Menelaos' (the name of Ptolemy I's brother), or 'Philon', 'Eirene', or 'Demo' attested among early Ptolemaic settlers (*P. Petrie*² I 14).

13 On the military milieu of Karanis, see Alston (1995: ch. 7). The Roman citizens included women as well as men; e.g. Rowlandson (1998: no. 71). The evidence for Karanis is so full that a complete analysis would be a major undertaking.

14 I assume that Bagnall's database was the whole name index of *P. Petaus* without distinguishing male from female names, although in note 38 he speaks as though the name index includes only males.

15 See *P. Petaus* 126; among the landholders was Mariamme daughter of Joseph, a rare Jewish name in the period following the Jewish revolt. Note also *P. Petaus* 1–2, declarations of birth for the daughter of a brother–sister marriage.

16 Rowlandson (1998: no. 226 = *P. Mil.* II 84; fourth century AD; see further no. 225 with introduction, and pp. 106, 120, 147, 294).

17 My impression is admittedly that many fewer Greek theophoric names than Egyptian ones carry a clear local reference, but refer to the most important or universal Graeco-Egyptian cults (not all anthropomorphic): Isis, Sarapis, Apis, Horus.

18 For the Ptolemaic period, see D.J. Thompson (2002: 142); Roman period, Bagnall *et al.* (1997: 98) with references to Bagnall and Frier (1994).

19 These points are most effectively brought out by Hopkins (1991).

20 Youtie (1971a: 175) cites an Alexandrian example; cf. the *kyrios* in *P. Oxy.* XII 1463 below.

21 The *ius liberorum*: *P. Oxy.* XII 1467, *P. Charite* 8 (= Rowlandson 1998: nos. 142, 179b). Handwriting: also Rowlandson (1998: 301–2).

22 The infrequency of references to translation between Greek and Egyptian is a puzzle as yet unsolved, not helped by ambiguity over the meaning of '*hermeneus*' (perhaps often 'broker' rather than 'interpreter'). Peremans (1983) and Rochette (1994) cite earlier bibliography.

23 Cf. the famous mummy portrait of 'Hermione, *grammatike*': Walker and Bierbrier (1997: cat. 11).

24 I do not know any certain cases of women literate in Demotic; the assumed literacy of the 'Serapeum twins' is based on a dream text which describes seeing them at school (*UPZ* I 78; cf. Lewis 1986: ch. 5), but dreams may be surreal. Ahwere, the magician's sister-wife in the (fictional) first Setne story, is represented as reading, but for writing relies on her more accomplished brother (Lichtheim 1980: 130–1). For women literate in Coptic centuries later, Wilfong (2002: 75–6).

25 For background, see Tait (1996); Depauw (1997).

26 See especially Montserrat (1993); Borg (1996).

27 For a detailed discussion, Germer *et al.* (1993). Doxiadis (1995: 64–5) gives colour plates, but misidentifies the children as two girls; the younger is, in fact, a boy.

28 Bernand (1975: no. 59). The Egyptian month Mesore began on 25 July. Walker (1997: 2) prefers to date the earliest portraits no earlier than the reign of Claudius.

29 Esp. Walker and Bierbrier (1997: cat. 74), a very traditional gilded mask inscribed 'Titus Flavius Demetrius'.

BIBLIOGRAPHY

Abu-Lughod, L. (1987) *Veiled Sentiments: Honor and Poetry in Bedouin Society*, Berkeley: University of California Press.

Alexiou, M. (1974) *The Ritual Lament in Greek Tradition*, Cambridge: Cambridge University Press.

Alic, M. (1986) *Hypatia's Heritage: A History of Women in Science from Antiquity to the Late Nineteenth Century*, London: Women's Press.

Alston, R. (1995) *Soldier and Society in Roman Egypt: a Social History*, London: Routledge.

Andreau, J. (1983) 'À propos de la vie financière à Pouzzoles: Cluvius et Vestorius', in M. Cébeillac-Gervasoni (ed.) *Les 'Bourgeoisies' municipales italiennes aux IIe et Ie siècles av. J-C.*, Naples: Bibliothèque de l'Institut français de Naples, 9–20.

Andreau, J. (1995) 'Affaires financières à Pouzzoles au Ie siècle ap. J-C.: les tablettes de Murecine', *RÉL* 73, 39–55.

Annas, J. (1996) 'Plato's *Republic* and Feminism', in J.K. Ward (ed.) *Feminism and Ancient Philosophy*, London: Routledge, 3–12.

Anzaldúa G. and Moraga, C. (eds) (1981, 1983) *This Bridge Called My Back: Writings by Radical Women of Color*, New York: Kitchen Table Press.

Applebaum, S. (1979) *Jews and Greeks in Ancient Cyrene*, Leiden: Brill.

Archer, L., Fischler, S. and Wyke, M. (eds) (1994) *Women in Ancient Societies*, Basingstoke: Macmillan.

Arjava, A. (1996) *Women and Law in Late Antiquity*, Oxford: Clarendon Press.

Astin, A.E. (1970) s.v. 'Cornelia' (1) in N.G.L. Hammond and H.H. Scullard (eds) *Oxford Classical Dictionary*, 2nd edn, Oxford: Clarendon Press, 291.

Aubert, J-J. (1994) *Business Managers in Ancient Rome*, Leiden: Brill.

Bacchielli, L. (1978) 'Aspetti dell'acculturazione dei libyi di Cirenaica', *Africa* 33, 605–22.

Bacchielli, L. (1987) 'La scultura libya in Cirenaica e la variabilità delle risposte al contatto culturale greco-romano', *QAL* 12, 459–88.

Bacchielli, L. (1994) 'Un Santuario di Frontiera, fra Polis e Chora', *Libyan Studies* 25, 45–59.

Badian, E. (1996) s.v. 'Cornelia' in S. Hornblower and A. Spawforth (eds) *Oxford Classical Dictionary*, 3rd edn, Oxford: Oxford University Press, 392.

Bagnall, R.S. (1997) 'The People of the Roman Fayum', in M.L. Bierbrier (ed.) *Portraits and Masks*, London: British Museum, 7–15.

Bagnall, R.S. (1998) 'Cults and Names of Ptolemais in Upper Egypt', in W. Clarysse, A. Schoors and H. Willems (eds) *Egyptian Religion: the Last Thousand Years*, vol. II, Leuven: Peeters, 1093–101.

Bagnall, R.S. and Frier, B.W. (1994) *The Demography of Roman Egypt*, Cambridge: Cambridge University Press.

Bagnall, R.S., Frier, B.W. and Rutherford, I.C. (1997) *The Census Register P. Oxy. 984: The Reverse of Pindar's Paeans*, *Pap. Brux.* 29, Brussels.

Baldwin, B. (1975) 'Olympiodorus of Thebes', *L'Antiquité Classique* 18, 85–97.

Barnes, J. (ed.) (1984) *The Complete Works of Aristotle*, vol. II, Princeton: Princeton University Press.

Barnes, J. (1987) *Early Greek Philosophy*, Harmondsworth: Penguin.

Bates, O. (1914) *The Eastern Libyans*, London: Macmillan.

Bauman, R.A. (1992) *Women and Politics in Ancient Rome*, London: Routledge.

Beer, J. (1995) 'Women, Authority, and the Book in the Middle Ages', in L. Smith and J. Taylor (eds) *Women, the Book, and the Worldly*, Cambridge: D.S. Brewer, 61–9.

Beran, M. (1998) *The Last Patrician: Bobby Kennedy and the End of American Aristocracy*, New York: St Martin's Press.

Bernand, E. (1975) *Receuil des inscriptions grecques du Fayoum*, vol. 1, Leiden: Brill.

Berubé, M. (1992) *Marginal Forces/Cultural Centers: Tolson, Pynchon, and the Politics of the Canon*, Ithaca: Cornell University Press.

Bieber, M. (1961) *The History of the Greek and Roman Theater*, 2nd edn, Princeton: Princeton University Press.

Bierl, A. (1997) *Die Orestie des Aischylos und der modernen Bühne: theoretische Konzeptionen und ihre szenische Realisierung*, Stuttgart: J.B. Metzler.

Bingen, J. (1991) 'Notables hermopolitains et onomastique féminine', *Chronique d'Egypte* 66, 324–9.

Bisi, A.M. (1985) 'Origine e diffusione del culto cirenaica do Zeus Ammon', in G.W.W. Barker, J.A. Lloyd and J. Reynolds (eds) *Cyrenaica in Antiquity*, Oxford: B.A.R., 307–18.

Black-Michaud (1975) *Cohesive Force: Feud in the Mediterranean and the Middle East*, Oxford: Blackwell.

Blockley, R.C. (1981) *The Fragmentary Classicising Historians of the Later Roman Empire: Eunapis, Olympiodorus, Priscus and Malchus*, vol. I, *ARCA* 6, Liverpool: Cairns.

Blockley, R.C. (1983) *The Fragmentary Classicising Historians of the Later Roman Empire: Eunapis, Olympiodorus, Priscus and Malchus*, vol. II, *ARCA* 10, Liverpool: Cairns.

Blok, J. (2001) 'Virtual Voices: Toward a Choreography of Women's Speech in Classical Athens', in A. Lardinois and L. McClure (eds) *Making Silence Speak: Women's Voices in Greek Literature and Society*, Princeton: Princeton University Press, 95–116.

Bluestone, N.H. (1987) *Women and the Ideal Society: Plato's Republic and Modern Myths of Gender*, Oxford: Berg.

Blundell, S. (1998) *Women in Classical Athens*, London: Bristol Classical Press.

Boardman, J. (1980) *The Greeks Overseas*, 2nd edn, Harmondsworth: Penguin.

Boatwright, M.T. (1991) 'Plancia Magna of Perge: Women's Roles and Status in Roman Asia Minor', in S. Pomeroy (ed.) *Women's History and Ancient History*, Chapel Hill: University of North Carolina Press, 249–72.

Boedeker, D. (1991) 'Euripides' *Medea* and the Vanity of LOGOI', *CPh* 86, 95–112.

Boedeker, D. (1997) 'Becoming Medea: Assimilation in Euripides', in J.J. Clauss and S.I. Johnston (eds) *Medea*, Princeton: Princeton University Press, 127–48.

Boehm, C. (1984) *Blood Revenge: the Anthropology of Feuding in Montenegro and Other Tribal Societies*, Lawrence, Kan.: University Press of Kansas.

Boethius, A. and Ward-Perkins, J.B. (1970) *Etruscan and Roman Architecture*, New Haven: Yale University Press.

Bongie, E.B. (1977) 'Heroic Elements in the *Medea* of Euripides', *TAPA* 107, 27–56.

Borg, B. (1996) *Mumienporträts: Chronologie und kultureller Kontent*, Mainz: P. von Zabern.

Borg, B. (1997) 'The Dead as a Guest at Table? Continuity and Change in the Egyptian Cult of the Dead', in M.L. Bierbrier (ed.) *Portraits and Masks*, London: British Museum, 26–32.

Bowman, A.K. and Rathbone, D.W. (1992) 'Cities and Administration in Roman Egypt', *JRS* 82, 107–27.

Bradley, K.R. (1985) 'Child Labour in the Roman World', *Historical Reflections* 12, 311–30.

Braund, S. (1997) 'A Passion Unconsoled? Grief and Anger in Juvenal's Satire 13', in S. Braund and C. Gill (eds) *The Passions in Roman Thought and Literature*, Cambridge: Cambridge University Press, 68–88.

Bremmer, J. (1983) 'The Importance of the Maternal Uncle and Grandmother in Archaic and Classical Greece and Early Byzantium', *ZPE* 50, 173–86.

Brion, M. (1960) *Pompeii annd Herculaneum*, London: Elek.

Brion, M. (1973) *Pompeii and Herculaneum, the Glory and the Grief*, trans. J. Rosenberg, London: Cardinal.

Brisson, L. and Meyerstein, F.W. (1995) *Inventing the Universe: Plato's* Timaeus*, the Big Bang, and the Problem of Scientific Knowledge*, Albany: State University of New York Press.

Brubaker, L. (1997) 'Memories of Helena: Patterns of Imperial Female Patronage in the Fourth and Fifth Centuries', in L. James (ed.) *Women, Men and Eunuchs*, London: Routledge, 52–75.

Brubaker, L. (forthcoming, 2004) 'Sex, Lies and Prokopius: the *Secret History* and the Rhetoric of Gender in Sixth-century Byzantium', in L. Brubaker and J. Smith (eds) *Gender and the Transformation of the Ancient World*, Cambridge: Cambridge University Press.

Burgess, R.W. (ed. and trans.) (1993) *Idatius. The Chronicle of Hydatius and Consularia Constantinopolitana*, Oxford: Clarendon Press.

Burkert, W. (1972) *Lore and Science in Ancient Pythagoreanism*, Cambridge, Mass.: Harvard University Press.

Burnett, A. (1973) '*Medea* and the Tragedy of Revenge', *CPh* 68, 1–24.

Burnett, A. (1998) *Revenge in Attic and Later Tragedy*, Berkeley: University of California Press.

Calame, C. (1977) *Les Choeurs de jeunes filles en Grèce archaïque*, vol. I, Rome: Edizioni dell'Ateneo & Bizzarri.

Calame, C. (1990) 'Narrating the Foundation of a City: the Symbolic Birth of Cyrene', in L. Edmunds (ed.) *Approaches to Greek Myth*, Baltimore: The Johns Hopkins University Press, 275–341.

Calci, C. (1984) *La Villa di Livia a Prima Porta*, Rome: De Luca.

Callus, D.A. (1944) *Introduction of Aristotelian Learning to Oxford, Proceedings of the British Academy* 29, London: H. Milford.

Calza, G. (1939) 'Epigrafe sepolcrale contenente disposizioni testamentarie', *Epigraphica* 1, 160–2.

Cameron, A. (1970) *Claudian Poetry and Propaganda at the Court of Honorius*, Oxford: Clarendon Press.

Cameron, A. (1990) 'Isidore of Miletus and Hypatia: On the Editing of Mathematical Texts', *GRBS* 31, 103–27.

Cameron, A. and Kuhrt, A. (eds) (1983) *Images of Women in Antiquity*, London and New York: Routledge.

Camodeca, G. (1999) *Tabulae pompeianae Sulpiciorum. Edizione critica dell'archivio puteolano dei Sulpicii*, (Vetera 12), Rome.

Camps, G. (1993) 'Liste onomastique libyque d'apres les sources latines', *Reppal* 7–8, 39–73.

Canducci, D. (1991) 'I 6475 cateci greci dell'Arsinoite: Prosopografia', *Aegyptus* 71, 121–216.

Caraveli-Chaves, A. (1980) 'Bridge between Worlds: the Greek Women's Lament as Communicative Event', *Journal of American Folklore* 93, 129–57.

Caraveli-Chaves, A. (1986) 'The Bitter Wounding: the Lament as Social Protest in Rural Greece', in J. Dubisch (ed.) *Gender and Power in Rural Greece*, Princeton: Princeton University Press, 170–94.

Carp, T. (1981) 'Two Matrons of the Late Republic', in H. Foley (ed.) *Reflections of Women in Antiquity*, New York: Gordon Breach Science Publ., 343–54.

Carson, A. (1990) 'Putting Her in Her Place: Women, Dirt, and Desire', in D. Halperin, J. Winkler and F. Zeitlin (eds) *Before Sexuality: the Construction of Erotic Experience in the Ancient Greek World*, Princeton: Princeton University Press, 135–70.

Case, S.-E. (1988) *Feminism and Theatre*, New York: Methuen.

Casini, P. (1984) 'Newton: the Classical Scholia', *History of Science* 22, 1–58.

Caspar, M. (ed.) (1938) *Gesammelte Werke: Johannes Kepler*, vol. I, Munich: C.H. Beck.

Caspar, M. (1959) *Kepler*, trans. C.D. Hellman, London: Abelard-Schuman.

Catani, E. (1987) 'Per un iconografia di Libya in età romana', *QAL* 12, 385–402.

Catto, J.I. (ed.) (1984) *The Early Oxford Schools* (*The History of the University of Oxford*, vol. 1), Oxford: Oxford University Press.

Chamoux, F. (1953) *Cyrène sous la monarchie des Battiades*, Paris: E. de Boccard.

Champlin, E. (1991) *Final Judgements. Duty and Emotion in Roman Wills, 200 B.C.–A.D. 250*, Berkeley: University of California Press.

Chaplin, J. (2000) *Livy's Exemplary History*, Oxford: Oxford University Press.

Christianson, J. (2003) *On Tycho's Island: Tycho Brahe, Science, and Culture in the Sixteenth Century*, Cambridge: Cambridge University Press.

Cixous, H. and Clément, C. (1986) *The Newly Born Woman*, trans. B. Wing, Minneapolis: University of Minnesota Press.

Clark, E.A. (1998) 'The Lady Vanishes: Dilemmas of a Feminist Historian after the "Lingusitic Turn",' *Church History* 67, 1–31.

Clark, G. (1993) *Women in the Ancient World: Greece and Rome*, Oxford: Oxford University Press.

Clarysse, W. (1992) 'Some Greeks in Egypt', in J.H. Johnson (ed.) *Life in a Multi-cultural Society*, Chicago: Oriental Institute of the University of Chicago, 51–6.

Cogman, P. (1992) *Mérimée: Colomba and Carmen*, London: Grant and Cutler Ltd.

Cohen, D. (1995) *Law, Violence and Community in Classical Athens*, Cambridge: Cambridge University Press.

Cohen, N. (1996) 'A Notice of Birth of a Girl', in R. Katzoff, Y. Petroff and D. Schaps (eds) *Classical Studies in Honor of David Sohlberg*, Ramat Gan: Bar-Ilan University Press, 385–98.

Colin, F. (2002) 'Les prêtresses indigènes dans l'Egypte hellénistique et romaine: une question à la croisée des sources grecques et égyptiennes', in H. Melaerts and L. Mooren (eds) *Le rôle et le statut de la femme en Égypte hellénistique, romaine et byzantine*, Leuven: Peeters, 41–122.

Compernolle, R. van (1983) 'Femmes indigenes et colonisateurs', in *Modes de contact et Processus de Transformation dans le Societés Anciennes*, Rome: Scuola normale superiore, 1033–49.

Constantinides, E. (1983) 'Ανδρειομάνη: the Female Warrior in Greek Folk-Songs', *Journal of Modern Greek Studies* 1, 63–72.

Cooper, K. (1992) 'Insinuations of Womanly Influence: an Aspect of the Christianisation of the Roman Aristocracy', *JRS* 82, 150–64.

Cooper, K. (1996) *The Virgin and the Bride: Idealised Womanhood in Late Antiquity*, Cambridge, Mass. and London: Harvard University Press.

Corbier, M. (1995) 'Male Power and Legitimacy through Women: the *domus Augusta* under the Julio-Claudians', in R. Hawley and B. Levick (eds) *Women in Antiquity: New Assessments*, London: Routledge, 178–93.

Corcella, A. and Medaglia, S.M. (1993) *Erodoto: Le Storie Libro IV. La Scizia e la Libia*, Milan: Fondazione Lorenzo Valla.

Courtney, E. (1999) *Archaic Latin Prose*, Atlanta: Scholars Press.

Crawford, D.J. (1971) *Kerkeosiris: an Egyptian Village in the Ptolemaic Period*, Cambridge: Cambridge University Press.

Cribiore, R. (2001) *Gymnastics of the Mind. Greek Education in Hellenistic and Roman Egypt*, Princeton: Princeton University Press.

Cribiore, R. (2002) 'The Women in the Apollonios Archive and their Use of Literacy', in H. Melaerts and L. Mooren (eds) *Le rôle et le statut de la femme en Égypte hellénistique, romaine et byzantine*, Leuven: Peeters, 149–66.

Crombie, A.C. (1953) *Robert Grosseteste and the Origins of Experimental Science 1100–1700*, Oxford: Clarendon Press.

Crombie, A.C. (1994) *Styles of Scientific Thinking in the European Tradition: the History of Argument and Explanation Especially in the Mathematical and Biomedical Sciences and Arts*, vol. I, London: Duckworth.

Crook, J.A. (1967) *Law and Life of Rome, 90 B.C.–A.D. 212*, London: Thames & Hudson.

Crook, J.A. (1986) 'Women in Roman Succession', in B. Rawson (ed.) *The Family in Ancient Rome: New Perspectives*, London: Croom Helm, 58–82.

Cumont, F. (1917) 'L'aigle funéraire d'Hierapolis et l'apothéose des emereurs', *Etudes Syriennes*, Paris: A. Picard, 37–118.

Cumont, F. (1942) *Recherches sur les symbolisme funeraire des Romains*, Paris: Geuthner.

Cuomo, S. (2000) *Pappus of Alexandria and the Mathematics of Late Antiquity*, Cambridge: Cambridge University Press.

d'Alverny, M.-T. (1982) 'Translations and Translators', in R.L. Benson and G. Constable (eds) *Renaissance and Renewal in the Twelfth Century*, Cambridge Mass.: Harvard University Press, 421–62.

d'Arms, J.H. (1980) 'Republican senators' involvement in commerce in the late Republic: some Ciceronian evidence', in J. H. d'Arms and E. C. Kopff (eds) *The Seaborne Commerce of Ancient Rome: Studies in Archaeology and History*, Rome: Memoirs of the American Academy in Rome, 36, 77–90.

d'Arms, J.H. (1981) *Commerce and Social Standing in Ancient Rome*, Cambridge, Mass: Harvard University Press.

Davesne, A. (1986) 'La divinité cyrénéenne au silphion', in *Iconographie classique et identité régionales*, BCH Suppl. 14, 195–204.

Davesne, A. and Garlan, Y. (1987) 'Découverte d'un lot de figurines grecques en terrcuite à Apollonia de Cyrénaique', *Libya Antiqua* 15–16, 199–26.

171

Davies, P.J.E. (2000) *Death and the Emperor: Funerary Monuments from Augustus to Marcus Aurelius, 28 B.C.–A.D. 193*, Cambridge: Cambridge University Press.

de Beauvoir, S. (1953) *The Second Sex*, trans. and ed. H.M. Parshley, New York: Random House/Vintage Books.

DeGrassi, A. (1962) 'La data della fondazione della colonia romana di Pola', in *Scritti Vari di Antichità* 2, Rome, 913–24.

Deliyanni, H. (1985) 'Blood Vengeance Attitudes in Mani and Corsica', unpublished typescript held by the Department of Sociology, University of Exeter.

DeMaria, S. (1988) *Gli Archi Onorari di Roma e dell'Italia Romana*, Rome: L'erma di Bretschneider.

Depauw, M. (1997) *A Companion to Demotic Studies*, Pap. Brux. 28, Brussels.

Desanges, J. (1981) 'The Proto-Berbers', in G. M. Mokhtar (ed.) *Ancient Civilizations of Africa*, Berkeley, CA: Heinemann, 423–40.

Dillon, J. (1986) 'Female Principles in Platonism', *Itaca* 1, 107–23.

Dixon, S. (1983) 'A Family Business: Women's Role in Patronage and Politics at Rome, 80–44 B.C.', *Classica et Medievalia* 34, 91–112.

Dixon, S. (1984a) 'Family Finances: Tullia and Terentia', *Antichthon* 18, 78–101 (reprinted in modified form as ch. 4, of B. Rawson (ed.) *The Family in Ancient Rome*, 1986, London: Croom Helm, 93–120).

Dixon, S. (1984b) '*Infirmitas Sexus*: Womanly Weakness in Roman Law', *Tijdschrift voor Rechtsgeschiedenis/Legal History Journal* 52, 343–71.

Dixon, S. (1985a) 'Polybius on Roman Women and Property', *AJP* 106, 147–70.

Dixon, S. (1985b) 'Breaking the Law to Do the Right Thing: the Voconian Law in Ancient Rome', *The Adelaide Review* 9, 519–34.

Dixon, S. (1985c) 'The Marriage Alliance in the Roman Elite', *Journal of Family History* 10, 353–78.

Dixon, S. (1988) *The Roman Mother*, London: Croom Helm.

Dixon, S. (1992) 'A Woman of Substance: Iunia Libertas of Ostia', *Helios* 19, 162–74.

Dixon, S. (1993a) 'The Meaning of Gift and Debt in the Roman Elite', *EMC/CV* 12, 451–64.

Dixon, S. (1993b) '"A Lousy Ingrate": Honour and Patronage in the American Mafia and Ancient Rome', *International Journal of Moral and Social Studies* 8, 61–72.

Dixon, S. (2001a) *Reading Roman Women. Sources, Genres and Real Life*, London: Duckworth.

Dixon, S. (2001b) 'How do you Count Them When They Aren't There? New Perspectives on Roman Textile Production', *Opuscula Romana* 25–6, 1–20.

Dixon, S. (2001c) '*Familia veturia*: towards a lower-class prosopography', in S. Dixon (ed.) *Childhood, Class and Kin in the Roman World*, London: Routledge, 100–27.

Dobbins, J.J. (1994) 'Problems of Chronology, Decoration, and Urban Design in the Forum at Pompeii', *AJA* 98, 629–94.

Dooley, W.E. (1989) *Alexander of Aphrodisias: on Aristotle Metaphysics One*, London: Duckworth.

Dougherty, C. (1993) *The Poetics of Colonization*, Oxford: Oxford University Press.

Dougherty, C. (1994) 'Archaic Greek Foundation Poetry: Questions of Genre and Occasion', *JHS* 114, 35–46.

Dover, K. (1974) *Greek Popular Morality in the Time of Plato and Aristotle*, Oxford: Basil Blackwell.

Doxiadis, E. (1995) *The Mysterious Fayum Portraits: Faces from Ancient Egypt*, London: Thames & Hudson.

Dubisch, J. (ed.) (1986) *Gender and Power in Rural Greece*, Princeton: Princeton University Press.

duBois, P. (2001) *Trojan Horses: Saving the Classics from Conservatives*, New York: New York University Press.

Dunand, F. (1979) *Religion populaire en Egypte romaine: Les terres cuites isiaques du Musée du Caire*, Leiden: Brill.

Duncan-Jones, R. (1974) *The Economy of the Roman Empire. Quantitative Studies*, Cambridge: Cambridge University Press.

Duras, M. (1985) *The Lover*, trans. Barbara Bray, New York: Pantheon Books.

Durham, M.E. (1909) *High Albania*, London: Edward Arnold.

Durham, M.E. (1928) *Some Tribal Origins, Laws and Customs of the Balkans*, London: George Allen & Unwin.

Dusanic, S. (1978) 'The *horkion ton oikisteron* and Fourth-century Cyrene', *Chiron* 8, 55–76.

Dzielska, M. (1995) *Hypatia of Alexandria*, Cambridge, Mass.: Harvard University Press.

Eastwood, B. (1987) 'Plinian Astronomical Diagrams in the Early Middle Ages', in E. Grant and J. Murdoch (eds) *Mathematics and its Applications to Science and Natural Philosophy in the Middle Ages*, Cambridge: Cambridge University Press, 141–72.

Echols, A. (1989) *Daring to be Bad: Radical Feminism in America 1967–1975*, Minneapolis: University of Minnesota Press.

Edwards, C. (1996) *Writing Rome: Textual Approaches to the City*, Cambridge: Cambridge University Press.

Edwards, M. (1995) *Greek Orators IV: Andocides*, Warminster: Aris and Phillips.

Eisenstein, H. (1983) *Contemporary Feminist Thought*, Boston: G.K. Hall.

Evans Grubbs, J. (1995) *Law and the Family in Late Antiquity*, Oxford: Clarendon Press.

Fabbricotti, E. (1987) 'Divinità greche e divinità libie in rilievi di età ellenistica', *QAL* 12, 211–44.

Fabré, G. (1981) *Libertus. Recherches sur les rapports patron-affranchi à la fin de la République romaine*, Rome: École française de Rome.

Fant, M.B. and Lefkowitz, M.R. (1977) *Women in Greece and Rome*, Toronto: Samuel Stevens.

Fantham, E., Foley, H., Kampen, N., Pomeroy, S. and Shapiro, H. (1994) *Women in the Classical World*, Oxford: Oxford University Press.

Farrell, J. (2001) *Latin Language and Latin Culture: From Ancient to Modern Times*, Cambridge: Cambridge University Press.

Fauvel, J., Flood, R., Shortland, M. and Wilson, R. (eds) (1988) *Let Newton Be!* Oxford: Oxford University Press.

Favro, D. (1992) '*Pater urbis*: Augustus as City Father of Rome', *JSAH* 51, 61–84.

Favro, D. (1996) *The Urban Image of Augustan Rome*, Cambridge: Cambridge University Press.

Fewster, P. (2002) 'Bilingualism in Roman Egypt', in J.N. Adams, M. Janse and S.C.R. Swain (eds) *Bilingualism in Ancient Society*, Oxford: Oxford University Press, 220–45.

Fikhman, I. (1996) 'On Onomastics of Greek and Roman Egypt', in R. Katzoff, Y. Petroff and D. Schaps (eds) *Classical Studies in Honor of David Sohlberg*, Ramat Gan: Bar-Ilan University Press, 403–14.

Findlen, P. (1993) 'Science as a Career in Enlightenment Italy: The Strategies of Laura Bassi', *Isis* 84, 441–69.

Finley, M.I. (1973) *The Ancient Economy*, Berkeley: University of California Press.

Finnegan, R. (1995) 'The Professional Careers: Women Pioneers and the Male Image Seduction', *Classics Ireland* 2, 1–3.

Fischler, S. (1994) 'Social Stereotype and Historical Analysis: the Case of the Imperial Women at Rome', in L. Archer, S. Fischler and M. Wyke (eds) *Women in Ancient Societies*, Basingstoke: Macmillan, 115–33.

Flory, M.B. (1984) '*Sic exempla parantur*: Livia's Shrine to Concordia and the Porticus Liviae', *Historia* 33, 309–30.

Foley, H. (1981) 'The Conception of Women in Athenian Drama', in H. Foley (ed.) *Reflections of Women in Antiquity*, London: Gordon and Breach Science, 127–68.

Foley, H. (1989) 'Medea's Divided Self', *Classical Antiquity* 8, 61–85 (reprinted in *Female Acts in Greek Tragedy*, 2001, 243–71).

Foley, H.P. (ed.) (1991) *Reflections of Women in Antiquity*, New York and London: Gordon and Breach Science.

Foley, H. (1993) 'The Politics of Tragic Lamentation', in A.H. Sommerstein, S. Halliwell, J. Henderson and B. Zimmerman (eds) *Tragedy, Comedy and the Polis*, Bari: Levante Editori, 101–43.

Foley, H. (2001) *Female Acts in Greek Tragedy*, Princeton: Princeton University Press.

Fora, M. (1992) 'Ummidia Quadratilla ed il restauro del teatro di Cassino', *ZPE* 94, 269–73.

Forbes, C.A. (1955) 'The Education and Training of Slaves in Antiquity', *TAPA* 86, 321–60.

Forlati Tamaro, B. (1947) *Inscriptiones Italiae, X. Regio X.1: Pola et Nesactium*, Rome: Libreria dello Stato.

Fowler, D. and Fowler, P. (1996) s.v. 'Virgil' in S. Hornblower and A. Spawforth (eds) *Oxford Classical Dictionary*, 3rd edn, Oxford: Oxford University Press, 1602–7.

Foxhall, L. (1996) 'The Law and the Lady: Women and Legal Proceedings in Classical Athens', in L. Foxhall and A. Lewis (eds) *Greek Law in its Political Setting*, Oxford: Clarendon Press, 133–52.

Frank, T. (1916) 'Race Mixture in the Roman Empire', *American Historical Review* 21, 689–708.

Frank, T. (1920) *An Economic History of Rome*, Baltimore: The Johns Hopkins University Press.

Frank, T. and Broughton, T.R.S. (eds) (1933–40) *An Economic Survey of Ancient Rome*, 5 vols, Baltimore: The Johns Hopkins University Press.

Fraschetti, A. (1983) 'La *pietas* di Cesare e la colonia di Pola', *Aion* 5, 77–102.

Friedl, E. (1967) 'The Position of Women: Appearance and Reality', *Anthropological Quarterly* 40, 97–108 (reprinted in J. Dubisch (ed.) *Gender and Power in Rural Greece*, 1986, Princeton: Princeton University Press, 42–52).

Friedrich, R. (1993) 'Medea *apolis*: On Euripides' Dramatization of the Crisis of the Polis', in A.H. Sommerstein, S. Halliwell, J. Henderson and B. Zimmerman (eds) *Tragedy, Comedy and the Polis*, Bari: Levante Editori, 219–39.

Gabriel, M.M. (1955) *Livia's Garden Room at Prima Porta*, New York: New York University Press.

Gagarin, M. (2001) 'Women's Voices in Attic Oratory', in A. Lardinois and L. McClure (eds) *Making Silence Speak*, Princeton: Princeton University Press, 161–76.

Galinsky, K. (1981) 'Augustus' Legislation on Morals and Marriage', *Philologus* 125, 126–44.

Galinsky, K. (1996) *Augustan Culture*, Princeton: Princeton University Press.

Gallo, L. (1983) 'Colonizazzione, Demografia e Strutture di Parentela', *Modes de contact et Processus de Transformation dans le Societés Anciennes*, Rome: Scuola normale superiore, 703–28.

Gardner, J. (1986) *Women in Roman Law and Society*, London: Croom Helm.

Gardner, J. (1995) 'Gender-role Assumptions in Roman Law', *EMC/CV* 39, 377–400.

Gardner, J. (1999) 'Women in Business Life: Some Evidence from Puteoli', in P. Setälä and L. Savunen (eds) *Female Networks and the Public Sphere in Roman Society*, Rome: Finnish Institute in Rome, 11–27.

Garnsey, P. (1976) 'Urban Property Investment', in M.I. Finley (ed.) *Studies in Roman Property*, Cambridge: Cambridge University Press, 123–37.

Garnsey, P. (ed.) (1980) *Non-Slave Labour in the Roman World*, Cambridge: Cambridge Philological Society (suppl. vol. 6).

Gasperini, L. (1987) 'Echi della componente autoctona nella produzione epigrafica cirenaica', *QAL* 12, 403–14.

Germer, R., Kischkewitz, H. and Lüning, M. (1993) 'Das Grab der Aline und die Untersuchung der darin gefundenen Kindermumien', *Antike Welt* 24, 186–96.

Geyer, U. (1967) *Der Adlerflug im römischen Konsekrationszeremoniell*, Diss. Bonn.

Giannini, P. (1990) 'Cirene nella poesia greca: tra mito e storia', in B. Gentili (ed.) *Cirene: Storia, mito, letteratura*, Urbino: QuattroVenti, 51–95.

Gilbert, J. (1999) 'Review of Burnett, *Revenge in Attic and Later Tragedy*', *Bryn Mawr Classical Review*, 9.2, 1–6.

Gilchrist, R. (1999) *Gender and Archaeology: Contesting the Past*, London and New York: Routledge.

Gillett, A. (1992) 'The Date and Circumstances of Olympiodorus of Thebes', *Traditio* 48, 1–29.

Gilligan, C. (1982) *In a Different Voice: Psychological Theory and Women's Development*, Cambridge, Mass. and London: Harvard University Press.

Ginat, J. (1987) *Blood Disputes among Bedouin and Rural Arabs in Israel – Revenge, Mediation, Outcasting and Family Honor*, Pittsburgh: University of Pittsburgh Press.

Glare, P.G.W. (ed.) (1982) *Oxford Latin Dictionary*, Oxford: Clarendon Press.

Gleason, M. (1995) *Making Men: Sophists and Self-Presentation in Ancient Rome*, Princeton: Princeton University Press.

Glotz, G. (1904) *La solidarité de a famille dans le droit criminel en Grèce*, Paris: A. Fontemoing.

Goldhill, S. (1990) 'The Great Dionysia and Civic Ideology', in J.J. Winkler and F.I. Zeitlin (eds) *Nothing to Do With Dionysos: Athenian Drama in its Social Context*, Princeton: Princeton University Press, 97–129.

Goldhill, S. (1994) 'Representing Democracy: Women at the Great Dionysia', in R. Osborne and S. Hornblower (eds) *Ritual, Finance, Politics: Athenian Democratic Accounts Presented to David Lewis*, Oxford: Clarendon Press, 347–69.

Goodchild, R. (1971) *Kyrene und Apollonia*, Zurich: Raggi Verlag.

Graf, F. (1997) 'Medea, the Enchantress from Afar: Remarks on a Well-Known Myth', in J.J. Clauss and S.I. Johnston (eds) *Medea*, Princeton: Princeton University Press, 21–43.

Graham, A.J. (1964) *Colony and Mother City in Ancient Greece*, Manchester: Manchester University Press.

Greene, K. (1986/1990) *The Archaeology of the Roman Economy*, Berkeley: University of California Press.

Griffith, M. (2001) 'Antigone and her Sisters: Embodying Women in Greek Tragedy', in A. Lardinois and L. McClure (eds) *Making Silence Speak: Women's Voices in Greek Literature and Society*, Princeton: Princeton University Press, 117–36.

Grubbs, J.E. (2002) *Women and the Law in the Roman Empire. A Sourcebook on Marriage, Divorce and Widowhood*, London: Routledge.

Guerrini, R. (1981) 'Tipologia di "Fatti e Detti Memorabili": dalla storia all'exemplum', in *Studi su Valerio Massimo*, Pisa: Giardini editori e stampatori, 11–28.

Hägg, T. (1983) *The Novel in Antiquity*, Berkeley: University of California Press.

Haigh, A. (1898) *The Attic Theatre*, 2nd edn, Oxford: Clarendon Press.

Hall, M. (ed.) (1997) *Raphael's 'School of Athens'*, Cambridge: Cambridge University Press.

Hallett, J.P. (1985) 'Queens, *Princeps* and Women of the Augustan Elite: Propertius' Cornelia-Elegy and the *Res Gestae Divi Augusti*', in R. Winkes (ed.) *The Age of Augustus*, Providence and Louvain-La-Neuve: Art and Archaeology Publications, Collège Erasme, 73–88.

Hallett, J.P. (1989) 'Woman as *Same* and *Other* in Classical Roman Elite', *Helios* 16, 59–78.

Hallett, J.P. (1996–97) 'Edith Hamilton (1867–1963)', *CW* 90, 107–47.

Hallett, J.P. (2002) '*Feminae Furentes*: The Frenzy of Noble Women in Vergil's *Aeneid* and the Letter of Cornelia, Mother of the Gracchi', in W.S. Anderson and L. Quartarone (eds) *Approaches to Teaching Vergil's Aeneid*, New York: the Modern Language Association of America, 159–67.

Halperin, D. (1990) 'Why is Diotima a Woman: Platonic *Eros* and the Figuration of Gender', in D. Halperin, J. Winkler and F. Zeitlin (eds) *Before Sexuality*, Princeton: Princeton University Press, 257–308.

Hanson, A.E. (1991) 'Ancient Illiteracy', in J.H. Humphrey (ed.) *Literacy in the Roman World*, *JRA* Suppl. 3, Ann Arbor, 159–98.

Harlow, M. (forthcoming, 2004) 'Clothes Maketh Man: Dress and the Elite Male in the Late Roman World', in L. Brubaker and J. Smith (eds) *Gender and the Transformation of the Ancient World*, Cambridge: Cambridge University Press.

Harries, J. (1994) *Sidonius Apollinaris and the Fall of Rome*, Oxford: Clarendon Press.

Harris, W.V. (1989) *Ancient Literacy*, Cambridge, Mass.: Harvard University Press.

Harris, W.V. (1993) 'Between Archaic and Modern: Some Current Problems in the History of the Roman Economy', in *The Inscribed Economy. Production and Distribution in the Roman Empire in the Light of the* Instrumentum domesticum, Ann Arbor: *JRA* (suppl. series 6), 11–31.

Hartmann, H. (1981) 'The Unhappy Marriage of Marxism and Feminism', in L. Sargent (ed.) *Women and Revolution: a Discussion of the Unhappy Marriage of Marxism and Feminism*, Boston: South End Press, 1–41.

Haskins, C.H. (1924) *Studies in the History of Mediaeval Science*, Cambridge, Mass.: Harvard University Press.

Hasluck, M. (1954) *The Unwritten Law in Albania*, Cambridge: Cambridge University Press.

Haury, A. (1956) 'Philotime et la vente des biens de Milon', *REL* 34, 179–90.

Hawass, Z. (2000) *Valley of the Golden Mummies*, London: Virgin.

Hawley, R. (1994) 'The Problem of Women Philosophers in Ancient Greece', in L. Archer, S. Fischler and M. Wyke (eds) *Women in Ancient Societies*, Basingstoke: Macmillan, 70–87.

Hawley, R. and Levick, B. (eds) (1995) *Women in Antiquity: New Assessments*, London: Routledge.

Headlam, W.G. (1906) 'Praelections Delivered before the Senate of the University of Cambridge, January 1906', *Cambridge Praelections*, Cambridge.

Hegel, G.W.F. (1977) *Phenomenology of Spirit*, trans. A.V. Miller, Oxford: Oxford University Press.

Helen, T. (1975) *Organization of Roman Brick Production in the First and Second Centuries A.D.*, Helsinki: Finnish Academy.

Hellegouarc'h, J. (1972) *Le vocabulaire latin des relations et des partis politiques sous la République*, Paris: Les Belles Lettres.

Herrmann, C. (1964) *Le role judiciare et politique des femmes sous la république romaine*, Collection Latomus 67.

Herzfeld, M. (1985) *The Poetics of Manhood: Contest and Identity in a Cretan Village*, Princeton: Princeton University Press.

Hobson, D.W. (1989) 'Naming Practices in Roman Egypt', *BASP* 26, 157–74.

Holst-Warhaft, G. (1992) *Dangerous Voices: Women's Laments and Greek Literature*, London and New York: Routledge.

Holst-Warhaft, G. (2000) *The Cue for Passion*, Cambridge, Mass.: Harvard University Press.

Holum, K.G. (1982) *Theodosian Empresses: Woman and Imperial Dominian in Late Antiquity*, Berkeley: University of California Press.

hooks, b. (1989) *Feminist Theory: From Margin to Center*, Boston, Mass.: South End Press.

Hopkins, K. (1978) *Conquerors and Slaves*, Cambridge: Cambridge University Press.

Hopkins, M.K. (1991) 'Conquest by book', in J.H. Humphrey (ed.) *Literacy in the Roman World*, *JRA* Suppl. 3, Ann Arbor, 133–58.

Hornblower S. and Spawforth A. (eds) (1996) *Oxford Classical Dictionary*, 3rd edn, Oxford: Oxford University Press.

Horsfall, N. (1989) *Cornelius Nepos: a Selection, Including the Lives of Cato and Atticus*, Oxford: Clarendon Press.

Howard, J.E. (1988) 'Crossdressing, the Theatre, and Gender Struggle in Early Modern England', *Shakespeare Quarterly* 39, 418–40.

Hultsch, F. (1876–8) *Pappi Alexandrini Collectionis quae supersunt*, Berlin: Apud Weidmannos.

Humphreys, S. (1993) *The Family, Women and Death: Comparative Studies*, 2nd edn, Ann Arbor: University of Michigan Press.

Huskinson, J. (1975) *Roman Sculpture from Cyrenaica in the British Museum*, London: British Museum Publications Ltd.

Huygens, R. (2000) *Ars Edendi: A Practical Introduction to Editing Medieval Latin Texts*, Turnhout: Brepols.

Instinsky, H.U. (1971) 'Zur Echtheitsfrage der Brieffragmente der Cornelia, Mutter der Gracchen', *Chiron* 1, 177–89.

Irigaray, L. (1985a) *Speculum of the Other Woman*, trans. G.C. Gill, Ithaca: Cornell University Press.

Irigaray, L. (1985b) *This Sex Which Is Not One*, trans. C. Porter with C. Burke, Ithaca: Cornell University Press.

Izbicki, T. and Christianson, G. (eds) (2000) *F. Edward Cranz: Nicholas of Cusa and the Renaissance*, Aldershot: Ashgate.

Jackson Knight, W.F. (trans.) (1958) *Virgil. The Aeneid*, Harmondsworth: Penguin.

Janko, R. (1998) 'The Homeric Poems as Oral Dictated Texts', *CQ* 48, 1–13.

Jashemski, W. (1979–93) *The Gardens of Pompeii, Herculaneum and the Villas Destroyed by Vesuvius*, 2 vols, New Rochelle, New York: Caratzas.

Jeffrey, L.H. (1961) 'The Pact of the First Settlers at Cyrene', *Historia* 10, 139–47.

Jenkins, G.K. (1974) 'Some Ancient Coins of Libya', *Libyan Studies* 5, 29–34.

Jones, A. (ed. and trans.) (1986) *Book 7 of the Collection: Pappus of Alexandria*, New York: Springer-Verlag.

Jones, A.H.M. (1960) 'The Cloth Industry under the Roman Empire', in P.A. Brunt (ed.) *The Roman Economy*, Oxford: Blackwell, 350–64 (reprinted from original article in *Economic History Review* 13, 1974, 183–92).

Jones, A.H.M. (1964) *The Later Roman Empire*, Oxford: Blackwell.

Jongman, W. (1988) *The Economy and Society of Pompeii*, Amsterdam: Gieben.

Joost-Gaugier, C.L. (2002) *Raphael's Stanza della Segnatura: Meaning and Invention*, Cambridge: Cambridge University Press.

Joshel, S. (1992) *Work, Identity and Legal Status at Rome. A Study of the Occupational Inscriptions*, Norman, London: University of Oklahoma Press.

Kähler, H. (1939) 'Triumphbogen', *RE* VII.

Kampen, N.B. (1981a) *Image and Status. Roman Working Women in Ostia*, Berlin: Mann.

Kampen, N.B. (1981b) 'Biographical Narration and Roman Funerary Art', *AJA* 85, 47–58.

Kampen, N.B. (1982) 'Social Status and Gender in Roman Art: the Case of the Saleswoman', in N. Broude and M. Garrard (eds) *Feminism and Art History*, New York: Harper & Row, 62–77.

Kampen, N.B. (1991) 'Between Public and Private: Women as Historical Subjects in Roman Art', in S.B. Pomeroy (ed.) *Women's History and Ancient History*, Chapel Hill: University of North Carolina Press, 218–48.

Kassis, K. (1979) Μοιρολόγια της Μέσα Μάνης, Athens: privately published.

Keller, E.F. (1985) *Reflections on Gender and Science*, New Haven: Yale University Press.

Keller, E.F. (1992) *Secrets of Life, Secrets of Death: Essays on Language, Gender and Science*, London: Routledge.

Keller, E.F. and Longino, H. (eds) (1996) *Feminism and Science*, Oxford: Oxford University Press.

Kellum, B. (1990) 'The City Adorned: Programmatic Display at the Aedes Concordiae Augustae', in K. Raaflaub and M. Toher (eds) *Between Republic and Empire*, Berkeley: University of California Press, 276–96.

Kellum, B. (1996) 'The Phallus as Signifier: the Forum of Augustus and Rituals of Masculinity', in N. Kampen (ed.) *Sexuality in Ancient Art*, New York: Cambridge University Press, 170–83.

Kennedy, M.T. (ed.) (1998) *Make Gentle the Life of This World: the Vision of Robert F. Kennedy*, New York, San Diego and London: Harcourt.

Kerber, L.K. (1988) 'Separate Spheres', *The Journal of American History* 75.1, 9–39.

King, H. (1995) 'Self-help, Self-knowledge: in Search of the Patient in Hippocratic Gynaecology', in R. Hawley and B. Levick (eds) *Women in Antiquity*, London: Routledge, 135–48.

Kingsley, P. (1995) *Ancient Philosophy, Mystery, and Magic: Empedocles and Pythagorean Tradition*, Oxford: Clarendon Press.

Kirshenbaum, A. (1987) *Sons, Slaves and Freedmen in Roman Commerce*, Jerusalem: Magnes Press.

Kleiner, D.E.E. (1992) *Roman Sculpture*, New Haven: Yale University Press.

Kleiner, D.E.E. (1996) 'Imperial Women as Patrons of the Arts in the Early Empire', in S. Matheson and D.E.E. Kleiner (eds) *I Claudia*, Austin: University of Texas Press, 28–39.

Kleiner, F.S. (1991) 'The Sanctuary of the Matronae Aufaniae in Bonn and the Tradition of Votive Arches in the Roman World', *Bonner Jahrbücher* 191, 199–224.

Kline, M. (1972) *Mathematical Thought from Ancient to Modern Times*, Oxford: Oxford University Press.

Knox, B. (1977) 'The *Medea* of Euripides', *YCS* 25, 193–225.

Knudson, A. (1988) 'Men Killed for Women's Songs', *Culture and History* 3, 79–97.

Koenen, L. (1993) 'The Ptolemaic King as a Religious Figure', in A.W. Bulloch, E.S. Gruen, A.A. Long and A. Stewart (eds) *Images and Ideologies*, Berkeley: University of California Press, 25–115.

Kohlstedt, S.G. (ed.) (1999) *History of Women in the Sciences: Readings from Isis*, Chicago: University of Chicago Press.

Kraeling, C.H. (1962) *Ptolemias. City of the Libyan Pentapolis*, Chicago: University of Chicago Press.

Kuhns, R. (1962) *The House, the City, and the Judge: the Growth of Moral Awareness in the Oresteia*, Indianapolis: Bobbs-Merrill.

La'da, C.A. (2002) 'Immigrant Women in Hellenistic Egypt: the Evidence of Ethnic Designations', in H. Melaerts and L. Mooren (eds) *Le rôle et le statut de la femme en Égypte hellénistique, romaine et byzantine*, Leuven: Peeters, 167–92.

Lambeck, P. (1665–79) *Commentarium de Bibliotheca Caesarea Vindobonensi libri VIII*, Vienna. (Re-edited by Kollar, 1766–82.)

Lambropoulou, V. (1995) 'Some Pythagorean Female Virtues', in R. Hawley and B. Levick (eds) *Women in Antiquity*, London: Routledge, 122–34.

Laqueur, T. (1990) *Making Sex: Body and Gender from the Greeks to Freud*, Cambridge, Mass.: Harvard University Press.

Lardinois, A. and McClure, L. (eds) (2001) *Making Silence Speak*, Princeton: Princeton University Press.

Laroche, R. (1995) 'Popular/Symbolic/Mystical Numbers in Antiquity', *Latomus* 54, 568–76.

Laronde, A. (1990) 'Greeks and Libyans in Cyrenaica', in J.P. Descoedres (ed.) *Greek Colonists and Native Populations*, Oxford: Clarendon Press, 169–80.

Lattimore, R.A. (1942) *Themes in Greek and Latin Epitaphs*, Urbana: University of Illinois Press.

Laurence, R. (1994) *Roman Pompeii. Space and Society*, London: Routledge.

Lawson-Tancred, H. (1998) *Aristotle: Metaphysics*, London: Penguin.

Lazzarini, M.L. (1987) 'Libyi nell'esercito di Cirene', *QAL* 12, 171–4.

LeGall, J. (1969) 'Métiers de Femmes au *Corpus Inscriptionum Latinarum*', *REL* 47, 123–30.

Levick, B. (1978) 'Concordia at Rome', in *Scripta Nummaria Romana. Essays presented to Humphrey Sutherland*, London: Spink and Son, 217–33.

Lévi-Strauss, C. (1969) *Elementary Structures of Kinship*, 2nd edn, trans. J.H. Bell, London, Boston: Eyre & Spottiswoode, Beacon Press.

Lewis, N. (1986) *Greeks in Ptolemaic Egypt*, Oxford: Clarendon Press.

Lewis, N. (1993) 'The Demise of the Demotic Document: When and Why', *JEA* 79, 276–81.

Lichtheim, M. (1980) *Ancient Egyptian Literature: a Book of Readings*, vol. III, Berkeley: University of California Press.

Lindberg, D. (1992) *The Beginnings of Western Science: the European Scientific Tradition in Philosophical, Religious, and Institutional Context, 600 BC to AD 1450*, Chicago: University of Chicago Press.

Litchfield, H. (1914) 'National *Exempla Virtutis* in Roman Literature', *HSCP* 25, 1–71.

Lloyd, G. (1993) *The Man of Reason: 'Male' and 'Female' in Western Philosophy*, 2nd edn, London: Routledge.

Lloyd, G. (1996) 'Reason, Science and the Domination of Matter', in E.F. Keller and H. Longino (eds) *Feminism and Science*, Oxford: Oxford University Press, 41–53.

Lloyd, G.E.R. (1987) *The Revolutions of Wisdom: Studies in the Claims and Practice of Ancient Greek Science*, Berkeley: University of California Press.

Lloyd, G.E.R. (1990) 'Plato and Archytas in the Seventh Letter', *Phronesis* 35, 159–73.

Lloyd, G.E.R. (1991) *Methods and Problems in Greek Science*, Cambridge: Cambridge University Press.

Lloyd-Jones, H. (1971) *The Justice of Zeus*, Berkeley: University of California Press.

Loane, H.J. (1938) *Industry and Commerce of the City of Rome (50 B.C.–200 A.D.)*, Baltimore: The Johns Hopkins University Press.

Longino, H. and Lennon, K. (1997) 'Feminist Epistemology as a Local Epistemology', *Proceedings of the Aristotelian Society* 71: suppl. vol., 19–54.

Longino, H.E. and Hammonds, E. (1990) 'Conflicts and Tensions in the Feminist Study of Gender and Science', in M. Hirsh and E.F. Keller (eds) *Conflicts in Feminism*, London: Routledge, 164–83.

Longo, O. (1990) 'Theater of the Polis', in J.J. Winkler and F.I. Zeitlin (eds) *Nothing to Do With Dionysos*, Princeton: Princeton University Press, 12–19.

Loraux, N. (1981) *Les enfants d'Athéna: idées athéniennes sur la citoyenneté et la division des sexes*, Paris: F. Maspero.

Loraux, N. (1986) *The Invention of Athens: the Funeral Oration in the Classical City*, trans. A. Sheridan, Cambridge, Mass.: Harvard University Press.

Loraux, N. (1998) *Mothers in Mourning*, trans. Corinne Pache, Ithaca: Cornell University Press.

Lorde, A. (1984) *Sister/Outsider: Essays and Speeches*, Trumansburg, NY: Crossings Press.

Loretto, F. (1977) 'Das Bild der Frau in Senecas philsophischen Schriften', *Ziva Antike* 27, 119–211.

Lovibond, S. (1994) 'An Ancient Theory of Gender: Plato and the Pythagorean Table of Opposites', in L. Archer, S. Fischler and M. Wyke (eds) *Women in Ancient Societies: an Illusion of the Night*, Basingstoke: Macmillan, 88–101.

McAuslan, I. and Walcot, P. (eds) (1996) *Women in Antiquity*, Oxford: Oxford University Press.

McClure, L. (1999) *Spoken like a Woman: Speech and Gender in Athenian Drama*, Princeton: Princeton University Press.

McDermott, E.A. (1989) *Euripides' 'Medea': The Incarnation of Disorder*, University Park: Pennsylvania State University Press.

McEvoy, J. (1982) *The Philosophy of Robert Grosseteste*, Oxford: Clarendon Press.

McEvoy, J. (2000) *Robert Grosseteste*, Oxford: Oxford University Press.

McGrayne, S.B. (1993) *Nobel Prize Women in Science*, Secaucus, NJ: Carol.

McHardy, F. (1999) *The Ideology of Revenge in Ancient Greek Culture*, unpublished PhD thesis, University of Exeter.

McHardy, F. (2004) 'From Treacherous Wives to Murderous Mothers: Filicide in Tragic Fragments', in D. Harvey, F. McHardy and J. Robson (eds) *Lost Dramas of Classical Athens*, Exeter: Exeter University Press.

MacKendrick, P. (1983) *The Mute Stones Speak*, 2nd edn, New York: Norton.

Mackridge, P. (1986) 'Popular Tradition and Individual Creativity: Pandelis Prevelakis (1909–1986)', *Modern Greek Studies Yearbook*, 143–52.

McManus, B. (1997) *Classics and Feminism: Gendering the Classics*, New York: Twayne Publishers.

MacMullen, R. (1959) 'Roman Imperial Building in the Provinces', *HSCP* 64, 207–35.

MacMullen, R. (1974) *Roman Social Relations 50 B.C. to A.D. 284*, New Haven and London: Yale University Press.

Manning, C.E. (1973) 'Seneca and the Stoics on the Equality of the Sexes', *Mnemosyne* 26, 170–7.

Marshall, E. (1999) 'Sex and Paternity: Gendering the Foundation of Kyrene', in L. Foxhall and J. Salmon (eds) *When Men were Men*, London: Routledge, 98–110.

Masson, O. (1976) 'Grecs et Libyens en Cyrénaïque d'aprés les téemoignages de l'epigraphie', in M. Pippidi (ed.) *Assimilation et résistance à la culture gréco-romaine dans le monde ancien*, Paris: Les Belles Lettres, 377–87.

Matthews, J. (1970) 'Olympiodorus of Thebes and the History of the West (AD 407–425)', *JRS* 60, 79–97.

Matthews, J. (1975) *Western Aristocracies and the Imperial Court AD 364–425*, Oxford: Clarendon Press.

Mattingly, D.J. (1994) *Tripolitania*, Ann Arbor: University of Michigan Press.

Mattingly, D.J. and Hitchner, R.B. (1995) 'Roman Africa: an Archaeological Review', *JRS* 85, 65–213.

Meier, C. (1993) *The Political Art of Greek Tragedy*, trans. A. Webber, Cambridge: Polity in association with Blackwell.

Mérimée, P. (1992) *Colomba*, Paris: Flammarion.

Meyer, E. (1894) *Untersuchungen zur Geschichte der Gracchen*, Halle: Niemeyer.

Millett, K. (1970) *Sexual Politics*, Garden City, NY: Doubleday.

Mitchell, B.J. (2000) 'Cyrene: Typical or Atypical', in R. Brock and S. Hodkinson (eds) *Alternatives to Athens*, Oxford: Oxford University Press, 82–102.

Moeller, W. (1969) 'The Male Weavers at Pompeii', *Technology and Culture* 10, 561–6.

Moeller, W. (1976) *The Wool Trade in Ancient Pompeii*, Leiden: Brill.

Mohler, S.L. (1940) 'Slave Education in the Roman Empire', *TAPA* 71, 262–80.

Montevecchi, O. (1970) 'Nerone a una polis e ai 6475', *Aegyptus* 50, 5–33.

Montevecchi, O. (2000) 'Gli ἀπὸ γυμνασίου di Λύκων πόλις', in S. Russo (ed.) *Atti del V Convegno Nazionale de Egittologia e Papirologia, Firenze 10–12 dicembre 1999*, Florence, 175–84.

Montserrat, D. (1993) 'The Representation of Young Males in "Fayum Portraits"', *JEA* 79, 215–25.

Montserrat, D. (1997) 'Death and Funerals in the Roman Fayum', in M.L. Bierbrier (ed.) *Portraits and Masks*, London: British Museum, 33–44.

Moretti, G. (1987–8) 'Analecta Epigraphica', *Rendiconti della Pontificia Accademia della Archeologia* 60, 237–51.

Mossman, J. (1995) *Wild Justice: a Study of Euripides' Hecuba*, Oxford: Clarendon Press.

Murdoch, J. (1987) 'Thomas Bradwardine: Mathematics and Continuity in the Fourteenth Century', in E. Grant and J. Murdoch (eds) *Mathematics and its Applications to Science and Natural Philosophy in the Middle Ages: Essays in Honor of Marshall Clagett*, Cambridge: Cambridge University Press, 103–37.

Murnaghan, S. (1999) 'The Poetics of Loss in Greece', in M. Beissinger, J. Tylus and S. Wofford (eds) *Epic Tradition in the Contemporary World*, Berkeley: University of California Press, 203–20.

Mustakallio, K. (1990) 'Some Aspects of the Story of Coriolanus and the Women Behind the Cult of Fortuna Muliebris', *Commentations Humanarum Litterarum* 91, 125–31.

Netz, R. (2002) 'Greek Mathematicians: A Group Picture', in C. Tuplin and T. Rihll (eds) *Science and Mathematics in Ancient Greek Culture*, Oxford: Oxford University Press, 196–216.

Nicholas, B. and Treggiari, S.M. (1996) s.v. *'patria potestas'*, in S. Hornblower and A. Spawforth (eds) *Oxford Classical Dictionary*, 3rd edn, Oxford: Oxford University Press, 1122–3.

Nichols, J. (1989) 'Patrona Civitatis: Gender and Civic Patronage', in C. Deroux (ed.) *Studies in Latin Literature and Roman History*, Brussels: Latomus, 122–4.

Nicolai, R. (1992) 'La Fondazione di cirene e i karneia cirenaici dell'Inno ad Apollo di Callimaco', *Materiali e Discussioni per l'Analisi dei Testi Classici* 28, 153–73.

Nixon, L. (1994) 'Gender Bias in Archaeology', in L. Archer, S. Fischler and M. Wyke (eds) *Women in Ancient Societies*, Basingstoke: Macmillan, 1–23.

Noble, D. (1992) *A World Without Women: The Christian Clerical Culture of Western Science*, New York: Knopf.

O'Meara, D. (1989) *Pythagoras Revived: Mathematics and Philosophy in Late Antiquity*, Oxford: Clarendon Press.

Oates, J.F., Bagnall, R.S. and Willis, W.H. (eds) (2001) *Checklist of Editions of Greek, Latin, Demotic and Coptic Papyri, Ostraca and Tablets*, 5th edn, *BASP* Suppl. 9, Oakville, Conn.

Ogilvie, R.M. (1965) *A Commentary on Livy, Books 1–5*, Oxford: Clarendon Press.

Oost, S.I. (1968) *Galla Placidia Augusta: a Biographical Essay*, Chicago and London: University of Chicago Press.

Orgel, S. (1996) *Impersonations: the Performance of Gender in Shakespeare's England*, Cambridge: Cambridge University Press.

Osborne, R. (1996) *Greece in the Making 1200–479 B.C.*, London: Routledge.

Paradisi, U. (1966) 'Prehistoric Art in Gebel'el'Akhdar', *Antiquity* 39, 95–101.

Paribeni, E. (1959) *Catalogo delle sculture di Cirene*, Rome: L'erma di Bretschneider.

Parisi Presicce, C. (1994) 'La dea con il silphio e l'iconographia di Panakeia a Cirene', in J. Reynolds (ed.) *Cyrenaican Archaeology. Libyan Studies* 25, 85–100.

Pateman, C. (1989) *The Disorder of Women: Democracy, Feminism and Political Theory*, Stanford: University of Stanford Press.

Paterson, J.J. (1982) 'Salvation from the Sea: Amphorae and Trade in the Roman West', *JRS* 72, 146–57.

Patterson, C. (1981) *Pericles' Citizenship Law of 452–50 B.C.*, Salem, NH: Ayer.

Patterson, C. (1986) *'Hai Attikai*: The Other Athenians', *Helios* 13, 49–68.

Pedersen, O. (1993) *Early Physics and Astronomy: a Historical Introduction*, revised edn, Cambridge: Cambridge University Press.

Pensabene, P. (1987) 'Statuine fittili votive della chora cirenea', *QAL* 12, 93–170.

Peradotto, J. and Sullivan, J.P. (eds) (1984) *Women in the Ancient World: the Arethusa Papers*, Albany: State University of New York Press.

Peremans, W. (1983) 'Les *hermeneis* dans l'Egypte gréco-romaine', in G. Grimm, H. Heinen and E. Winter (eds) *Das römisch-byzantinische Ägypten*, Mainz am Rhein: P. von Zabern, 11–17.

Peters, E. (1967) 'Some Structural Aspects of the Feud Among the Camel-Herding Bedouin of Cyrenaica', *Africa* 37.3, 261–82.

Pitt-Rivers, J. (1965) 'Honour and Social Status', in J.G. Peristiany (ed.) *Honour and Shame*, London: Weidenfeld & Nicolson, 19–77.

Podlecki, A. (1990) 'Could Women Attend the Theater in Ancient Athens? A Collection of Testimonia', *AW* 21, 27–43.

Pomeroy, S.B. (1975) *Goddesses, Whores, Wives and Slaves: Women in Classical Antiquity*, New York: Schocken.

Pomeroy, S.B (ed.) (1991) *Women's History and Ancient History*, Chapel Hill and London: University of North Carolina Press.

Prevelakis, P. (1989) Ο ήλιος του θανάτου, 6th edn, Athens: Estias.

Price, S. (1987) 'From Noble Funerals to Divine Cult: the Consecration of Roman Emperors', in D. Carradine (ed.) *Rituals of Royalty: Power and Ceremonial in Traditional Societies*, New York: Cambridge University Press, 56–105.

Purcell, N. (1985) 'Wine and Wealth', *JRS* 75, 1–19.

Quaegebeur, J. (1982) 'De la préhistoire de l'écriture Copte', *Or. Louv. Per.* 13, 125–36.

Quilici, S. (1981) 'Annotazioni topografiche sul tempio della Fortuna Muliebris', *MEFRA* 93, 547–63.

Rabinowitz, N. (1976) 'From Force to Persuasion: Aeschylus' Oresteia as Cosmogonic Myth', unpublished thesis, University of Chicago.

Rabinowitz, N. (1981) 'From Force to Persuasion: Aeschylus' *Oresteia* as Cosmogony', *Ramus* 10, 159–91.

Rabinowitz, N. (1993) *Anxiety Veiled: Euripides and the Traffic in Women*, Ithaca: Cornell University Press.

Rabinowitz, N. (1998) 'Embodying Tragedy: the Sex of the Actor', *Intertexts* 2.1, 3–25.

Rapp, S. (1998) 'A Woman Speaks: Language and Self-representation in Hildegard's Letters', in M. Burnett McInerney (ed.) *Hildegard of Bingen: A Book of Essays*, London: Garland Publishing, 3–24.

Rattansi, P. (1988) 'Newton and the Wisdom of the Ancients', in J. Fauvel, R. Flood, M. Shortland and R. Wilson (eds) *Let Newton Be!* Oxford: Oxford University Press, 185–202.

Rawson, E. (1976) 'The Ciceronian Aristocracy and its Properties', in M.I. Finley (ed.) *Studies in Roman Property*, Cambridge: Cambridge University Press, 85–102.

Ray, J.D.C. (1994) 'How Demotic is Demotic?', in E. Bresciani (ed.) *Acta Demotica. Acts of the Fifth International Conference for Demotists* (= *Egitto e Vicino Oriente* 17), Pisa: Giardini, 251–64.

Reeder, E.D. (1995) *Pandora: Women in Classical Greece*, Princeton: Princeton University Press.

Reiter, R.R. (ed.) (1975) *Toward an Anthropology of Women*, New York: Monthly Review Press.

Reynolds, J. (1987) 'Libyans and Greeks in Rural Cyrenaica', *QAL* 12, 379–84.

Richlin, A. (1992) 'Julia's Jokes, Galla Placidia and the Roman Use of Women as Political Icons', in B. Garlick, S. Dixon and P. Allen (eds) *Stereotypes of Women in Power*, New York: Greenwood Press, 65–91.

Riedweg, C. (1997) '"Pythagoras hinterliess keine einzige Schrift" – ein Irrtum? Anmerkungen zu einer alten Streitfrage', *Museum Helveticum* 54, 65–92.

Roberts, P.C. (1997) '"One of our Mummies is Missing": Evaluating Petrie's Records from Hawara', in M.L. Bierbrier (ed.) *Portraits and Masks*, London: British Museum, 19–25.

Robins, G. (1993) *Women in Ancient Egypt*, London: British Museum Press.

Robinson, E.S.G. (1927) *A Catalogue of the Greek Coins of Cyrenaica*, London: British Museum.

Rochette, B. (1994) 'Traducteurs et traductions dans l'Egypte gréco-romaine', *Chronique d'Egypte* 69, 313–22.

Roes, A. (1949) 'L'aigle psychopompe de l'époque impériale', *Mél. Ch. Picard* 2, Paris, 881–91.

Rohrbacher, D. (2002) *The Historians of Late Antiquity*, London: Routledge.

Rome, A. (1926) 'Le troisième livre des commentaires sur l'Almageste par Théon et Hypatie', *Annales de la Societié de Bruxelles* 46, 1–14.

Rosaldo, M.Z. (1980) 'The Uses and Abuses of Anthropology: Reflections on Feminism and Cross-cultural Understanding', *Signs* 5, 389–417.

Rosaldo, M.Z. and Lamphere, L. (eds) (1974) *Woman, Culture, and Society*, Stanford: University of Stanford Press.

Rosenbloom, D. (1995) 'Myth, History, and Hegemony in Aeschylus', in B. Goff (ed.) *History, Tragedy, Theory*, Austin: University of Texas Press, 91–130.

Ross, W.D. (1924) *Aristotle's Metaphysics*, Oxford: Clarendon Press.

Rowan, J.P. (1981) *Commentary on Aristotle's Metaphysics: St. Thomas Aquinas*, Indiana: Dumb Ox Books.

Rowlandson, J.L. (1995) 'Beyond the Polis: Women and Economic Opportunity in Early Ptolemaic Egypt', in A. Powell (ed.) *The Greek World*, London: Routledge, 301–22.

Rowlandson, J.L. (ed.) (1998) *Women and Society in Greek and Roman Egypt*, Cambridge: Cambridge University Press.

Rubin, G. (1975) 'The Traffic in Women', in R.R. Reiter (ed.) *Toward an Anthropology of Women*, New York: Monthly Review Press, 157–210.

Rykwert, J. (1988) *The Idea of the City*, 2nd edn, Cambridge, Mass.: MIT Press.

Saller, R. (1982) *Personal Patronage under the Roman Empire*, Cambridge: Cambridge University Press.

Saller, R. (2003) 'Women, Slaves, and the Economy of the Roman Household', in C. Osiek and D. Balch (eds) *Early Christian Families in Context*, Grand Rapids, Mich.: Eerdman.

Samuel, D.H. (1981) 'Greeks and Romans at Soknopaiou Nesos', in R.S. Bagnall, G.M. Browne, A.E. Hanson and L. Koenen (eds) *Proceedings of the Sixteenth International Congress of Papyrology*, Chico, Calif.: Scholars Press, 389–403.

Santoro L'Hoir, F. (1992) *The Rhetoric of Gender Terms: 'Man', 'Woman' and the Portrayal of Character in Latin Prose*, Leiden: Brill.

Schaps, D. (1982) 'The Women of Greece in Wartime', *CPh* 77, 193–213.

Scheidel, W. (1995) 'Incest Revisited: Three Notes on the Demography of Sibling Marriage in Roman Egypt', *BASP* 32, 143–55.

Schiesaro, A. (1997) 'Passion, Reason and Knowledge in Seneca's Tragedies' in S. Braund and C. Gill (eds) *The Passions in Roman Thought and Literature*, Cambridge: Cambridge University Press, 89–139.

Schmitt, C.B. (1973) 'Towards a Reassessment of Renaissance Aristotelianism', *Hist. Sci.* 11, 159–93.

Schmitt, C.B. (1983) *Aristotle and the Renaissance*, Cambridge, Mass.: Harvard University Press.

Seaford, R. (1987) 'The Tragic Wedding', *JHS* 107, 106–30.

Seaford, R. (1994) *Reciprocity and Ritual: Homer and Tragedy in the Developing City-State*, Oxford: Clarendon Press.

Selden, D. (1998) 'Alibis', *CA* 17.2, 299–412.

Seremetakis, N. (1991) *The Last Word: Women, Death and Divination in Inner Mani*, Chicago: University of Chicago Press.

Setälä, P. (1977) *Private Domini in Roman Brick Stamps of the Roman Empire*, Helsinki: Finnish Academy (= *Annales Academiae Scientiarum Fennicae. Dissertationes Humanarum Litterarum* 10).

Setälä, P. (1998) 'Female Property and Power in Imperial Rome', in L. Larsson Lovén and A. Strömberg (eds) *Aspects of Women in Antiquity*, Jonsered, Sweden: Paul Åstrom, 96–110.

Shatzman, I. (1975) *Senatorial Wealth and Roman Politics*, Brussels: Latomus (Coll. vol. 142).

Shaw, B. (1984) 'Bandits in the Roman Empire', *Past and Present* 105, 3–52.

Shaw, B. (1987) 'The Age of Roman Girls at Marriage: Some Reconsiderations', *JRS* 77, 30–46.

Shinn, T. (1980) 'Orthodoxy and Innovation in Science: the Atomist Controversy in French Chemistry', *Minerva* 18, 539–55.

Sirks, A.J.B. (1980) 'A Favour to Rich Freed Women (*libertinae*) in 51 A.D. On Suet. *Cl.* 19 and the *Lex Papia*', *RIDA* 27 (ser. 3): 283–93.

Sissa, G. (1990) 'Maidenhood without Maidenhead: the Female Body in Ancient Greece', in D. Halperin, J. Winkler and F. Zeitlin (eds) *Before Sexuality: the Construction of Erotic Experience in the Ancient Greek World*, Princeton: Princeton University Press, 339–64.

Sivan, H. (1996) 'Why not Marry a Barbarian? Marital Frontiers in Late Antiquity', in R. Mathisen and H. Sivan (eds) *Shifting Frontiers in Late Antiquity*, Aldershot, 136–45.

Skidmore, C. (1996) *Practical Ethics for Roman Gentlemen: the Work of Valerius Maximus*, Exeter: University of Exeter Press.

Skinner, M.B. (1983) 'Clodia Metelli', *TAPA* 113, 273–87.

Skinner, M.B. (1987) 'Introduction', in *Rescuing Creousa: New Methodological Approaches to Women in Antiquity* (special issue of *Helios* 13.2), 1–8.

Skydsgaard, J.-E. (1976) 'The Disintegration of the Roman Labour Market and the *clientela* Theory', *Studia Romana in Honorem Petri Krarup Septuagenarii*, Odense, 44–8.

Smith, B. (ed.) (1983) *Home Girls: a Black Feminist Anthology*, New York: Women of Color Press.

Smith, B., Hull, G.T. and Bell Scott, P. (eds) (1982) *All the Women are White, all the Blacks are Men: But Some of Us Are Brave*, New York: The Feminist Press.

Smith, R.M. and Porcher, E.A. (1864) *History of the Recent Discoveries at Cyrene made during an Expedition to the Cyrenaica 1860–61*, London: Day & Son.

Smith, R.R.R. (1999) 'Late Antique Portraits in a Public Context: Honorific Statuary in Aphrodisias in Caria; AD 300–600', *JRS* 89, 155–89.

Sommerstein, A.H., Halliwell, S., Henderson, J. and Zimmermann, B. (eds) (1993) *Tragedy, Comedy and the Polis*, Bari: Levante.

Sorabji, R. (ed.) (1990) *Aristotle Transformed: the Ancient Commentaries and their Influence*, London: Duckworth.

Sourvinou-Inwood, C. (1995) 'Male and Female, Public and Private, Ancient and Modern', in E. Reeder (ed.) *Pandora: Women in Classical Greece*, Princeton: Princeton University Press, 111–20.

Sourvinou-Inwood, C. (1997) 'Medea at a Shifting Distance: Images and Euripidean Tragedy', in J.J. Clauss and S.I. Johnston (eds) *Medea*, Princeton: Princeton University Press, 253–96.

Spender, D. (1990) *Man Made Language*, 2nd edn, London: Pandora.

Stanford, W.B. (1942) *Aeschylus in his Style: a Study in Language and Personality*, Dublin: The University Press.

Stehle, E. (1997) *Performance and Gender in Ancient Greece: Nondramatic Poetry in its Setting*, Princeton: University of Princeton Press.

Steinby, M. (1993–2002) *Lexicon Topographicum Urbis Romae*, Rome: Quasar.

Stephens, S.A. (2003) *Seeing Double: Intercultural Poetics in Ptolemaic Alexandria*, Berkeley: University of California Press.

Stucchi, S. (1967) *Cirene 1957–67*, Tripoli: Istituto Italiano di Cultura di Tripoli.

Stucchi, S. (1975) *Architettura Cirenaica*, Rome: L'erma di Bretschneider.

Tait, W.J. (1996) 'Demotic Literature: Forms and Genres', in A. Loprieno (ed.) *Ancient Egyptian Literature*, Leiden: Brill, 175–87.

Taub, L. (2002) 'Instruments of Alexandrian Astronomy: the Uses of the Equinoctial Rings', in C. Tuplin and T. Rihll (eds) *Science and Mathematics in Ancient Greek Culture*, Oxford: Oxford University Press, 133–49.

Taylor, L.R. (1961) 'Freedmen and freeborn in the epitaphs of Imperial Rome', *AJP* 82, 113–32.

Thomas, R. (1992) *Literacy and Orality in Ancient Greece*, Cambridge: Cambridge University Press.

Thompson, D.J. (1992) 'Language and Literacy in Early Hellenistic Egypt', in P. Bilde, T. Engberg-Pedersen, L. Hannestad and J. Zahle (eds) *Ethnicity in Hellenistic Egypt*, Aarhus: Aarhus University Press, 39–52.

Thompson, D.J. (1994) 'Literacy and Power in Ptolemaic Egypt', in A.K. Bowman and G. Woolf (eds) *Literacy and Power in the Ancient World*, Cambridge: Cambridge University Press, 67–83.

Thompson, D.J. (1997) 'The Infrastructure of Splendour: Census and Taxes in Ptolemaic Egypt', in P. Cartledge, P. Garnsey and E. Gruen (eds) *Hellenistic Constructs*, Berkeley: University of California Press, 242–57.

Thompson, D.J. (2001) 'Hellenistic Hellenes: the Case of Ptolemaic Egypt', in I. Malkin (ed.) *Ancient Perceptions of Ethnicity*, Washington, DC: Center for Hellenic Studies, 301–22.

Thompson, D.J. (2002) 'Families in Early Ptolemaic Egypt', in D. Ogden (ed.) *The Hellenistic World: New Perspectives*, Swansea: Classical Press of Wales and Duckworth, 137–56.

Thompson, E.A. (1944) 'Olympiodorus of Thebes', *CQ* 38, 43–52.

Thompson, H. (1934) *A Family Archive from Siut from Papyri in the British Museum*, Oxford: Oxford University Press.

Thomson, G. (1950) *Aeschylus and Athens: a Study in the Social Origins of Drama*, 2nd edn, London: Lawrence & Wishart.

Tong, R. (ed.) (1989) *Feminist Thought*, London: Unwin Hyman.

Traub, V. (1992) *Desire and Anxiety: Circulations of Sexuality in Shakespearean Drama*, London, New York: Routledge.

Traversari, G. (1971) *L'arco dei Sergi*, Padua: CEDAM.

Treggiari, S. (1975) 'Jobs in the Household of Livia', *Publications of the British School at Rome* 43, 48–77.

Treggiari, S. (1976) 'Jobs for Women', *AJAH* 1, 76–104.

Treggiari, S. (1979) 'Lower Class Women in the Roman Economy', *Florilegium* 1, 65–86.

Treggiari, S. (1991) *Roman Marriage*, Oxford: Clarendon Press.

Tuana, N. (ed.) (1994) *Feminist Interpretations of Plato*, University Park: Pennsylvania State University Press.

Turner, V. (1969) *The Ritual Process: Structure and Anti-Structure*, Chicago: Aldine Publishing Company.

Valone, C. (2001) 'Matrons and Motives: Why Women Built in Early Modern Rome', in S. Reiss and D. Wilkins (eds) *Beyond Isabella, Sixteenth Century Essays and Studies* 54, Kirksville, Mo.: Truman State Press.

van Bremen, R. (1996) *The Limits of Participation. Women and Civic Life in the Greek East in the Hellenistic and Roman Periods*, Amsterdam: J.C. Gieben.

van Gennep, A. (1960) *Rites of Passage: a Classic Study of Cultural Celebrations*, trans. M.B. Vizedom and G.L. Caffee, Chicago: University of Chicago Press.

van Houts, E. (1999) *Memory and Gender in Medieval Europe 900–1200*, Basingstoke: Macmillan.

van Minnen, P. (1998) 'Did Ancient Women Learn a Trade Outside the Home?', *ZPE* 123, 201–3.

van Minnen, P. (2002) 'ΑΙ ΑΠΟ ΓΥΜΝΑΣΙΟΥ: "Greek" Women and the Greek "Elite" in the Metropoleis of Roman Egypt', in H. Melaerts and L. Mooren (eds) *Le rôle et le statut de la femme en Égypte hellénistique, romaine et byzantine*, Leuven: Peeters, 337–53.

Vandorpe, K. (2002) 'Apollonia, a Businesswoman in a Multicultural Society (Pathyris, 2nd–1st centuries B.C.)', in H. Melaerts and L. Mooren (eds) *Le rôle et le statut de la femme en Égypte hellénistique, romaine et byzantine*, Leuven: Peeters, 325–36.

Ver Eecke, P. (1982) *La collection mathématique: oeuvres traduites pour la première fois du Grec en Francais avec une introduction et des notes*, Paris: Desclée.

Verboven, K. (2002) *The Economy of Friends. Economic Aspects of* Amicitia *and Patronage in the Late Republic*, Brussels: Coll Latomus, 269.

Vidèn, G. (1993) *Women in Roman Literature: Attitudes of Authors under the Early Empire*, Göteborg: Acta Universitatis Gothoburgensis.

Vlastos, G. (1991) *Socrates: Ironist and Moral Philosopher*, Cambridge: Cambridge University Press.

von Mercklin, E. (1844) *Dissertatio de Cornelia vita moribus et epistolis*, Dorpat.

Vuillemin-Diem, G. (1987) 'La Traduction de la Métaphysique d'Aristote par Guillaume de Moerbeke et son Exemplaire Grec: Vind. Phil. Gr. 100 (J)', in J. Wiesner (ed.) *Aristoteles: Werk und Wirkung*, vol. 2, Berlin: De Gruyter, 434–86.

Waithe, M.E. (ed.) (1987) *A History of Women Philosophers*, vol. I, Boston: Kluwer Academic Publishers.

Walker, S. (1997) 'Mummy Portraits in their Roman Context', in M.L. Bierbrier (ed.) *Portraits and Masks*, London: British Museum, 1–6.

Walker, S. and M. Bierbrier (1997) *Ancient Faces: Mummy Portraits from Roman Egypt*, London: British Museum.

Wallace-Hadrill, A. (ed.) (1989) *Patronage in Ancient Society*, London: Routledge.

Walters, K. (1993) 'Women and Power in Classical Athens', in M. DeForest (ed.) *Woman's Power, Man's Game*, Wanconda, Ill.: Bolchazy-Carducci, 194–214.

Walton, M.J. (1980) *Greek Theatre Practice*, Westport, Conn.: Greenwood Publishing Group.

Waltz, R. (1955) *Seneca, Dialogi*, Paris: les Belles Lettres.

Waltzing, J.-P. (1895–1900) *Étude historique sur les corporations professionnelles chez les romains depuis les origines jusquà' la chute de l'Empire d'Occident*, 4 vols, Louvain: Peeters.

Walzer, R. (1962) *Greek into Arabic: Essays on Islamic Philosophy*, Cambridge, Mass.: Harvard University Press.

Wanis, S. (1992) 'A New Relief from Cyrene with a Libyan Scene', *Libyan Studies* 23, 41–4.

Ward, J.K. (ed.) (1996) *Feminism and Ancient Philosophy*, London: Routledge.

Warner, M. (1999) 'Normal and Normaller: Beyond Gay Marriage', *GLQ* 5.2, 119–71.

Webster, T.B.L. (1970) *Greek Theatre Production*, 2nd edn, London: Methuen.

Wertheim, M. (1997) *Pythagoras' Trousers: God, Physics, and the Gender Wars*, London: Fourth Estate.

White, D. (1976) 'Excavations in the Sanctuary of Demeter and Persephone at Cyrene. Fourth Preliminary Report', *AJA* 80, 165–81.

White, D. (1987) 'Demeter Libyssa: Her Cult in Light of the Recent Excavations', *QAL* 12, 67–84.

Whitehead, J. (1984) *Biography and Formula in Roman Sarcophagi*, unpublished PhD dissertation, Yale University.

Whitlock-Blundell, M. (1989) *Helping Friends and Harming Enemies. A Study in Sophocles and Greek Ethics*, Cambridge: Cambridge University Press.

Wild, J.P. (1976) 'Textiles', in D. Strong and D. Brown (eds) *Roman Crafts*, London: Duckworth, 167–77.

Wiles, D. (1997) *Tragedy in Athens: Performance Space and Theatrical Meaning*, Cambridge: Cambridge University Press.

Wilfong, T.G. (2002) *Women of Jeme: Lives in a Coptic Town in Late Antique Egypt*, Ann Arbor: University of Michigan Press.

Williams, G. (1958) 'Some Aspects of Roman Marriage Ceremonies and Ideals', *JRS* 48, 16–29.

Wilson, M. (1997) 'The Subjugation of Grief in Seneca's Epistles', in S. Braund and C. Gill (eds) *The Passions in Roman Thought and Literature*, Cambridge: Cambridge University Press, 48–67.

Wilson, S. (1988) *Feuding, Conflict and Banditry in Nineteenth Century Corsica*, Cambridge: Cambridge University Press.

Winkler, J.J. (1985) 'The Ephebes' Song: *Tragôidia* and *Polis*', *Representations* 11, 26–62.

Winkler, J.J. (1990) *Constraints of Desire: the Anthropology of Sex and Gender in Ancient Greece*, New York, London: Routledge.

Wiseman, T.P. (1971) *New Men in the Roman Senate 139 B.C.–A.D. 14*, Oxford: Oxford University Press.

Wittig, M. (1992) *The Straight Mind and Other Essays*, Boston: Beacon Press.

Wohl, V. (1998) *Intimate Commerce: Exchange, Gender, and Subjectivity in Greek Tragedy*, Austin: University of Texas Press.

Woodhull, M. (1999) *Building Power: Women as Architectural Patrons during the Early Roman Empire, 30 B.C.E. to 68 C.E*, unpublished PhD dissertation, Austin: University of Texas.

Woodhull, M. (2003) 'Engendering Space: Octavia's Portico in Rome', *Aurora. The Journal of Art History* IV, Fall 2003.

Woods, E. and Woods, N. (1978) *Class Ideology and Ancient Political Theory: Socrates, Plato, and Aristotle in Social Context*, Oxford: Basil Blackwell.

Woolf, G. (1994) 'Becoming Roman, Staying Greek: Culture, Identity and the Civilizing Process in the Roman East', *PCPS* 40, 116–43.

Woolf, V. (1957) *A Room of One's Own*, New York: Harvest/Harcourt Brace Jovanovich.

Wyke, M. (1992) 'Augustan Cleopatras: Female Power and Poetic Authority', in A. Powell (ed.) *Roman Poetry and Propaganda in the Age of Augustus*, London: Bristol Classical Press, 98–140.

Yont, L. and Brown, N. (eds) (1999) *A to Z of Women in Science and Math*, New York: Facts on File Inc.

Youtie, H.C. (1971a) 'ΑΓΡΑΜΜΑΤΟΣ. An Aspect of Greek Society in Egypt', *HSCP* 75, 161–76 (= *Scriptiunculae* II, 611–27).

Youtie, H.C. (1971b) 'Βραδέως γράφων: Between Literacy and Illiteracy', *GRBS* 12, 161–76 (= *Scriptiunculae* II, 629–51).

Youtie, H.C. (1975a) 'ΥΠΟΓΡΑΦΕΥΣ: the Social Impact of Illiteracy in Graeco-Roman Egypt', *ZPE* 17, 201–21(= *Scriptiunculae posteriores* I, 17–34).

Youtie, H.C. (1975b) 'Because they do not Know Letters', *ZPE* 19, 101–8 (= *Scriptiunculae posteriores* I, 255–62).

Yoyotte, J. (1969) 'Bakhthis: religion égyptienne et culture grecque à Edfou', in P. Derchain (ed.) *Religions en Égypte hellénistique et romaine*, Paris: Presses universitaires de France, 127–41.

Zauzich, K.-T. (1983) 'Demotische Texte römischer Zeit', in G. Grimm, H. Heinen and E. Winter (eds) *Das römisch-byzantinische Ägypten*, Mainz am Rhein: P. von Zabern, 77–80.

Zeitlin, F.I. (1978) 'The Dynamics of Misogyny in the *Oresteia*', *Arethusa* 11: 149–84.

Zeitlin, F.I. (1985) 'Playing the Other: Theater, Theatricality, and the Feminine in Greek Drama', *Representations* 11, 63–94.

Zeitlin, F.I. (1996) *Playing the Other: Gender and Society in Classical Greek Literature*, Chicago: University of Chicago Press.

Zhmud, L. (1989) ' "All is Number"?: "Basic Doctrine" of Pythagoreanism Reconsidered', *Phronesis* 34, 270–92.

Zimmermann, K. (1996) 'Zum Personennamen Libys/Libyssa', *Chiron* 26, 349–71.

INDEX